Starr: *A Reassessment*

Starr
A Reassessment

BENJAMIN WITTES

Yale University Press   *New Haven & London*

Designed by James J. Johnson and set in Janson type by Keystone Typesetting, Inc.
Printed in the United States of America.

Library of Congress Cataloging-in-Publication Data

Wittes, Benjamin.
Starr : a reassessment / Benjamin Wittes.
     p. cm.
Includes bibliographical references and index.
ISBN 0-300-09252-0 (alk. paper)

1. Starr, Kenneth, 1946– Interviews. 2. Special prosecutors – United States –
Interviews. 3. Governmental investigations – United States. 4. Clinton, Bill,
1946 – Impeachment. 5. Lewinsky, Monica S. (Monica Samille), 1973– I. Title.
KF5076.C57 W58 2002
345.73'01 – dc21   2001057401

A catalogue record for this book is available from the British Library.

The paper in this book meets the guidelines for permanence and durability of the
Committee on Production Guidelines for Book Longevity of the Council on
Library Resources.

10 9 8 7 6 5 4 3 2 1

Contents

Preface

It is a rare public figure in Washington who willingly subjects his judgment and decision-making during a controversial five-year term in office to hours of on-the-record cross-examination by a journalist known to view that tenure skeptically. Kenneth W. Starr, his enthusiasts and critics will agree, was a most unusual public official. He is possessed of both an old-school sense of accountability for his decisions and a media-age need to explain himself to a society that, in large measure, regards as a delusion his continued belief that he performed admirably in office. Although his office's contacts with the press during the Monica Lewinsky investigation drew much fire, moreover, he became convinced that one of his great errors was a failure to justify and explain his investigation to the public as it was going on. Consequently, when I approached him a few days after he stepped down as independent counsel and asked him to let me interrogate him about his conduct in office, he consented without a moment's hesitation.

I had, before asking him to sit for these interviews, met him only once. Over the course of his investigation, I had spoken frequently to members of his staff. But Starr himself was little more than a name and a face to me until shortly before he resigned, when we met at the bland suite of offices on Pennsylvania Avenue that housed his investigation. The meeting was notable in exactly one respect: Starr seemed human, thoughtful, and surprisingly open to criticism. He seemed, in fact, so different from the cartoonish images of him that dominated public discussion of his work that I, shortly thereafter, proposed exploring what had really motivated his conduct and why he acted as he did.

In a series of interviews, Starr and I spent approximately ten hours discussing the history of his investigation. My aim in these conversations was to examine the question of whether Starr's reputation as an out-of-control independent counsel was fair. Was the aggressive direction his probe took, particularly as the Lewinsky affair erupted in 1998, an inevitable structural consequence of the independent counsel law itself, or was it due to decisions Starr made? If the latter, which of Starr's decisions ought we fault? Was Starr being blamed for faithfully implementing the policy choices that Congress had made when it adopted the statute, policy choices he had always opposed? Or was the law itself a victim of his alleged crusade against the Clintons?

Underlying these questions lay my conviction that the common understandings of Starr's tenure lacked adequate complexity. Portrayals of Starr tended to paint him either as a demon or a saint, though neither image easily accounts for the voluminous public record of an investigation that dragged on for so many years. As both a psychological and political matter, the caricatures seem unrealistic. Not many public servants walk into office determined to pursue a partisan agenda, abuse the power of the federal government, violate ethical rules, flout the public interest, and thereby risk their own professional reputations. Likewise, not many emerge from public life as such a savior of the Republic as conservative opinion now regards Starr. As a historical matter, the unrealism of the portraits presents an acute problem: whole swaths of his behavior become inexplicable if one is too doctrinally committed to the caricatures. My purpose throughout my interviews with Starr was to seek a more plausible analysis.

The theory that underlies my reporting, in some respects, itself gives Starr more credit than other writers — and, in all likelihood, many readers — have been willing to contemplate. The idea, simply put, is that Starr himself is a significantly underexploited source of truthful information about his own thinking and decision-making during his investigation. Starr, as best I have been able to discern, is not a liar, and his memory is excellent. While there are questions he cannot legally answer, one can learn an enormous amount about his investigation merely by listening to him carefully. Given the degree to which the motives and purposes behind individual investigative steps have come under the microscope, it seems only fair to ask Starr what he was thinking, lay out his answers fairly, and then reflect seriously upon them. With all the ink that has been spilled on the Starr investigation, such a discussion has not been attempted.

A comprehensive and balanced evaluation of the independent counsel's office is glaringly absent from the current literature on the Clinton scandals. Richard Posner, in one chapter of his quixotic work *An Affair of State*, attempts an evaluation of Starr's performance during the Lewinsky phase of the investigation, but his treatment of the subject is underdeveloped. Posner's discussion is both limited to the Lewinsky phase and based only on the public record of the investigation. *An Affair of State* is generally defensive of Starr, and Posner spends a good deal of time rebutting various charges made against the Office of Independent Counsel. Starr's excesses, in Posner's view, lay chiefly in the extremity of portions of his impeachment referral and in certain unnecessary lines of questioning his prosecutors pursued before the grand jury. Posner's book represents one of the earliest serious efforts to make sense of the Lewinsky episode and contains numerous useful observations throughout. His discussion of Starr, however, is cursory and ultimately unsatisfying — a function, perhaps, of the fact that it represents only one component of Posner's far more ambitious project, which is to use the larger scandal as a test case for his theories about the interaction of morality, moral and constitutional theory, and law.

By contrast, Starr's investigation is the sole focus of Susan Schmidt and Michael Weisskopf's book, *Truth at Any Cost*, which tells in significant and useful detail the story of the office's investigation of the Monica Lewinsky episode. Though Schmidt and Weisskopf treat their subject with obvious sympathy, their book does not attempt a systematic assessment. Rather, it is simply a narrative in which Starr's defenders and critics alike will find grist for their arguments. Similarly, Michael Isikoff's riveting book, *Uncovering Clinton*, offers no analysis of Starr's behavior, but, rather, tells the broader story of the Clinton sex scandals and the narrower one of Isikoff's involvement in their unfolding. James Stewart, in his 1996 book, *Blood Sport*, tells the story of Whitewater and the other pre-Lewinsky Clinton scandals, but he focuses largely on the behavior of the Clintons and their supporters; any assessment of the investigation at the time he was writing would, in any event, have been premature. Bob Woodward, in the portion of his book *Shadow* that deals with Starr, likewise brings a pile of data to the table — mostly about the White House's approach to the scandals — and leaves it largely unanalyzed. Peter Baker's account, *The Breach*, focuses on Clinton's impeachment and Senate trial, not on the probe that produced them. At this point, the story of the scandals, including the tale of important portions of the Starr investigation, has been well told. The narrative, however, is far better developed than our understanding of it.

Other books that have attempted to situate or evaluate Starr have been, to one degree or another, overtly political. Jeffrey Toobin's *A Vast Conspiracy* encapsulates a series of pre-existing caricatures of the Starr probe and perpetuates them by filling them out in rich, albeit sadly selective, detail. Joe Conason and Gene Lyons's work, *The Hunting of the President*, contains some useful reporting about the activities of Clinton haters in Arkansas, but its unremitting hostility to Clinton's foes and its tendency to see them as part of a coordinated conspiracy make its discussions of the Starr investigation all but useless. These books, and the countless articles written under similar theories, are largely in the business of perpetuating simplistic understandings of the investigation, and these understandings are precisely what need revisiting.

Evaluating the Starr investigation, not retelling its story, is my objective in these pages. The work that has emerged from my conversations with Starr is one of unapologetic revisionism that examines his investigation through the particular lens of his understanding and interpretation of his role under the independent counsel statute. My argument is that Starr's great error was not one of malicious motive or evil tactics, but, rather, that he fundamentally misconceived his role, taking a statute designed to authorize a conventional criminal investigation and finding in it license to conduct the broadest of inquiries, an investigation that he never intended to use chiefly as a vehicle for punishing crimes. Starr saw the independent counsel as a kind of truth commission—a conception of the role that, while adopted in good faith, was entirely wrongheaded. His view of the statute, moreover, had a profound effect on key decisions he made throughout the investigation and tended to push him in exactly the wrong direction: away from restraint and toward ever-mounting confrontation with the executive branch. In looking to explain the uncontrolled direction the probe took in 1998 in terms of Starr's relationship with the statute, I have tried to tell a story of a decent man who honestly set out to avoid the excesses of his predecessors, yet whose efforts to do so were so misguided that they not only ensured his failure but helped cause him to eclipse those excesses. This book is an attempt, at once, to persuade Starr's more strident critics that they need not ascribe to him unethical conduct or improper political motivations in order to account for his behavior, and to persuade his more faithful defenders that the rejection of the many unsupportable charges against Starr does not necessarily vindicate his investigation generally. It is an effort, in other words, to reformulate the critique of Starr in what I hope will prove, over time, a more defensible construction than the angry denunciations to date have offered.

The first chapter summarizes the prevailing views of Starr, both the demonologies and the hagiographies, and sketches out the inadequacies of these explanations of his behavior. It then introduces my own thesis: that Starr, despite his long-standing and principled opposition to the independent counsel law, adopted a vision of the statute — which I term the truth commission vision — that heightened, rather than minimized, its inherent problems.

The second chapter describes Starr's background and history of concern for the separation of powers, and his resulting distaste for the independent counsel statute. It then describes his far-too-modest efforts, upon taking office, to mitigate the evils of the law, and explains his interpretation of the statute itself as authorizing a kind of truth commission. It proceeds to evaluate that vision against the statute's legislative history, in which Starr grounds his view, and demonstrates why that history in no sense supports Starr's interpretation.

The third chapter attempts to trace the manner in which Starr's vision influenced his investigation of scandals surrounding Clinton's investment in the Whitewater Development Corporation, the White House Travel Office, and the White House's access to FBI files of Republican former officials. It illustrates the significant delays that the truth commission vision caused during the various components of the investigation, particularly the probe of the death of Deputy White House Counsel Vincent Foster Jr. It then argues that, during the Whitewater investigation in particular, Starr's vision of his role precluded restraint in his dealings with witnesses whom he believed had not fully cooperated with his prosecutors.

The fourth chapter shows how, along with other unnecessarily aggressive interpretations of the law, the truth commission vision prevented moderation on the part of Starr's office during the Monica Lewinsky saga. It argues that, faced with a scandal that presented a limited set of viable criminal questions and a far more pressing congressional interest in gathering information relevant to possible impeachment proceedings, Starr's view of the statute forced him to become Congress's agent in the impeachment process, rather than letting the legislature take responsibility for its own constitutional functions and focusing narrowly on the prosecutorial interests the case presented.

The final chapter attempts to draw some lessons from Starr's experience for the future of public integrity investigations involving allegations of high-level misconduct, arguing that the truth-seeking function and the prosecutorial function need to be rigorously separated.

My work on this subject has left me with two strongly felt

impulses toward Starr: frustration and sympathy. Which of these sentiments should, on the whole, serve as the noun and which the adjective — whether the proper position, in other words, ought to be sympathetic frustration or frustrated sympathy — I will leave to the reader to decide. When examining the component parts of the larger mosaic, however, the balance necessarily shifts depending on which tile is under study. The ethical allegations against Starr and the assumption — so often stated yet always unproven — that he was on a political crusade or a personal vendetta to "get" President Clinton, for example, deserve little patience and do not hold up under serious scrutiny. Moreover, Starr was subjected to a truly vicious campaign of attacks and, generally speaking, operated under extreme pressures that made his job nearly impossible. A certain awareness of the extraordinary difficulty of his position ought to pervade and temper one's discussion and judgment of his performance, even where that performance falls short — in some cases, widely short — of what would have been desirable. At the same time, a truly fair evaluation of Starr is not flattering. While his motives and his intentions were no doubt decent, his conduct of the investigation was nonetheless maddening. The more closely one focuses on Starr's behavior, rather than the public discussion of it, the more grounds one finds for criticism and the fewer for sympathy.

In the analysis that follows I discuss the evidence against Clinton, and Clinton's behavior itself, only to the degree that doing so is necessary to evaluate Starr's decision-making. I do not mean, in focusing on Starr at Clinton's expense, to put the weight of the evil here on the prosecutor or to let Clinton off of the hook for his misconduct. The behavior of the president is a portion of the overall story that has been better and more richly told than the portion that focuses on Starr. The honest evaluation of Clinton's contribution to the conflagration, moreover, is a relatively simple one. His behavior was consistently venal and self-serving. His lies were offensive and, by the end of his presidency, inarguable. His non-cooperation with investigators would have tested any prosecutor. Because my purpose here is not to tell the full story of the war between Clinton and Starr and apportion blame between them, I deal with Clinton's behavior only to the extent I need to.

One of the subtle barriers to a fuller public understanding of Starr's tenure has been the unaccountability of so much of the media coverage of the office. Writing in real time, it is almost impossible to attribute credibly each fact one chooses to report. Reporters tend to rely on background sources, a decision that allows them to offer substantially more information to their readers than they could if they relied only on what was offered on the record. The reliance on background sourcing, in this instance, gave the public that benefit, but it also had considerable negative effects. Innocuous facts that appeared in newspapers without clear attribution were assumed to be improper prosecutorial leaks, for example. In addition, as I shall argue, a great deal of writing became permeated with factual assumptions about the motives and purpose of the office that were never supported and, indeed, could not have been supported. I am in the happy position, publishing somewhat later, to provide a more comprehensive account of my own sourcing. I have endeavored to attribute and justify every sentence in this book, except those that are either composed solely of my own analysis or involve only common knowledge of the sort that requires no documentation. My efforts to make my reporting as transparent and reproducible as possible tend to mask, at times, the diversity of the book's sources, since many people interviewed for it preferred not to be named. In addition to the interviews with Starr himself, I spoke with many prosecutors who served during different periods of his office's existence. Several of those conversations were on the record, and their fruits appear discernibly throughout these pages, but my many conversations with Starr's staff also inform the countless judgments I have made. In a few instances I have cited material from these interviews, while protecting the identity of the source who offered it. Each of these cases was the result of a specific decision that the individual comment was valuable enough to warrant its inclusion even in the absence of named attribution.

This project would have died on the vine at several points without the timely intervention of people owed more thanks than I can offer here. *The New Republic* was kind enough to publish an early version of my thesis, and the magazine's legal affairs editor, Jeffrey Rosen, encouraged me to expand the argument I outlined in that article in longer form, read the manuscript, and offered useful comments on it. Akhil Reed Amar, whose work has greatly influenced my views of executive power and the independent counsel structure, likewise encouraged me to expand the thesis and championed this project in a manner that would do any literary agency proud. John Covell and Larisa Heimert of Yale University Press offered invaluable assistance in shepherding the project from proposal to publication. Fred Hiatt, editorial page editor of *The Washington Post*, offered unstinting support and tolerance while I was writing. Without all of their help, this book simply would not exist.

A special word of thanks goes to a panel of former prosecutors and alumni of independent counsels' offices I assembled to serve as a sounding board for Starr's comments and my initial thinking about his claims. John Barrett, who also read and commented on the manuscript, Gerard Lynch, Alexia Morrison, and Ronald Noble provided a consistently thoughtful check both against my own prejudices and presumptions and against the often seductive logic of Starr's argumentation. The manuscript also benefited significantly from the thoughtful comments of Peter Berkowitz, Alejandro Manevich, David Glenn, Bruce Brown, and Neal Katyal, whose review of the manuscript for Yale University Press significantly aided my efforts to revise the book.

I received invaluable research assistance from Elizabeth Gelner, who spent the better part of a month combing the Library of Congress to check and correct countless of my assertions. Though it was far outside her job description, Melody Blake, research librarian for the *Post*'s editorial page, could not resist helping out on occasion. Jenna Beveridge spent generous amounts of her spare time transcribing taped interviews.

Years ago, my mother dedicated her dissertation to my sister and me "for being such good babies." Having spent the last year trying to write with a two-year-old named Miriam running around the house — a two-year-old who took to, as she put it, "bouncing down the stairs" to find me and cut short my early-morning work sessions — I am no longer certain I understand how even a good baby facilitates the completion of lengthy projects. That said, I can improve upon the dedication only by adding to it my wife, Tamara Cofman Wittes, who made sure I had blocks of time to get the project done and who also somehow found time both to edit much of the manuscript and to listen and respond to the many thoughts — good, bad, and truly terrible — with which I flirted while working on it.

CHAPTER 1

Images of Starr

"I know no method to secure the repeal of bad or obnoxious laws so
effective as their stringent execution."

ULYSSES S. GRANT

The Howard Johnson's that the Watergate burglars used
as an observation post during their ill-fated adventure across
Virginia Avenue in Northwest Washington was purchased by
George Washington University and converted into a dormi-
tory, but it still looked like a HoJo's. At least on the seventh
floor, its role in history remained very much alive for the
freshmen who lived there as part of an extracurricular seminar
on Watergate and its legacy during the Fall 1999 semester.
The room Richard Nixon's minions had once stocked with
eavesdropping equipment was decked out with Watergate
memorabilia. In a small auditorium on the ground floor, various Watergate figures spoke to the group. And on an evening
in early November, they heard Kenneth W. Starr attack one of
Watergate's most important legislative offspring: the now-
defunct independent counsel law under which Starr himself
had served for the previous five years.

Watching this pedantic intellectual teach a class, I struggled to envision him as the half-crazed, partisan crusader-
pornographer whose image his name still evoked. His famous
moralism showed itself now and again, as when he concluded
the event by saying that G. Gordon Liddy, who had previously

addressed the class, "should be ashamed." He betrayed, however, no signs of zealotry. The man who pursued President Clinton over five years and tens of millions of dollars seemed downright jovial, even goofy. He asked each of the students where he or she came from, and made a good show of caring about the answer. He clearly wanted to connect with them. More specifically, he wanted to persuade them of something he fervently believed: the independent counsel law was a "profoundly misguided" response to Watergate, one that falsely promised "a process that was utterly devoid of and divorced from politics."

"We have now been through two extraordinarily controversial investigations, the [Lawrence] Walsh [Iran-Contra] investigation in the 1980s and then a certain not-to-be-named investigation in the 1990s," he said, referring to his own. "There was real power and insight at the founding of the American Republic when Mr. Madison and others [were] thinking very hard about structures. . . . And the independent counsel [law] — noble experiment — was a very useful demonstration to us that you need structures that are compatible with the original design at the Founding." The independent counsel statute, he argued, was not such a structure.

Starr attempted to convince the students of something else too, something a touch more controversial than his now widely shared skepticism of a law that few today still defend. Starr believed the statute set him up to be attacked for running amok as independent counsel. Not being selected by the attorney general, he complained, left him isolated from the protective bosom of the executive branch and consequently vulnerable to White House criticism. To succeed, he said, any system must have "accountability by the executive branch. So that if the independent counsel should be fired, fire the independent counsel, but if the independent counsel should not be fired, then don't allow attacks [by the executive branch] to go on."[1] The law, in his view, made it impossible for him to conduct his investigation with the public confidence it deserved.

Starr's distaste for the statute may seem like a convenient, retroactive self-justification, given the low esteem in which the public holds his performance in office. In truth, however, Starr always hated the statute and saw it as a dangerous affront to the separation of powers, as he explained in a conversation later that evening. While serving at the Justice Department in the early 1980s, he helped formulate the Reagan administration's opposition to its reauthorization. As a judge, he watched in dismay as the Supreme Court overwhelmingly upheld it in 1988. And when he talked about a man named Whitney North Seymour Jr., he sounded like one of the innumerable naysayers who clucked disapprovingly about his own conduct. Seymour was the independent counsel who prosecuted former Ronald Reagan aide Michael Deaver on perjury charges and who touched off an international incident by attempting to subpoena then–Canadian Ambassador Allan Gotlieb, in violation of the norms of diplomatic protocol. When Starr recalled the incident, his dismay still seemed fresh: "There was, as I saw the litigation as a judge, what I felt was a mono-maniacal quality to this determination to get the facts no matter what." He added, only half jokingly, "Sound familiar?"[2]

Starr knew that he long ago captured whatever space in the public mind Seymour might ever have occupied as the poster boy for everything excessive and dangerous about the independent counsel law. It is an irony he described as "un-delicious."[3] For Starr believed his very sensitivity to the law's dangers helped make him an appropriate independent counsel in the first place. In fact, his goal when he became independent counsel — one he articulated even in retrospect with no

small passion — was "that we maintain balance, that we maintain perspective, that we would not go to the ends of the
earth, . . . that we would exercise, as best we could, prudent
judgment while being aggressive."[4]

Kenneth W. Starr believes he did that.

The contemporary debate about Starr and his investigation of President Clinton has become a competition among
caricatures, none of which accounts well for the awesome conflagration that enveloped this country's political culture for
more than a year. Both during and after his service, Starr was
that unusual public servant whose work was almost never evaluated soberly on its merits. Instead, among both his detractors
and his supporters, he became a symbol. Treating Starr as an
icon, of either good or evil, served the political needs of both
camps, because both sides wished to portray the drama that
led to Clinton's impeachment as a morality play. The dominant view, that of Clinton's defenders, saw the events of 1998
as an anticonstitutional revolt, in which the president's opponents deployed the American legal system as a weapon against
the president.[5] This narrative left no room for complexity in
the chief villain, except perhaps in the fashion that an Iago
or a Richard III can be complicated. Complexity could arise
only in the specific qualities of his evil. Starr's malevolence itself was never questioned. To hear Starr's critics describe him,
he represented a symbol of all that is intrusive and prurient
in a culture of scandal that reached its apex under his grin-
ning watch.

On the other side, Clinton's foes proved only too happy
to concur in portraying Starr as the stark antithesis of the
president — only in their narrative, he was riding a white horse
in defense of the rule of law. Starr's generally conservative
defenders made him into an emblem of virtue in a society,

typified by its president, that embraced situational ethics at the expense of truth. For them, Starr was the man who drew a line in the sand and insisted upon a limit even to Clinton's abuses of the law and morality. For them too, Starr was simple.

The trouble with both of these portrayals is that Starr's performance as independent counsel was not simple. The caricatures of him were politically convenient, but they were bad history, or, rather, not history at all. They represented, instead, a kind of cognitive shorthand for values and conduct we admire or abhor. In reality, the mixture of laudable and dangerous traits that constituted Starr's investigation do not distill easily into some sort of discernible archetype. To reduce him to a mythical figure of any kind is to overlook important aspects of his investigation — and, for that matter, of his character. To demonize him is to miss the fact that explanations for all of his actions, other than some nefarious political motivation, are readily available, and that his earnest sincerity makes any claim of improper motivation seem implausible in the extreme. To lionize him, by contrast, is to ignore, or to rationalize, the genuinely terrifying qualities of his investigation: its boundlessness and lack of perspective, its seeming removal from the norms under which federal prosecutors operate. Starr's great error, I shall argue, lay neither in his intentions nor in his motives nor in any specific misconduct, but in a far subtler failure of self-discipline in reading the statute he so hated. In several related respects, Starr fundamentally misunderstood his role as independent counsel.

The caricatures of Starr are, at this point, so entrenched, and the interests in maintaining them — both political and professional — so strong, that it is worth stepping back and scrutinizing them. The salient fact that emerges from such an exercise is just how much of the ink spilled on the subject of

Starr has been wasted. There were, to be sure, complex and rich portraits of the man by authors of varying degrees of sympathy for his project.[6] Far more common and influential, however, was work that repackaged the same handful of themes, which became accepted not through persuasive argumentation but as a result of endless repetition.

Three dominant themes make up the demonic caricature of Starr: first, that Starr was politically motivated, intent on bringing Clinton down at all costs; second, that he was at once puritanical and moralistic — using the criminal law to enforce a right-wing vision of sexual morality — yet simultaneously prurient and sex-obsessed; and third, that he was unethical as an attorney, both in that he allegedly had conflicts of interest and in that the specific conduct of his investigation violated rules of legal ethics. These themes often overlap, bleeding into one another and forming an indiscernible melange of Starr's supposed malevolence.

Incidences of the demonic caricature in the work of respected journalists, academics, and public intellectuals are too numerous to list. One example, a 1998 article in *The New York Review of Books* by the late Lars-Erik Nelson, illustrates well the interaction of all three of the major themes and shall serve to represent a class. The familiarity of both its tone and its facts — several of them false or highly misleading — testifies to the pervasiveness of the portrayal of Starr that the article presents:

> In his legal briefs, courtroom arguments, and exchanges of letters with opposing lawyers, Starr makes it clear that he plays under no known rules. First, he effectively answers to no one. Theoretically, the President or the Attorney General can fire him; politically, they cannot. He is not bound by federal guidelines on conflict of interest because he is an outside employee and therefore can represent, say, tobacco

and defense companies in their disputes with the federal government. He is not barred from using hearsay testimony or obliged to follow federal rules of evidence because he is gathering evidence for the Congress, which also need not follow standard rules of evidence. . . . Given [Starr's] disregard of the rules that most of us, especially non-lawyers like myself, believe protect us from arbitrary government, it is chilling that Starr, in his courtroom presentations against the President, is formally known as "the United States."

It is equally chilling to see Lewinsky stripped naked in these pages [of evidence, released by the House of Representatives]. Starr and his deputies probed literally into the deepest recesses of her mind and body.

Later in the same article, Nelson insisted that the thousands of pages of evidence released by the House was "most noteworthy for its sheer bulk, embodying the thousands of hours of investigative work, at a cost of $4 million, that Starr has devoted to proving that the President lied in Paula Jones's civil lawsuit. The effort seems wildly disproportionate to the offense, but makes sense if *Starr's goal was, in advance, to bring down the President at all costs*" (emphasis added). Nelson declared that "Starr's behavior throughout these four years — his appointment by a conservative three-judge panel, his continuing ties to tobacco companies, his speeches to right-wing audiences, his obvious and admitted leaks of secret grand jury information to the press, his threats to imprison uncooperative witnesses (plus the two-year detention of Clinton's onetime real estate partner, Susan McDougal) — deserve serious, impartial examination."[7]

Each of the themes is starkly stated: Starr was on a right-wing vendetta against Clinton; he was sex-obsessed and prurient; and he was willing to violate all known rules to get his man. Proponents of the demonic vision of Starr often seemed convinced they had tapped his mind and understood his purpose. "His abuses were driven by an obsessive — and, for a prosecutor, entirely inappropriate — determination to force President Clinton from office by any means available. That was the purpose of the leaks and of his grossly salacious impeachment report to the House," wrote *New York Times* columnist Anthony Lewis in October 1998.[8] It is hard to fathom how a journalist could so confidently make claims about Starr's motives in the absence of either Starr's or his confidantes' having verified the nefarious intentions being attributed to him. To the Starr-haters, however, those motives could simply be inferred from the totality of Starr's behavior. Their failure to justify their confidence speaks loudly, for despite its widespread acceptance, the demonic caricature always stood on weak footing. Indeed, none of its three constituent themes was ever persuasively demonstrated, and the purveyors of the caricature seldom even attempted to make a case for them.

The evidence that Starr harbored some improper political motivation, for example, was incredibly thin. Critics drew this conclusion on the basis of Starr's being a conservative and consorting with other conservatives, his having kept clients who had interests different from those of the Clinton administration, his having once consulted with Paula Jones's lawyers on the issue of temporary presidential immunity from civil suits, and his having conducted a particularly vigorous and intrusive investigation of the president. These facts taken together, however, far from supported the edifice built upon them. In our conversations, Starr at times displayed a certain contempt for Clinton. He made no secret of his shock and disapproval at how the White House responded to his investigation. His contempt for Clinton, however, was pedestrian, not the stuff of a political crusade, and his shock, in any event, postdated the advent of the alleged crusade. One cannot, of course, disprove the allegation of political motivation. Those of us who object to breezy claims about Starr's secret thoughts on the part of writers who could not possibly know them should not turn around and claim to know those thoughts ourselves. The case, however, was never made that Starr sought corruptly to depose the president because he disagreed with him politically. There is, quite simply, no evidence that Starr was acting in bad faith.

The depiction of Starr as a sex-obsessed puritan stood on weaker footing still. Starr's alleged sex obsession was promoted most famously by Maureen Dowd of *The New York Times*, in a September 1998 column whose clever construction made the reader believe its subject was the president:

> He couldn't stop thinking about the thong underwear. He couldn't believe Monica had pulled up her jacket to show it off. It so inflamed his imagination. At meetings, at briefings, at the most unlikely times, his mind suddenly reverted to the image of those straps, quickening his pulse, making him catch his breath.
>
> But it was the cigar that undid him. He was driven by the thought of what had been done with it. Suddenly the capital became a city of cigars. He saw them wherever he went. They ignited his desire. When he was alone or talking to other people, he took secret pleasure in letting smoke rings drift through his mind.

Only at the end of the article does Dowd let on that her target is not actually Clinton, but his prosecutor:

> His acolytes and subordinates became agents of shamelessness. It seemed that everyone around him, everyone in the city, everyone in the country, was talking about what he wanted to hear. All of them had become his collaborators in perversity. He was spending millions and millions of dollars to drag an entire nation down to his twisted level.
>
> He knew how strong he was. He was the most powerful man in the land. He could reach into every recess of the

Government to satisfy himself. And the prospect of impeachment didn't frighten him.

In fact, the more he fixated on the strap of that thong, the more certain he was that he could hang Bill Clinton with it. And, of all those naughty words he loved to hear, none filled him with more pleasure than "impeachment."

After all, nobody could impeach him. He was Ken Starr.[9]

Dowd's evocative writing and beautifully constructed argument disguised the fact that her thesis was completely fanciful.[10] To be sure, Starr investigated a matter related to President Clinton's sex life. He included many unnecessary sexual details in his referral to Congress, which then made those details public without his approval. In the course of his investigations, his prosecutors surely asked intrusive questions to witnesses, Lewinsky in particular. But as Richard Posner has argued, this is not necessarily evidence of an obsession with sex:

> It is no doubt the case, given his religious beliefs, that [Starr] disapproves of extramarital sex. But it is a bit much to argue that anyone who disapproves of extramarital sex must be a puritan, let alone that he must be obsessed with sex — a repressed pervert incapable of maintaining a professionally detached attitude in investigating conduct that involves sex. Nothing is known about Starr's personal life that would support such a theory; nothing in his marathon testimony before the House Judiciary Committee on November 19, 1998, or in his television interview by Diane Sawyer shortly afterward, was suggestive of sexual obsession.
>
> Even the gratuitous sexual details . . . in the Starr Report do not require a postulate of sexual obsession (or "mere" puritanism, or partisan zealotry) to explain.[11]

Posner proposes that the aggressiveness of the investigation derived from straightforward prosecutorial hardball, rather than sexual pathology on Starr's part. He then suggests that the attacks on Starr and his staff may have reinforced this inclination: "It is only speculation that Starr, whose demeanor is phlegmatic and who remained at least outwardly imperturbable throughout the ordeal (and it *was* his ordeal, as well as Clinton's), was furious [about the attacks], or that if he was this influenced his conduct of the investigation. It is, however, a much more plausible if less colorful speculation than that he is obsessed with sex. It is an especially plausible conjecture that his subordinates, feeling that their reputations as prosecutors were at stake, redoubled their efforts to "nail" Clinton. The harder they fought, the harder he and his supporters, some unscrupulous, fought back."[12]

Once one sheds the assumption that Starr was politically motivated, the silliness of the sex-obsession charge snaps into focus. Why would a man obsessed with sex spend years investigating complex bank-fraud allegations? Why, for that matter, would he have served for years on a court specializing in dense administrative law questions — time he might have better spent immersed in pornography? Accusing Starr of puritanical sex obsession merely reduced the evaluation of Starr to an ad hominem attack. Instead of isolating and analyzing what he may actually have done wrong, the argument simply labeled him a pervert.

The third claim — that Starr behaved unethically — is by its nature more easily tested than the various allegations about his motives. Starr's probe spawned numerous allegations of unethical conduct both on his part and on the part of his staff. A few, as of this writing, remain publicly unresolved, though these seem generally unconvincing. A comprehensive evaluation of the ethical claims against Starr may have to await their final public adjudication, if that ever happens. In the meantime, it is worth noting that none of the complaints that have been fully adjudicated have been found to have merit.

To start with the most famous alleged ethical infractions, Starr took a beating for supposedly leaking grand jury information, but to this day there exists not a single confirmed incident of a grand jury leak by Starr or his staff. I do not mean necessarily to vindicate the office of the charge of leaking grand jury information. Starr's office clearly talked to the press a great deal. Some of these contacts certainly crossed lines of propriety, and some of them could have crossed ethical or legal lines as well. Without convincing the reporters who ran stories about the grand jury's operations to reveal their sources, one simply cannot be certain. That said, the leaks charge was pretty clearly overblown. David Kendall, President Clinton's personal lawyer, accused Starr's office in 1998 of "a deluge of leaks" that violated "Rule 6(e) of the Federal Rules of Criminal Procedure, case law, Department of Justice Guidelines, rules of court and well-established ethical prohibitions,"[13] and went to court asking for a contempt citation against the office. Journalist Steven Brill, writing in the inaugural issue of his magazine *Brill's Content* later that year, contended that "Starr himself conceded to me that he . . . often talked to . . . reporters, and he has all but fingered [Deputy Independent Counsel Jackie Bennett Jr.] as 1998's Deep Throat. Moreover, his protestations that these leaks — or 'briefings,' as he calls them — do not violate the criminal law, and don't even violate Justice Department or ethical guidelines if they are intended to enhance confidence in his office or to correct the other side's 'misinformation,' is not only absurd, but concedes the leaks."[14]

Chief Judge Norma Holloway Johnson of the U.S. District Court for the District of Columbia adopted a sweeping interpretation of grand jury secrecy rules and, using it, found that "the serious and repetitive nature of disclosures to the media of Rule 6(e) material strongly militates in favor of conducting a show cause hearing" to determine if the office should be held in contempt.[15] She then appointed a special master, Senior Appeals Court Judge John Kern III, to investigate the charges.[16] The D.C. Circuit Court of Appeals, however, rejected her broad vision of the secrecy rules,[17] and Kern — whose report on the matter has never become public — reportedly did not find grand jury violations by the office, though he apparently did find inappropriate disclosures.[18] Two and a half years after her famous orders suggesting Starr had illegally leaked, Chief Judge Johnson — with the assent of both the office and Clinton's legal team — quietly dismissed the case.[19] It is reasonable to imagine that the record of this litigation, which is still sealed as of this writing, is unflattering to Starr and his staff, but the allegations of grand jury leaks appear to have petered out.

Ironically, the only serious leak ever credibly pinned on Starr's operation was tied to the independent counsel's office by the office itself. A *New York Times* story in January 1999 disclosed that Starr had concluded that he had the constitutional authority to indict the president before Clinton's term in office ended.[20] An internal investigation by the independent counsel's office traced some of the information in the story — which the D.C. Circuit later found, incidentally, not to involve grand jury information[21] — to Starr's then-spokesman, Charles Bakaly III. Bakaly had filed an affidavit denying that he had leaked the material in connection with the contempt proceedings before Chief Judge Johnson. Starr asked him to step down and also referred the matter of the affidavit to the Justice Department for possible criminal prosecution.[22]

The other ethical allegations against Starr are easier to dismiss. The suspicion that Starr's office acted in cahoots with Paula Jones's lawyers in an effort to entrap the president is unsupported factually. Starr's critics contended somewhat

vaguely that a group of conservative lawyers who were covertly working on Jones's case exploited ties to Starr's staff to
route Linda Tripp and her explosive story to the independent
counsel. This was, in general terms, true, but the story's details in no sense suggest any impropriety on the part of Starr
or the staff.[23] The critics' accusation, in any event, lapses at
that point into incoherence, with Starr somehow seeking to
induce the president to lie. The Justice Department examined
this and a number of other instances of alleged misconduct by
Starr, including the infamous initial hotel-room encounter
between Starr's office and Lewinsky. Around the time that
Starr stepped down, the department dismissed these allegations as not warranting Starr's removal from office. One specific question — whether the office's discussion of immunity
with Lewinsky in the absence of her attorney violated department rules — was referred back to the Office of Independent
Counsel for internal investigation.[24] In the same vein, special
investigative counsel Michael Shaheen Jr. found no merit to
the allegation that Starr's chief Whitewater witness, David
Hale, had been paid for testimony with money from right-
wing philanthropist Richard Mellon Scaife.[25] Moreover, in
May 2000, U.S. District Judge John Nangle refused to order
an inquiry into any of a long series of ethical complaints
against Starr brought by Connecticut lawyer Francis Mandanici. On Mandanici's contention that Starr had sought to
solicit false testimony from two of Starr's indictees, Julie Hiatt
Steele and Susan McDougal, Judge Nangle wrote, "there is
no support for the allegation that Starr or the OIC attempted
to solicit false testimony." On the charge that Starr had conflicts of interest with respect to Scaife and the offer to become
a dean at Pepperdine University, the judge scoffed: "This is
the stuff that dreams are made of. . . . This court has never
heard a more absurd argument." On the allegation that Starr

had a conflict of interest in investigating Whitewater because his law firm, Kirkland & Ellis, was sued by the Resolution Trust Corporation in connection with its representation
of a Colorado thrift, Judge Nangle — acknowledging that a
technical conflict may at one time have existed — held that,
"contrary to Mandanici's assertion, the evidence he presents
clearly indicates that there was no suggestion of bias or conflict in Starr's handling of the matter involving the RTC."
Judge Nangle also dismissed the allegation that Starr's ties to
the tobacco industry represented a conflict of interest, noting,
"The court finds this allegation to be nonsense."[26]

Even if one assumes that the common allegations against
Starr and his office have merit, there is no reason to think the
alleged infractions would have affected the direction the investigation ultimately took. If, for example, Starr's office did
leak grand jury information, it surely leaked nothing that was
not eventually disclosed more fully by the House of Representatives. In retrospect, would the course of the impeachment
have been different had it refrained? If anything, the allegations contained in the referral would likely have been more
shocking had they not been sketched out elaborately in the
press over the preceding months. Similarly, it is hard to imagine that President Clinton would have fared better had Starr's
team handled the initial encounter with Lewinsky differently.
The president's interests were served, not hindered, by the
manner in which the approach was made. Had things gone
differently, after all, Lewinsky might have ended up cooperating much sooner than she did and the president would not
have had so many months to gear up his defense machine. The
result of any hypothetical misconduct was only to prevent
Lewinsky from reaching an early agreement with the independent counsel, an agreement that would have been devastating for Clinton.

Ultimately, the demonic portrait of Starr presumes the truth of a series of allegations — some of which are demonstrably false and none of which is demonstrably true — and then assumes the most ungenerous possible motives for the alleged behavior. For those of us unwilling to claim insight into Starr's inner thoughts, the caricature is quintessentially nonfalsifiable. It fails completely, however, to explain the Starr investigation. A truly demonic independent counsel had many opportunities for mischief that Starr passed up — such as indicting the president or Mrs. Clinton or submitting an impeachment referral in 1997 concerning Whitewater.[27] The demonic portrait offers no good explanation for the many instances in which Starr displayed restraint.

An important variation of the demonic caricature painted Starr as a bumbling incompetent who, by virtue of having no prosecutorial experience, became a tool of his ill-motived staff. The intellectual benefit of this view was that Starr himself could be acquitted of the worst of the malfeasance, while his office could still be painted as unrelentingly villainous. This sleight of hand allowed for Starr's positive qualities without modifying the fundamental judgment of his work. In its more extreme forms, Starr himself appeared to be almost a victim of his handlers. By deflecting the demonization onto the staff, this vision of the office diffused the portrayal among several people and thereby avoided vesting unrealistic quantities of evil in a single human vessel.

This version was quite commonly accepted among officials of Janet Reno's Justice Department, where some of Starr's staff — particularly deputy independent counsel and department veteran Jackie Bennett Jr. — were deeply unpopular. *New Yorker* writer Jeffrey Toobin also promoted it famously in a best-selling book about the Clinton sex scandals. Toobin describes Starr as a dupe, a man who took over the

Whitewater investigation without knowing anything about criminal prosecution and who had the wrong people whispering in his ear. "Until he was hired by the Special Division to investigate the president of the United States, Starr had never prosecuted or defended a criminal case," Toobin writes. He was "a consummate Washington careerist who navigated the capital more by self-interest than by ideology. His defining attribute — more important even than his piety (which was real), his intelligence (which was considerable), or his energy (which was phenomenal) — was his ability to attract powerful mentors." Yet Starr was also a "committed political conservative" who, while "no ideologue himself . . . had always surrounded himself with them." That, according to Toobin, was what concerned then–Deputy Attorney General Philip Heymann when he considered asking Starr to be the Whitewater special prosecutor — the job that Attorney General Janet Reno eventually offered to Robert Fiske Jr.:

> No one doubted Starr's intelligence or his integrity. But Heymann also heard a warning: Look at the people around him. Starr was a man who had never prosecuted a case in his life. Someone would have to teach him the rules. As Heymann and anyone else with experience in the criminal justice system knew, many of these rules — about fairness, judgment, and proportionality — weren't written down, and some prosecutors followed them more closely than others. Starr would be more dependent than most potential prosecutors on the people he hired. More than almost any independent counsel in history, Starr's destiny would be in the hands of his staff.
>
> Where, Heymann worried, would Starr get his advice?[28]

Toobin's answer to this question was that, initially, he got it from "experienced, thoughtful lawyers who had worked as defense attorneys as well as prosecutors" and who "managed the investigation in the time-honored professional manner: begin by prosecuting the mid-level players, in the hope that they will turn against the top people." As the investigation proceeded, however, and the Whitewater probe lost steam, these people "did what veterans usually do in such circumstances. They gave up — or, to put it another way, they moved on. Because of their professional reputations and experience, the original Starr group had job opportunities in the private sector; they knew when it was time to quit. For better or worse, the case against the Clintons, they recognized, was over." The ones who remained, Toobin claims, "generally fell into one (or both) of two categories — the unemployable and the obsessed."[29] It was these people more than Starr himself, in Toobin's version, who harbored the dark political agendas.

This explanation of the investigation both was subtler than the demonic caricature and contained significant elements of truth. Starr is not shy about admitting that his lack of prosecutorial experience concerned him when he initially took over the probe and that he depended on the advice of his prosecutors.[30] This inexperience proved fateful in that, as I shall argue, he lacked the instincts to constrain himself narrowly to vindicating real prosecutorial interests. The course he took was one that a better-disciplined prosecutor would have instinctively resisted, and both his predecessor, Fiske, and his successor, Robert Ray, in fact pursued different and less ambitious approaches. The office did, in addition, change over time. The investigation had been winding down throughout late 1997, and a certain self-selection process took place, in which those who stayed on tended to be the prosecutors who were most committed to the investigation's hitting pay dirt, and who lacked first-class opportunities in the private sector. The prosecutors who headed the Lewinsky investigation — Jackie Bennett, Solomon Wisenberg, and Robert

Bittman — were surely a more aggressive lot than some of those who had handled earlier portions of the probe, people like John Bates and Mark Tuohey III. They were also considerably less respected in the Washington legal world. The average prosecutor in the office by 1998 was probably also more politically conservative than during earlier incarnations of the office, although such things cannot be measured precisely. It is a plausible hypothesis that the earlier staff would have handled the Lewinsky affair differently.

Starr's inexperience, however, only explains so much, and it is certainly wrong to assume that he was not in control of his investigation or that everything would have been different had the earlier staff stayed on. The earlier staff might well have done certain things differently. It might, for example, have thought more carefully than the later staff did before hauling White House aide Sidney Blumenthal before the grand jury to discuss his contacts with the press or before forcing Marcia Lewis to testify about her daughter's sex life. Though these investigative steps loomed large in the public mind, however, they were actually little more than window dressing on the probe. It is hard to imagine that Starr, had he been advised differently, would have declined jurisdiction over the Lewinsky matter, conducted a narrower investigation of it, or written his referral to Congress differently. These key decisions reflected Starr's own character and idiosyncratic priorities for his investigation. It, therefore, only makes sense that Starr has always displayed such comfort with them and has balked so vehemently at the idea that Bennett's accession to deputy independent counsel fundamentally changed the office. "Jackie did very well in our office. He was a go-to guy. There's no question," Starr said. "But to suggest that Jackie somehow, in contrast to John Bates or Mark Tuohey, was now entirely running the show, that judgments now were going to be made in a different way, I think frankly is unfair to the office. It's inaccurate. It's unfair to me."[31]

In Senate testimony, likewise, Starr insisted that "It is not true that I relied unduly or gave undue weight to the professional judgment of one or two prosecutors. I made these assessments myself. I'm responsible for them."[32] There is no reason to disbelieve him on this point. Indeed, Starr showed himself willing to reverse staff decisions with which he disagreed — as when he vetoed the immunity agreement that the office had worked out with Lewinsky's first lawyer, William Ginsburg, in February 1998.[33] Starr's modus operandi was to hold long meetings at which he heard the views of every member of his staff on important decisions — but, by most accounts, he made the final decisions himself. The staff, including its evolution in the latter stages of the investigation, ought to be seen as a reflection of Starr's priorities, which were themselves conditioned by his inexperience. While that inexperience surely contributed to his errors, the evidence suggests that his prosecutors were doing his will, not the other way around.

I have focused so far on the inadequacy of the arguments put forth by Starr's critics, because these together constitute by far the strongest voice in the public debate about his investigation. His defenders, however, also advanced a flawed image of Starr. Starr's admirers did not actually spend much energy defending him. The conservative press generally assumed his virtue and spent its time attacking Starr's attackers or dwelling on the president's misbehavior. That the criticisms of Starr were frivolous was, in this world, a given. Still, a clear image of Starr emerged, often in subtext or in passing references. To his admirers, Starr was, in every sense, the antithesis of Clinton: he was honest, faithful to duty and truth, and loyal to the rule of law. He was sincerely religious. He was a family man. By possessing all of these virtues — and by being reviled for possessing them — Starr revealed in its full ugliness the character of the man whom he investigated. *The Weekly Standard*, in an editorial in September 1998, rhapsodized, "What Kenneth Starr has done — suffering relentless White House assaults on his reputation with a dogged loyalty to mission that looks positively heroic in retrospect — is add a devastating measure of finality and weight and *obligation* to [Washington's] judgment against the president" (emphasis in original).[34] Robert Bork, speaking at a dinner in Starr's honor a year later, said that Starr "spread upon the record for all time the nature of the man who holds the office of president. And that is a salutary and important achievement — an important achievement for our democracy. A man has obligations to truth, to history, and to honor. Ken, you have discharged those obligations nobly, and in doing so you give full credit to your family and the rest of the Starrs in supporting you and making this possible."[35]

Starr's defenders, in short, made him into a martyr to the rule of law, and the religious quality of his martyrdom lay only barely beneath the surface. Bork, in one article, called him "the mildest and most judicious of men."[36] In the above-referenced speech, he joked that Starr "displays what can only be called — if the courts allow it — Christian charity in dealing with those who have told endless lies about him." In both the article and the speech, Bork portrayed Starr's mildness and generosity toward his critics as maddeningly decent, a way of highlighting that Starr, Christlike, turned the other cheek where a normal human would not. In the speech, for example, Bork said he had tried to display similar charity toward those who attacked Starr unfairly, but could not. "The closest I can come is this: I wish these folks no harm, but if they should ever feel an overwhelming desire to drown themselves, they need not hold back on my account."[37]

Among the purest and most developed examples of the hagiographic image of Starr is a September 1998 editorial in *The Wall Street Journal* that began by asking, "Who better to bring Bill Clinton to justice than a hymn-singing son of a fundamentalist minister?" The *Journal* noted Starr's impressive legal credentials and stated that liberal opinion has found something "off-putting and reprehensible" about him. "What something? We would go so far as to suggest that the 'something' about Ken Starr that so rubbed many opinion-makers the wrong way was the clear understanding that he was not just prosecuting Bill Clinton; he was prosecuting the entire culture that gave birth to what Bill Clinton represents." The editorial went on to mock the criticisms of Starr and portray him as a living rebuke to his foes:

> He wasn't "fair," they said. . . . Mr. Starr wasn't very "nice." In short, he isn't one of us.
>
> That's for sure. Quick case in point: He never aspired to be dean of, say, Yale Law School; instead, he desired, and was vilified for, preferring Pepperdine — wherever that is. What the Pepperdine episode showed was that Mr. Starr really was not at all part of the world his critics lived in and dominated.
>
> These, of course, are the same two worlds that now compete for primacy in American politics. One pleads for re-establishing commonly held rules of the road. The other insists that social and moral diversity has rendered such commonality impossible — and, as they like to add, get used to it.

The ultimate point was that Starr's character is the opposite of Clinton's. He is a man for whom values are absolute and who has not allowed 1960s relativism to erode the sanctity of moral values and the rule of law:

What drives him, we are inclined to say, is nothing more complicated than a sense of political and legal duty.

In the world Mr. Starr represents the law does not "spin"; it stands still, at its best defending civilized behavior against moral chaos. Throughout the Clinton investigations, Mr. Starr was, in effect, asked repeatedly to let it go, to accept the chaos of one President's turbulent life. He said no.[38]

Starr's defenders converted him, in other words, from a prosecutor and investigator into a symbol of resistance to moral decline and relativism.

It was, of course, a conversion that no reasonable prosecutor could have embraced. The *Journal* could adopt an adulatory tone toward this supposedly larger function or effect of the Starr investigation, but its portrayal of Starr as a fighter in a larger culture war was only the mirror image of the notion that Starr harbored some sort of political motivation. Were it true, it would be altogether damning, no subject for praise. There is, however, no evidence to support this notion, and Starr, of course, would be the last to concede that his investigation had aims beyond examining the subjects within his mandate, let alone the prosecution of an entire culture.

More to the point, the sanctification of Starr ignored those aspects of his investigation that were genuinely troubling and raised issues toward which conservatives had, in other contexts, displayed considerable sensitivity. One might expect that those who had so railed against Lawrence Walsh for his pursuit of minor figures in the Iran-Contra scandal might have been concerned by the prosecution of Julie Hiatt Steele, a Richmond woman with only the most marginal of connections to the Lewinsky scandal.[39] Those conservatives who once fretted about fraying the unity of the executive branch by letting a figure unaccountable to the president supervise prosecutions seemed not to mind when Starr effectively ran an independent branch of government that was increasingly at odds with the executive branch of which it was nominally a part. They hardly blinked when he repeatedly sought information that he could get only by curtailing presidential confidentiality with respect to Clinton's most intimate advisers and guardians. Those who had so presciently warned about the capacity of the independent counsel law to warp law enforcement priorities seemed often gleeful at the horrific invasions of privacy that the Lewinsky investigation inflicted. Making Starr into a symbol of virtue presented hardly less of an impediment to understanding what really happened during his investigation than did demonizing him. At a human level, the portrayal was unrealistic. At a historical level, it left us no answer to the question of why the Starr investigation so viscerally offended so many Americans.

The challenge of evaluating Starr is reconciling the truths for which the demonizers and hagiographers cannot account and asking how an ethical lawyer with good intentions could nonetheless have produced such a terrifying probe. Even Starr candidly admits that the Lewinsky investigation was dreadful: "The whole thing was horrible for everyone, and you couldn't tune out. . . . Everyone was just saying, 'Please, do we have to have this? Do we have to have an investigation? Do we have to have twenty-four-hour news coverage? Do we have to have' — as it was called at the U.S. courthouse — 'Monica Beach?' "[40] Starr's own efforts to reconcile his belief in the fundamental virtuousness of his investigation with its troubling results are, however, only minimally persuasive. When pressed, Starr always described the three-ring circus his investigation became as beyond his control, either a result of the president's malfeasance or someone else's folly, or an inevitable consequence of the independent counsel statute. Starr's point has some merit.

To a certain extent, the die was cast the moment a prosecutor — using some of the president's own powers — set out to
investigate a specific allegation against a president who sought
to prevent the truth of that allegation from becoming known.
The situation so inherently tests the governmental structure
the Constitution envisions that it almost guarantees a major
conflagration.

In convincing himself that everything that seemed awry
about his investigation was simply an inevitable outgrowth of
the independent counsel law, however, Starr ignores his own
role as interpreter of that law. Indeed, it was in his interpretations of the statute that Starr's original sin lay. For even if Starr
was not a politically motivated or unethical zealot, his fundamentally radical vision of the role of the independent counsel
pushed his investigation toward ever-greater aggressiveness.
A striking feature of Starr's tenure, in fact, was that for a man
who understood so well the dangers of the independent counsel law, he nonetheless repeatedly interpreted the statute in
fashions that heightened, rather than minimized, its ill effects.
Instead of seeking to soften the law through readings that filed
off its rough edges, Starr submitted to its excesses in a fashion that seemed positively passive-aggressive. In retrospect,
whether talking about the timing and style of his impeachment referral to Congress, his decision to continue doing legal work for private clients, or some of the invasive steps his
investigators took, Starr has portrayed himself as the slave of a
law that, in reality, made him master of many more fates than
his own.

No less an authority on life as a reviled independent counsel than Lawrence Walsh fingered Starr's grandiose understanding of his role as peculiar shortly after the Lewinsky
scandal broke. Deep in an essay about Starr, Walsh wrote in
March 1998 that "Starr's activity . . . is not consistent with that

of a professional prosecutor. Perjury cases are difficult. Regularly appointed prosecutors generally eschew perjury prosecutions except when the perjury blocks a criminal investigation. They avoid intrusion into civil litigation and they are very wary of being drawn into private civil litigation concerning conflicting claims of sexual activity. Starr's somewhat sanctimonious pronouncement at his recent press conference that he was interested in 'truth' seems to reveal an overblown conception of his responsibility."[41] Walsh mentioned only in passing this idea that Starr had somehow misconceived his role as a search for truth; he appeared not to have attached a great deal of analytical importance to the point. Walsh's observation, however, was actually quite profound, and, unlike the demonic caricatures of Starr, it offered considerable insight into why the Starr investigation proceeded as it did. In fact, when I finally asked Starr about his vision of the statute, he effectively declared that he did not believe he ever was, first and foremost, a prosecutor at all. Critics have long accused him of behaving like a kind of minister of truth. Starr, it turned out, did not really dispute this description. He contended, rather, that it encapsulated the true nature of the office Congress created.

The troubles with Starr's view of his role, I shall argue, were myriad. At the level of statutory construction, it was an ahistorical conception of the independent counsel law that finds little support in the statute's text and cannot reasonably be reconciled with its legislative history either. Despite Starr's strenuous — and I believe sincere — efforts to frame his vision as a disinterested reading of congressional will, his reading was rooted instead in the character of a man profoundly offended by lies and in whose pantheon of social goods, truth seems to loom larger even than justice. It was an understanding that recast the law — and the prosecutorial process along with it — in his own image.

In practical terms, Starr's vision led to all sorts of mischief that — particularly in combination with Clinton's own obstructionism — had profound, if subtle, consequences for the fate of the Clinton presidency. Reading the law as authorizing an inquest more akin to Archbishop Desmond Tutu's South African Truth and Reconciliation Commission than to a typical federal criminal investigation caused Starr to distort his investigative priorities far beyond the distortion that the statute itself actually compelled. Truth commissions, such as the South African one, are a complicated undertaking, and it is not my intention in these pages to evaluate their merits. It is important to understand, however, that a truth commission is, both in theory and in operation, profoundly different from the normal prosecutorial project. Most important, the truth commission generally offers amnesty in exchange for truth, thereby clearly resolving any confusion between the competing aims of justice and disclosure in favor of the latter. The independent counsel law, I shall argue, makes no such judgment. In contrast to Starr's understanding, in fact, the legislative judgment that lay behind the statute was the insistence that a conventional criminal probe against high-level executive branch officials, one oriented toward punishing crimes, was both possible and desirable. At key junctures, however, Starr took fateful steps not for such traditional prosecutorial reasons as to punish wrongdoing, but to reach some reified notion of the truth, a project more typically the province of journalists and historians than prosecutors. Starr did this despite the discomfort of some members of his staff, who did not believe that the statute implied a truth-seeking function. By pushing the goals and, consequently, the behavior of his office away from prosecutorial normalcy, Starr's vision magnified the separation-of-powers problems inherent in the law. His vision also encouraged the independent counsel's office to become increasingly inward-looking, and to focus on prosecuting people for alleged failures to cooperate fully with its search for truth. Starr's vision, thereby, had the perverse effect of creating a class of crimes against truth that became focal to the independent counsel as the investigation wore on, but which would have been exceedingly marginal to a prosecutor chiefly interested in punishing crimes in the real world. My point is not to disparage the pursuit of truth, which is surely as noble a pursuit as exists in the world. It is, rather, that the pursuit of truth for its own sake is a project different from — though related to — that of the prosecutor, for whom truth is an instrument toward justice, not an end in itself. The confusion of the two roles — prosecutor and truth-seeker — gravely altered and, I shall argue, ultimately compromised Starr's mission.

Starr's story is ultimately one of self-fulfilling prophecy, of how Starr's deep belief in the statute's evil helped blind him to the ways in which he could have ameliorated that evil. For in the end, as we shall see, Starr's great error was in divesting himself of the discretion to behave with discretion. Though Starr denies it, a more modest reading of the law was possible, a reading that would have been more in keeping with Congress's original intent in passing the statute, and that would have given Starr greater flexibility to behave with restraint.

CHAPTER 2

Taming the Statute

"I think someone with the power the [independent counsel's] office
confers should have a tolerance for the idea that you cannot rectify all
the wrongs in the world; you can't pursue all the leads that come to
you; and you've got to have the courage to close the investigation in
spite of the fact that just when you're ready to close it, you get a letter
from somebody who says that he has the goods on your man — he's got
the goods and he will produce a woman in your office 10:30 tomorrow
morning to blow this investigation wide open.

"That's after you've been in office for, let's say, three months.

"And suppose he's got the goods.

"Well, he's got you, but you've got to have the courage to say, 'We're
through, we're closing down.'"

FORMER INDEPENDENT COUNSEL JACOB STEIN, 1997

The public's suspicions about Kenneth Starr, which began
almost immediately upon his appointment in 1994, lend in
retrospect some sense of inevitability to his subsequent behavior. Starr attracted this skepticism chiefly because of the
peculiar circumstances of his appointment: the sudden sack-
ing of the well-regarded Robert Fiske Jr. following the infamous lunch between Judge David Sentelle, the presiding
judge on the special court that names independent counsels,
and conservative senators Jesse Helms and Lauch Faircloth.[1]
To make matters worse, Starr had taken a public position
against presidential immunity from civil actions — then the

pressing question in the Paula Jones suit—and had, at the
time of his appointment, been considering filing an amicus
brief in the case on behalf of a conservative women's group.
Such activities, combined with his conservative politics and
service in the previous two Republican administrations, exac-
erbated the perception that the court was stacking the deck
against the president. Within days of praising his appointment, *The New York Times* was calling for Starr's resignation,
picking up on the suggestion of the president's civil lawyer,
Robert Bennett.[2] The mini-firestorm helped mark Starr in
the public mind as a potential partisan troublemaker.[3]

It also, however, distorted Starr's actual reputation at the
time. In truth, few in the legal world then dissented from
the belief that Kenneth W. Starr was a judicious, fair-minded,
and relatively moderate conservative, whose tenure on the
bench had been that of a conciliator on a divided court and
whose service as solicitor general had been respectable. As
legal journalist Stuart Taylor Jr. had written in 1993, before
the controversy surrounding the appointment, Starr "is liked
and respected, with an extraordinary degree of unanimity,
by lawyers and judges of all political stripes all across the
country—among them, most (and perhaps all) of the justices
of the Supreme Court."[4] Starr was sufficiently well-regarded
that, only a few months before becoming independent counsel, his service to the Senate ethics committee in reviewing the
diaries of Senator Bob Packwood, who was then under investigation for sexual misconduct, was entirely uncontroversial.[5]
Whatever may be said in retrospect, nothing in Starr's background suggested recklessness. To the contrary, his views
about executive power and his attitude toward the independent counsel law itself both indicated that Starr would be a
cautious special prosecutor keen to avoid running amok.

Starr came to Washington at the beginning of the Reagan

administration as counselor to then–Attorney General William French Smith, with whom he had previously practiced law. These were heady days for conservatives, and among the young conservative lawyers the Reagan years brought to Washington, the rehabilitation of traditional executive powers was a cause of its own. Watergate and Vietnam had spurred Congress to try to rein in the imperial presidency, and the result had been the rise of increasingly aggressive congressional oversight, extensive executive branch reporting requirements, and a series of laws—the War Powers Resolution, for example—that directly insinuated Congress into executive decision-making. "There was this sense when we came into office in the Justice Department that the president's prerogatives . . . had been badly diminished. And we were a bit Hamiltonian [and believed] that these incursions into the rightful province of the president should be resisted," Starr recalled. "One of the points in the Federalist Papers that was very much part of our breath was the Madisonian insight about each branch being given the prerogatives or the incentives and the [means] to resist encroachments by the other branches. And so we would say [that] we at the Justice Department have to protect the prerogatives of the executive branch and the dignity of the executive branch. . . . We should be able, within our province, to carry on our work."[6]

Starr remembered the battles of that era the way combat veterans reminisce about their tours of duty. He talked, for example, with evident pride about the stand Smith's Justice Department took in opposition to the legislative veto—the then-common practice under which a single house of Congress used to stop executive agency actions. Reagan's policy staffers saw the legislative veto as a weapon against the federal bureaucracy and regulation generally, Starr recounted. Their theory was that "we've got these agencies out here burdening

the American economy. If we can get some subcommittee to
overrule those regulations, to veto them, that's terrific." The
department, however, had long regarded the legislative veto as
unconstitutional, and when a regulatory reform proposal arose
that contained a legislative veto provision, Smith saw it as his
duty to defend the executive branch's prerogatives even at the
expense of Reagan's policy priorities. "The attorney general
personally studied [and] looked at it — and he wasn't just reading memos. [He] personally wrestled with this. I was studying
it. I was wrestling with it. And he came to the view that the
Justice Department's traditional position was correct as a matter of constitutional law. And he goes over and he tells the
president, 'Mr. President. You need to veto this law, because it
contains a legislative veto.' " Reagan's political advisers, Starr
recalled, "went ballistic." The president, they pointed out, had
campaigned on regulatory reform and had supported the legislative veto. Reagan, however, unequivocally backed up his attorney general. As Starr recounted with undisguised admiration, he told his advisers simply that "the attorney general has
concluded that it's unconstitutional. That's it. That's the end of
it."[7] In 1983, the Supreme Court struck down the legislative
veto in the case of *INS v. Chadha*, a decision Starr still remem-
bers with relief and a considerable measure of vindication.[8]

To someone of Starr's executive-power sensibilities, the
independent counsel law was especially offensive. By giving
judges the authority to appoint prosecutors, it deprived the
president — through the attorney general — of power over a
core function of the executive branch: the investigation and
prosecution of crimes. It created a prosecutor who did not
answer to the rest of the executive branch hierarchy and who
could not be dismissed at the whim of the president. Starr's
personal involvement with the statute began when it came up
for renewal early in the Reagan administration, and he helped

formulate the administration's opposition to its reauthorization. Starr's objections to the statute at that time were, as he put it, grounded in a "formalistic approach" to the separation of powers: Congress simply cannot deprive the president of law enforcement powers, judges generally cannot appoint prosecutors, and executive officials must be removable by the president. The Justice Department's position, Starr said, was driven both by these concerns and, more generally, by the same sensibility that animated the opposition to the legislative veto. The objections were "born not just from constitutional theory but [from] a sense that there was a growing and noteworthy imbalance in the structure of government as between Congress and the executive and that we had to stand up and be counted."[9]

By the time the law was actually challenged, Starr was on the bench, serving as a judge on the D.C. Circuit Court of Appeals. The D.C. Circuit heard the case that later went to the Supreme Court as *Morrison v. Olson*, but Starr did not take part in the decision.[10] The man challenging the law, former Reagan Justice Department official (and current solicitor general) Theodore Olson, was a close friend, so Starr would have recused himself had he been assigned to the case. He followed the case with interest, however, and was distressed when the Supreme Court ultimately upheld the law, particularly so by the fact that Chief Justice William Rehnquist—whom he had long regarded as a comrade-in-arms in the battle to restore executive power—wrote the opinion.[11] "I would have thought that, at a minimum, the chief would have been in dissent, that he would not have authored this almost painfully balancing, analytically unrigorous opinion [that] simply identif[ies] the arguments and then . . . say[s] almost in *ipse dixit* form, 'Well, we're not satisfied that that is enough of an intrusion [into presidential powers] in order to invalidate the statute,'" he

recalled, using the Latin term for an assertion that is made but
not proven. Rehnquist's conclusion that the encroachment on
executive power was — as Starr caricatured it — "not that big
of a deal" was particularly premature, Starr believed, because
the case did not deal with an investigation of the president
personally. Starr correctly suspected that the law's encroachment on presidential powers "could at any moment prove to
be an enormous deal when it goes to a high visibility investigation of the president himself."[12]

Seeing the conduct of the independent counsels whom
the law spawned only magnified Starr's distrust of the statute.
In our conversations, Starr carefully avoided criticizing Iran-
Contra prosecutor Lawrence Walsh, on whom he said he had
trouble passing judgment. He displayed no such courtesy,
however, toward Whitney North Seymour Jr., the man who
prosecuted Michael Deaver and tried to subpoena Canadian
Ambassador Allan Gotlieb. Starr described this incident as the
"monomaniacal pursuit of prosecutorial goals at the expense
of other important goals," and he expressed dismay at the
degree to which Seymour's tactics trampled on other important governmental interests. The attempt to force Ambassador Gotlieb's testimony, he said, "put the State Department
into fits and paroxysms of anger and outrage. The Canadian
government, at the very highest levels, was expressing more
than concern, a sense of genuine diplomatic anger."[13] Watching how the statute worked in practice only convinced Starr
that his formalistic approach toward the separation of powers
had been right, that bad structure had yielded bad results.

For those who feared runaway independent counsels,
Starr's sensitivity to the problems the law created for the
executive branch — both at an analytical and at a practical
level — ought to have been reassuring. When he took over the
Whitewater investigation, of course, these concerns were not

widely known, though they are hardly surprising given his conservative pedigree. Still, all things considered, Starr's attitude toward the statute — specifically, his deep sensitivity to its design flaws — seemed nearly ideal for service under it and should have enabled him to avoid the pitfalls into which his predecessors had fallen. This was certainly Starr's goal. "If there is one thing that my background lends itself to, it's the creation of careful procedures and structures that will safeguard against that no-no in governmental life, . . . arbitrary and capricious governmental action," he told me.[14] Indeed, well into his tenure, even long after the attacks against him had begun, thoughtful observers who looked closely at the investigation were impressed that he was doing just that. Legal journalist Jeffrey Rosen, writing as late as 1997, noted,

> Overextended or not, Starr has assembled an able staff of conscientious prosecutors in Little Rock and Washington. There is, for those attuned to these anthropological distinctions, a difference in prosecutorial culture between Starr's staff and that hired by his Whitewater predecessor. Robert Fiske had assembled a group in which former Federal prosecutors from New York were heavily represented; Starr's younger prosecutors are more likely to have roots in Washington and to be former Supreme Court clerks and members of the conservative Federalist Society.
>
> But it would be wrong to conclude that Starr's office is a simmering caldron of partisan enthusiasm, determined to bring down the President. The Federalist Society culture is suspicious of the independent counsel on principled, constitutional grounds and is resolved not to repeat the excesses of Lawrence Walsh. This helps to explain why Starr has set up such an elaborately deliberative pre-indictment review process, in which every lawyer in the office sits around a large conference table (the Little Rock staff often listens in by conference call) to debate the merits of every potential indictment.[15]

Rosen here has briefly and aptly summarized Starr's strategy for ensuring that he remained under control. Starr's idea was that Seymour and his ilk had gone astray by focusing too narrowly on the immediate needs of their investigations. He, by contrast, would create an office whose depth of experience would enable his staff to mimic the decision-making process of the Justice Department, which factors the government's nonprosecutorial interests into its investigative and prosecutorial decisions. By creating what he termed a "microcosm of the Justice Department," Starr believed he could avoid the loss of perspective that plagued his predecessors.

He sought, as he later described, to "build in structures that [would] reflect, in essence, the Justice Department at its very best." This included the elaborate pre-indictment review process to which Rosen referred, which was designed to ensure that the independent counsel's office was not subjecting its targets to a different standard of justice than normal federal prosecutors would employ. Starr described this process as "a very collegial and quite egalitarian agora where individuals [were] given standing in our office to speak up and to say, 'I have this problem and that other problem,' even though they were . . . not on the trial team [and] they [didn't] know the case all that well." Starr also sought to staff his investigation with people whose backgrounds would reflect the experience and concerns of the prosecutors within the department. Though Starr's staff was much criticized — as too aggressive, as too Republican, and as bumbling — in Starr's description, his prosecutors sounded like the very model of professionalism: "I said, 'I want the best prosecutors I can find and I know who they are. And I'm going to go after them.' So I had two [Justice Department] John Marshall Award winners. I had corruption unit chiefs. I had people with very elaborate experience and demonstrated records of success. I said, 'I want people who are respected by the judges before whom they try cases and who have a demonstrated record of success in front of juries.' "16

Starr's strategy was probably flawed on its own terms, since the creation of a real microcosm of the Justice Department is virtually impossible. Starr's pre-indictment review process was, to be sure, rigorous and serious. The pre-indictment review process in complex cases brought by Main Justice, however, is multilayered and infused with the institutional memory of long-serving career officials. Under the best of circumstances, this is extremely difficult to replicate in an ad hoc office, and as Starr's experience showed, the independent counsel law is far from the best of circumstances. The self-selection process involved in the assembly of an independent counsel's staff does not lend itself to re-creating the diversity of concerns that the full staff of the Justice Department displays. Republicans tended to be more interested in investigating Clinton than Democrats, and those who disliked Clinton most were apt to stick around the longest. That meant that, particularly as the investigation wore on, the office — always with notable exceptions — tended to be increasingly monochromatic politically and increasingly dominated by the more aggressive prosecutors. There is nothing intrinsically wrong with either of these tendencies. No mathematical formula, after all, can pinpoint some magic mean of aggressiveness in a prosecutorial office. Starr's shop was, to boot, not the first special prosecutor's office to be composed predominantly of members of one political party. Such political composition is arguably, in fact, in keeping with the history and purpose of the independent counsel statute. It does not, however, make for a microcosm of the Justice Department.

Even if one accepts that Starr succeeded in creating and maintaining such a microcosm, his vision was still woefully incomplete for a man who believed the law to be as dangerous as Starr did. Assembling a good, thoughtful staff ought to be a given, something any independent counsel would want to do. It provides no layer of assurance to the public that citizens ought not expect from any government office. Similarly, a rigorous pre-indictment review is hardly the sort of additional check that would prevent an independent counsel from going astray. The independent counsel is, under the law, generally obligated to follow Justice Department policies and proce-dures.[17] Having some process by which people familiar with departmental practice thrash out whether a particular indict-ment is warranted seems more like a baseline than an unusual layer of protection against a dangerous law.

In reality, as Starr well knows, the statute itself invites excess. Because of the awesome power and lack of oversight the law grants them, independent counsels who want — as Starr badly wanted — to avoid becoming a law unto them-selves have to interpret the law in a fashion that lessens its impact and intrusiveness. Consider, for example, the com-ments of Jacob Stein, quoted at the outset of this chapter. Stein served as one of the independent counsels for Edwin Meese III, and his tenure is widely regarded as among the most judicious and responsible investigations to take place under the law. Speaking at the Fourth Circuit's Judicial Con-ference in 1997, Stein said, "My experience is that I had un-limited authority as an independent counsel. . . . I had no limits. I was astonished at the authority I had, and I felt it was a personal test of my own sanity in the exercise of that author-ity. . . . I had more authority than anybody should have. I was reviewing myself." His response, he said, was to focus nar-rowly on the matter he had been assigned — even to the point of ignoring other information that the FBI presented to the investigators. The idea, he said, quoting Italo Calvino, was to avoid approaching his investigation like a novelist for whom "the least thing is seen as the center of a network of relationships that the [investigator] cannot restrain himself from following, multiplying the details, so that his descriptions and digressions become infinite. Whatever the starting point, the matter in hand spreads out and out, encompassing ever vaster horizons, and if it were permitted to go further and further in every direction, it would end by embracing the entire universe."[18] In other words, only by interpreting the wide discretion the law gave him as authorizing him to ignore matters that might arise could Stein beat the statute into some sort of uneasy submission.

Starr, however, made no effort to tame the law itself. Paradoxically, the same hard-line separation-of-powers purism that made him so hostile to it in the first place also committed him (in his own mind, anyway) to enforcing it rigorously. No matter how much he disagreed with it, he explained, "I respected the Supreme Court's resolution of the issue and the fact that it was so overwhelming and that the voice of the court was the voice of the chief justice."[19] At another interview, he stressed that the "clear delineation between those who articulate the law and those who simply execute the law" is "my mother's milk professionally." In accepting the position of independent counsel, he became "a creature of the statute, [with] a duty to accept this obligation that this statute imposes. . . . I am to execute it, and I should not be engaged in a quasi-judicial function of narrowing what seems so clearly to be my responsibilities as outlined by the attorney general of the United States and the Special Division. It would be . . . a form of a partial veto."[20]

This may sound principled in theory, but it is also impossible in practice. The independent counsel law was so poorly written that it inevitably required interpretations with

a legislative feel from the special prosecutors serving under it.
Starr himself amended the statute through interpretation
many times. One particularly poignant example was when he
submitted a report on the death of White House lawyer Vincent Foster Jr. Starr conceded that "there is no provision [in
the law] for a non-final report," yet he submitted one anyway
because "the exigencies were such that we needed to get that
report out." Starr said he could only "thank goodness" that
nobody had standing to challenge his move or the Special
Division's decision to accept the report.[21] Given the suspicions among conservatives that Foster had been murdered,
Starr probably made the right call in releasing an interim
report on the case. It is hard to square the admittedly extratex-
tual rule of necessity he and the Special Division crafted for
that circumstance, however, with his protestations that any
unilateral softening of the statute on his part would have been
a usurpation of congressional legislative power. Starr had no
choice but to fill in the gaps in the law. His trouble was not
that he did so, but that — with certain exceptions, of which the
Foster report was one — he tended to push the law in exactly
the wrong direction. Instead of adopting interpretations that
would allow him to coexist more easily with the executive
branch, he adopted interpretations that pushed his investigation toward ever-mounting confrontation.

Before evaluating Starr's understanding of the statute, it
is worth describing in some detail the independent counsel
mechanism itself. The independent counsel law, until it lapsed
in 1999, required the attorney general to conduct a ninety-
day "preliminary investigation" whenever confronted with
specific information from a credible source alleging a crime —
other than a Class B or C misdemeanor — by an official covered by the act.[22] The attorney general was required to decide whether or not to open such a preliminary investigation

within thirty days of receiving the allegations.[23] The group of people covered by the law included the president, the vice president, the chairman and treasurer of the president's campaign committee, and a raft of senior administration officials, as well as former officials who had left government within the previous year.[24] In addition to the mandatory trigger, the law gave the attorney general discretion to launch a preliminary investigation against noncovered persons "when the Attorney General determines that an investigation or prosecution of a person by the Department of Justice may result in a personal, financial, or political conflict of interest."[25] The attorney general was also authorized to open an inquiry against a member of Congress upon determining "that it would be in the public interest" to do so.[26] If a preliminary investigation was opened, the attorney general then had "no authority to convene grand juries, plea bargain, grant immunity, or issue subpoenas" during the course of that investigation.[27] The preliminary investigation could be extended once for sixty days.[28] After that, however, the statute required the attorney general to seek an independent counsel unless he or she concluded that there were "no reasonable grounds to believe that further investigation is warranted."[29] The attorney general was barred from determining that no reasonable grounds existed for further investigation on the basis that the subject of the preliminary investigation lacked criminal intent, unless there was "clear and convincing evidence that the person lacked such state of mind."[30] If the attorney general declined to seek an independent counsel, moreover, the law required that an explanation be given.[31] The judiciary committee of either house of Congress or a majority of committee members of either party were permitted to request that the attorney general seek an independent counsel, and the attorney general was, in such circumstances, required to file a report on whether or not he had

opened a preliminary investigation in response to the information they submitted.[32]

Once the attorney general determined that further investigation was warranted following the preliminary investigation, the law required him to apply to a special division of the
U.S. Court of Appeals for the D.C. Circuit for the appointment of an independent counsel.[33] The law granted the court
wide discretion to name "any individual who has appropriate
experience and who will conduct the investigation and any
prosecution in a prompt, responsible, and cost-effective manner," as long as that person does not hold "any office of profit
or trust under the United States."[34] The Special Division was
further authorized to define the prosecutor's mandate and was
instructed to "assure that the independent counsel has adequate authority to fully investigate and prosecute the subject
matter with respect to which the Attorney General has requested the appointment of the independent counsel," and all
matters related to that subject matter.[35] The Special Division
could, on a request of the attorney general, expand the jurisdiction of an independent counsel.[36] It was also empowered to
replace independent counsels who died or resigned or were
removed from office.[37] The court was permitted to award
attorneys' fees to subjects of an independent counsel investigation whose fees would not have been incurred but for their
having been investigated by an independent counsel, as opposed to a normal federal prosecutor.[38]

Once an independent counsel investigation commenced,
the Justice Department was obliged to suspend "all investigations and proceedings" regarding the matters in question.[39]
Independent counsels were given, with limited exceptions,
"full power and independent authority to exercise all investigative and prosecutorial functions and powers of the Department of Justice, the Attorney General, and any other of-

ficer or employee of the Department of Justice."[40] They were entitled to assemble a staff and to "appoint, fix the compensation, and assign the duties of such employees as such independent counsel considers necessary."[41] They were entitled, on request, to assistance from the Justice Department, including the detailing of departmental personnel to their offices.[42] They were also entitled to request that the Special Division or the attorney general refer to them matters related to their jurisdiction.[43] They were required to "comply with the written or other established policies of the Department of Justice," but not if "to do so would be inconsistent with the purposes" of the independent counsel statute.[44] They had authority to dismiss matters without conducting a probe if doing so would be consistent with departmental practice.[45] They also had a variety of reporting obligations: expenditure reports to be filed every six months, annual reports to Congress on their activities, a final report before termination of their offices, and the obligation of referring to Congress any information that might constitute grounds for an impeachment.[46] Congress gave itself oversight jurisdiction over independent counsel investigations.[47] It also permitted the attorney general to remove an independent counsel "for good cause," although it required a report from the attorney general justifying such dismissals and it gave the independent counsel judicial review of any removal action.[48] Finally, the act allowed the office to be terminated either when the independent counsel determined that he or she was done and filed a final report or when the Special Division decided that the office's work was substantially done and could be taken over by the Justice Department.[49] The statute, at least on its face, says nothing about truth.

The interpretive excess that lay at the heart of Starr's problem, however, was his understanding of the very nature and purpose of the independent counsel statute itself. Within the statute exists an embedded tension between a vision of the independent counsel as a prosecutor like any other and a vision of the independent counsel as a kind of one-person truth commission. On one side of the equation, Congress required that independent counsels follow the Justice Department's policies and evinced clear concern during its various debates over the statute's reauthorization that targets of independent counsel probes not be subjected to tougher standards of justice than those applied to targets of other criminal investigations. On the other side is the structure of the law, which asks the prosecutors to look at a single issue, gives them unlimited time and resources to address it, and then requires them to file a report at the end. The conventional approach to this tension — at least in theory — is to resolve it in favor of behaving like a traditional prosecutor with a somewhat peculiar obligation to write a report at the end of the probe. In practice, the truth commission vision risks insinuating itself into the conduct of investigations, largely as a consequence of the final report requirement.

Acknowledging as a regrettable reality that the statute subtly encourages prosecutors to behave like truth commissioners, however, is very different from embracing the notion that the truth commission side of the spectrum should *properly* dominate the prosecutorial side. Starr, however, believes that truth-seeking is the statute's core ambition, and in our conversations he made no bones about its taking precedence over the independent counsel's prosecutorial function. "While the independent counsel is to follow Justice Department practice and procedure, I think there's an unusual burden uniquely placed on an independent counsel. I think the independent counsel uniquely has an obligation to get to the bottom as best he or she can of the matters that have been entrusted to him,"

Starr explained. "That separates out the function of the independent counsel and distinguishes it from the much more general law enforcement set of responsibilities that the Justice Department generally or a U.S. attorney's office more specifically would have."

Starr analogized the independent counsel to a prosecutor who has been instructed that a particular investigation is so important as to merit the diversion of resources from other priorities. In his view, Congress made the policy judgment when the law was passed that matters investigated under it warrant particularly vigorous examination. This fact, he believes, greatly constrains the discretion of the independent counsel to cut an investigation short by deciding that the allegations are not important enough to justify a giant federal probe. The message from the statute's architects, as Starr understood it, was that "you all are to go out here and get the dadgum facts. It's not important to the public welfare whether you secure convictions or not. Can you imagine a district attorney that never gets convictions?" Starr said he used to tell defense lawyers that "I do not really want to see people being sent off to jail. I want the facts, want the facts, want the facts." Starr insisted, in fact, that "every experienced defense lawyer in this town knew full well" that he had this attitude toward the law. In dealing with defense lawyers, he said, "I was quite consistent throughout the investigation. My goal, above all, is to gather the facts. I want the truth, and then along the way to be just and to be fair."[50] Starr's emphasis in this particular formulation is critical to understanding the totality of his investigation. The core of his project was fact-gathering and reporting. Justice was almost an afterthought — something to be obtained "along the way." Placing fairness and justice in the service of truth, of course, precisely inverts the normal prosecutorial approach, which sees fact-gathering as a means

of securing justice. Starr's comment, however, was not a slip of
the tongue but a succinct distillation of the hierarchy of his
priorities as he explained and defended them throughout our
talks. Ironically, given his reputation as a conservative partisan, Starr claimed he was greatly influenced in placing the
truth-finding function of the law ahead of the prosecutorial
function by his former ethics adviser, Samuel Dash. Dash, a
law professor at Georgetown University, is something of a
liberal icon. He served as chief counsel to the Senate's Watergate investigation, which was responsible for uncovering the
Nixon tapes. He was also an influential voice when the independent counsel statute was originally passed, and proudly
calls himself "the father of the independent counsel law."[51]
Starr said that when his investigation was first getting off the
ground, he flew Dash down to Arkansas to have him brain-
storm with the staff. Dash's message, as Starr summarized it,
was that the office must "make sure" to track down and talk
to all conceivably "knowledgeable witnesses." The office, he
said, would not "be able to stand in the face of history" if it
failed to get to the truth.[52]

Interestingly, when asked about these remarks, Dash both
rejected Starr's truth commission understanding of the law
and denied Starr's suggestion that he encouraged it. Dash has
argued in his writings that "an independent counsel under the
1994 Act is no more and no less than a federal prosecutor in
the U.S. Department of Justice."[53] His speech to Starr's staff,
he contended, was no different. Starr, he said, "asked me to
come to Little Rock and give a lecture on my perception of the
role of the independent counsel. I was very happy to do that
because I believe the independent counsel law is an important
statute but can be misused, and I wanted to shape their understanding of the role they were to play." According to Dash, he
told the staff that "the independent counsel is nothing other

than an alternative federal prosecutor. . . . You have to bend over backwards to be fair and open prosecutors and follow the law religiously. . . . You should be a model for what a prosecutor should be — but you're just another prosecutor." Dash said he has never believed that independent counsels have some special truth-seeking function that separates them from other prosecutors. "There is nothing in the statute, the legislative history of [the law], in the reasons we brought it into existence, or in anything I told him that should have led Ken to this idea he had that he had to get the truth. That's his self-appointed role. That's his self-perception, and it came out of his lack of experience as a prosecutor. He brought with him a whole slew of values as to what he was and what he wanted to do."[54]

Starr actually laments the truth-finding function he believes lies at the law's heart. It places, he believes, "an undue and imbalanced emphasis on the criminal law mechanism as opposed to other mechanisms for ensuring public accountability and the public trust." Had he been a policymaker, he told me, he would have never supported such a law: "Stepping back and viewing it from a public policy perspective, it would be far better for there to be a truth commission that then says, 'Amnesty for all! We want to know what happened.' "[55] Starr, however, was not a policymaker, just an executor of existing policy. The law, as he read it, offered him no alternative but to deploy his office to examine the matters within his jurisdiction with a thoroughness that, he admits, went considerably beyond what a normal prosecutor would contemplate.

Starr's interpretation of the independent counsel's mission does not appear to be merely a retroactive self-justification. A review of his speeches and public statements suggests that he has long considered the search for truth a central concern. In October 1996, for example, he said, "We want all the facts, we want all the truth," and that "That is what the investigation is about, that's what the mandate is and that's what we're seeking to achieve."[56] At the press conference at which he retracted his resignation as independent counsel following his ill-fated courtship with Pepperdine University in 1997, Starr said that "My commitment is to the people and to the pursuit of the truth. As we say frequently, we want the facts. And I will seek to fulfill that responsibility to the best of my ability and for as long as it takes. And I regret, I deeply regret, any action on my part that has called into question my commitment in that respect."[57] If Starr has been inconsistent, in fact, it is only in his insistence that truth-finding is a particular concern of the independent counsel, as distinct from other federal prosecutors or, indeed, lawyers generally. At a commencement address at Duke University School of Law in 1995 — the speech at which Starr first laid out his vision of the independent counsel's office as a microcosm of the Justice Department — he spoke at length about the need for the independent counsel's office "to mirror the existing practices and mechanisms of accountability at the Department of Justice." In this speech, he gave no indication that he viewed an independent counsel's mission as profoundly different from that of a Justice Department probe. The decisions, he said, "whether to subpoena certain documents, to investigate certain issues, to grant immunity, to indict, or to agree to a plea bargain" are "the life of a federal prosecutor's office, and an independent counsel's office is no different. With one crucial distinction: unlike other federal prosecutors, an independent counsel does not report to the Attorney General or the President."[58] At the Pepperdine press conference, he declared, "We want to get the truth. And that's what a good U.S. attorney's office is interested in doing."[59] At a speech in 1998 in North Carolina, he went one step further, suggesting that the bar generally should be more committed to the pursuit of truth:

> We still have to concede that the profession has changed, and we face a host . . . of both economic and structural issues quite familiar to everyone in the room. But now to speak personally, none of these issues has been as baleful to our profession as its apparent loss of respect for truth. . . .
>
> When a search for truth is not in the client's interest, which value should guide the lawyer's conduct? Lawyers have faced this question for some time, indeed, I would say for generations. But the balance that the modern-day profession strikes appears to me to have changed. . . .
>
> Now this choice, to the extent it is being made each day, is most unfortunate. It goes to the basic moral foundation of our system. Truth indeed is intended to be the primary goal of our judicial system, because without truth as a foundation, justice cannot predictably be achieved.[60]

One could conclude from such remarks, with some fairness, that Starr regards truth-seeking as the obligatory concern of lawyers generally, and certainly of all prosecutors. Indeed, his contention that truth represents the central concern of the judicial system and, by extension, all actors within that system, reflects an austere vision of the lawyer's role that many would dispute. If his public comments have sometimes masked the distinction, however, Starr clearly believes as well — even within this truth-oriented vision of the legal system generally — that the statute created a special and deeper truth-seeking burden for the independent counsel.

Starr's vision of the independent counsel law contrasts sharply with that of his predecessor, Robert Fiske Jr. Fiske, of course, was not operating as an independent counsel under the statute, but as an ad hoc special prosecutor under Justice

Department regulations during a period in which the independent counsel law had lapsed. Fiske said, however, "I viewed the powers and the responsibility I had as identical with what they would have been if I had been appointed by the three-judge court" under the statute. Truth, he insisted, was not his project. "I definitely conceived of myself as a prosecutor, doing exactly what the Justice Department would do if there had not been circumstances requiring me to do it rather than them. I felt I was functioning exactly as I was as a U.S. attorney."[61] Starr's successor as independent counsel, Robert Ray, likewise described a far more modest vision of his role under the statute than Starr had conceived, though he declined to criticize Starr's reading explicitly: "There is a view of the independent counsel statute that is kind of the report view: shine a spotlight and gather the facts. I am not going to shine a spotlight unless it is going to bring me facts with which I can bring a case. All other things are ancillary. My principal role is to bring cases. I am not a congressional committee, nor am I a newspaper. I am a prosecutor. I turn a spotlight on to see if there are crimes to prosecute, and when I decide I don't have a case, I turn the spotlight off, because my tools are dangerous tools."[62]

Even Walsh, whose Iran-Contra investigation was much criticized for alleged excesses, professes a far narrower vision of the role of independent counsel than Starr's. "The only power that the independent counsel has to compel testimony is through the grand jury, so you come down to [the question of] what is the grand jury's role in compelling testimony," Walsh explained. "I never used the grand jury simply as a broad truth-seeking agency." Walsh said the question of whether he should function as a truth commissioner arose during his tenure, particularly in the wake of the elder President George Bush's pardon of former Defense Secretary Caspar Weinberger. Walsh considered bringing Bush before the grand jury, both because he felt that Bush had broken a promise to give him a deposition after the election and because he was interested in whether the pardon had been prompted by the president's "concern about being a witness himself." Walsh's staff, however, restrained him, insisting that "simply wanting to know what happened is not what a grand jury is for. Much as I would have liked to use the grand jury to find out what had happened with the pardon or, more generally, what [Bush] knew about Iran-Contra, the grand jury is not a device to answer your questions."[63]

Decrying the search for truth may seem like an odd objection to Starr's approach. After all, the public, and particularly the press, has come to expect independent counsels to clean up scandals by pronouncing truth from on high about public misconduct. Starr's understanding of the statute mirrored those expectations, which require enormous self-discipline to resist. No matter how often editorial pages demand the appointment of an independent counsel so that the truth can be known, however, the experienced prosecutor fights the urge to oblige. As Gerard Lynch, now a U.S. district judge in New York, explained, the functions of truth commissioner and prosecutor are different, and the coercive tools available to prosecutors were not designed to accomplish generalized oversight. The truth "is enormously complex, involving social and political pressures, deep psychological understanding of individuals, the relationships among different people and events. Journalists naturally want the 'whole story,' as do historians, sociologists, [and] the public. But the criminal process is designed to decide whether an individual, at a particular moment in time, violated a very specific social norm without qualifying for any of a limited number of particular defenses, and subject to a standard of proof beyond a reasonable doubt,"

Lynch said. "To confuse the power to prosecute for crimes with the power to broadly investigate malfeasance in office is terribly dangerous."[64]

Starr's vision, in fact, sparked incredulity in a number of the prosecutors I asked to evaluate it. "I frankly do not agree with — or even understand the basis for — the truth commission view," said former Independent Counsel Alexia Morrison, whose investigation of former Assistant Attorney General Theodore Olson led to the Supreme Court litigation in which the independent counsel statute was upheld. "There may be plenty of room for complaint . . . about aspects of the law . . . and some of the judgments that have been made under it . . . but the thrust of the position created by the law simply does not seem to me to be open to debate."[65] Others were blunter. "Starr's is a bad — almost a crazy bad — reading of the law," said John Barrett, who served under Walsh and has written extensively about the independent counsel law. Barrett acknowledged that elements of a truth commission are latent in the statute, but he argued that emphasizing this side of the statute ignores what the law actually says. While its terms clearly describe a prosecutor, Barrett argued, "The independent counsel law itself doesn't contain the truth-finding duty Starr is describing."[66] Added Ronald Noble, a former prosecutor and head of the Treasury Department's law enforcement agencies, Starr's "view is simply radically different from the view of most experienced prosecutors."[67]

As I noted above, Starr frankly acknowledged the dangers of a prosecutor's functioning as a truth commissioner and considered them strong policy arguments against the statute. He likewise acknowledged that an independent counsel could not constitutionally use the grand jury mechanism to write a report in the absence of any potential criminal question. He seemed, however, to have no reservations about inferring from the court's action in *Morrison v. Olson* that the coercive powers of the grand jury could reasonably be deployed undiminished even where the prosecutorial interests are almost entirely pre-textual and the project at hand is more akin to congressional oversight than to criminal prosecution. He consistently dismissed the notion that he should have taken a more minimalist view of his role, saying that such a reading "robs the independent counsel structure of its need for being, in terms of a special mechanism appointed by a three-judge panel and all these indicia to have these sort of ultra-assurances of independence." All of that is unnecessary, he argued, "if really what you want is just some prosecutor out there who is somewhat independent and who just goes out and does what the Justice Department does. That's not the mechanism at all."[68]

Starr's claim is that the truth commission vision of the statute, while it may not appear in the law's text, flows out of its legislative history.[69] In his view, "Congress in 1978 said public integrity [in] a certain kind of a case is so vitally important, that we want to cabin the discretion of the attorney general and that we want to create a special office.... The matter is of sufficient importance to us that we want a specially designated officer who will then get to the bottom of this and will give then, at a minimum, a report to the public of what he has done. That, in my view, is what the independent counsel mechanism was designed to do—for better or for worse." Congress, he said, "wanted thoroughness," and even after it attempted, during the subsequent reauthorizations of the statute, to prevent the final reports from being used to smear people's reputations, "the statute [still] requires, without making accusations, [the prosecutor] to tell as full a story as you can." Even after these amendments, he said, the committee report still "talks in terms of fully" reporting the facts. "I view the report-writing function as something that is always there as one is going about one's work and simply informs in a holistic and unifying way the need to get the truth." The statute, seen in light of its legislative history, Starr believed, represents "a coherent effort to gather all of the relevant information and to provide as much public information about that subject matter as possible."[70]

Starr's view of the statute's history is wrong. The independent counsel law was not written to enable prosecutors to pursue and disclose the truth about executive branch conduct, but because its drafters feared an inherent conflict of interest when the executive branch supervised prosecutions of its own high-ranking staff. The drafters' goal was not, as Starr suggests, to treat these cases differently from garden-variety ones; rather, it was precisely the opposite, to treat them the same way.

To be sure, isolated passages in the original law's legislative history can be read to support Starr's view. One can, for example, read the Senate Government Operations Committee's report on an early draft of the special prosecutor law as contemplating a sprawling, exhaustive probe where it observes that, "temporary special prosecutors may result in the investigation and prosecution of some matters which in the past were not even known to the public and were never pursued. When we have used a temporary special prosecutor every few decades, they have discovered and prosecuted additional crimes that we might never have known about if they had not been appointed."[71] Likewise, one can read a 1978 House Judiciary Committee report on a later draft of the bill as supporting Starr's idea that Congress intended special prosecutors to examine matters with uncommon vigor. The report notes that "the legislation vests a special prosecutor with enough authority and independence to investigate and prosecute *vigorously and thoroughly*" (emphasis added).[72] The original legislation, in addition, waffled on the question of whether or not the independent counsel was bound by Justice Department policies, saying that a special prosecutor should follow those policies only "to the extent that such special prosecutor deems appropriate."[73] Starr is also correct that the independent counsel's final report — at least as described in the original law — seems like an expansive project. Until the so-called "declination clause" was changed in 1994, the special prosecutor was required to file a report that "set forth fully and completely a description of the work of the special prosecutor, including the disposition of all cases brought, *and the reasons for not prosecuting any matter within the prosecutorial jurisdiction of such special prosecutor which was not prosecuted*" (emphasis added).[74] Read outside of their full context, such passages make a reasonable case for Starr's point of view.

Starr's position also finds some support in the behavior of some other independent counsels — if not in the theoretical framework they embraced — and in the Special Division's own opinions. In particular, the decisions awarding attorneys' fees to subjects of the Iran-Contra probe are quite frank that, in the judgment of the court, Walsh did not behave like a traditional prosecutor. The Special Division determined, to the contrary, that what it deemed the very premise of the Walsh probe — that the circumvention of laws prohibiting aid to the Nicaraguan Contras should be treated as a criminal matter — would never have been adopted by a traditional federal investigation.[75] More significantly, the Special Division has also seemed to recognize that the final report will be an exhaustive document that tells a story. The Special Division struggled with its release of Walsh's final report, which it described as laden with judgments of criminality on the part of people who had gone unindicted or who were acquitted or had their convictions reversed. Some of the report's subjects objected to the

release of Walsh's report, as it impugned them, in their judgment, unfairly. The Special Division ultimately ordered the
report released but did so with evident discomfort:

> The Independent Counsel, though not the normal type of
> federal prosecutor, is a federal prosecutor. . . .
>   Consistent with the power and responsibility of their
> office, prosecutors do not issue reports, and they do not
> pronounce persons guilty of crimes who have not been in-
> dicted, tried, and convicted. The filing of reports by Inde-
> pendent Counsels is "a complete departure from the au-
> thority of a United States Attorney" and is "contrary to the
> practice in federal grand jury investigations." . . .
>   Unfortunately for movants, and perhaps for the tradi-
> tion of fairness, the statute does require that the Indepen-
> dent Counsel file a report.[76]

It is important to note, however, that these opinions never
state that the final-report requirement binds together some
cohesive oversight-oriented understanding of the statute.
They represent, instead, expressions of the Special Division's
frustration with Walsh's report. The court, far from accepting
the notion that Walsh's expansive report reflected the actual
nature of the statute, all but openly clucked at his choices.

Indeed, notwithstanding Starr's attempts to ground his
vision of the statute in its legislative history, Starr's interpretation of the law is really a projection onto that history of the
peculiar structure of the office the law created. Giving a prosecutor unlimited time and money to investigate a specific
matter and requiring him or her to issue a final report certainly tolerates and supports a prosecutor's behaving like a
truth commissioner. Even that portion of the legislative history that most strongly supports the truth commission understanding of the law, however, does so only by implication, as
the quotations above illustrate. The committee reports reflect

no clear congressional understanding that the mandate of the independent counsel is to seek and report the truth. In attempting to glean the true meaning of the law, Starr read far too much into these implications and failed to account either for the strong countervailing currents in the legislative history or for the extent to which Congress subsequently sought to clarify that it was after justice, not truth. The totality of the legislative history contradicts any idea that Congress was seeking to deflect some portion of its oversight function onto the special prosecutor. As former Independent Counsel Alexia Morrison put it, "Any serious reflection on the history, law and practice of independent counsel leaves me with no room for conclusion that anything but a prosecutor was intended."[77] Senator Carl Levin, a Michigan Democrat who played a leading role in the reauthorizations of the statute, emphasized as well that, "as far as the type of investigation, [Starr is] exactly wrong as a matter of history. We wanted an investigation that treated [the covered official] no better than an average citizen and no worse than an average citizen — no different, in other words. We thought we were writing in safeguards. We tightened the safeguards. The whole direction of the history of the bill was towards reining in the independent counsels."[78]

Any assessment of the truth commission vision should begin by acknowledging that neither the statute itself nor the legislative history of the original special prosecutor legislation explicitly describes any truth-seeking function. Congress's overriding concern was ensuring the independence of the special prosecutor and addressing the conflict of interest on the part of the Justice Department in investigating the administration of which it is a part. The act grew out of the October 1973 firing of Watergate special prosecutor Archibald Cox — the so-called Saturday Night Massacre — and the consequent fear that the executive branch would be able to control or stymie investigations of high-level officials. The purpose of the special prosecutor law was to guarantee both that special prosecutors would be appointed to investigate serious allegations of executive branch wrongdoing and that, once appointed, they could proceed unencumbered. The congressional reports on the bill never directly discuss the specific nature of the investigations being authorized—which is evidence in itself that Congress was not contemplating anything extraordinary. The House Judiciary Committee, for example, described the "purpose of the legislation" as providing "a mechanism for the court appointment of a temporary special prosecutor when necessary in order to eliminate the conflict of interest inherent when the Department of Justice must investigate and prosecute high-level executive branch officials."[79] The previous year, the Senate Governmental Affairs Committee, in detailing the powers and responsibilities of the special prosecutor, noted, "The whole purpose of this chapter is defeated if a special prosecutor is not independent and does not have clear authority to conduct a criminal investigation and prosecution without interference, supervision, or control by the Department of Justice."[80] There is no great reason to read these sentences as meaning anything broader than their plain text suggests: that Congress meant to create an office that would not answer to the attorney general but that would conduct a traditional, albeit thorough, prosecutorial inquiry.

Even the final-report requirement is more complicated than Starr's reading allows. While Congress did request a full and complete account of the independent counsel's investigation and that report was clearly intended to include a discussion of the evidence, the purpose of this report was not, as Starr seems to believe, to make as much information public about the conduct under investigation as possible. Congress designed the reporting mechanism as a putative check on the special prosecutors. The statute's own language, which required a final report that "set forth fully and completely *a description of the work of the special prosecutors,*" clearly contemplated a report on the activity of the independent counsels themselves, more than a discussion of the subject matter they investigated. The legislative history is clear on this point as well. As the Senate Governmental Affairs Committee put it, "This mandatory final report is considered by the Committee to be very important to ensure the accountability of a special prosecutor. The Committee is well aware of the enormous power and responsibility which a special prosecutor has because of all the protections provided in this chapter to make sure that the special prosecutor is independent. This final report will provide a detailed document to permit *the evaluation of the performance of a special prosecutor* at an appropriate time" (emphasis added).[81]

The House Judiciary Committee expressed a similar objective: "The committee recognizes that a special prosecutor will possess a good deal of power and that it is important to make that special prosecutor accountable for the exercise of that power. The [final report provisions] are intended to achieve that accountability. A special prosecutor will know that the conduct of his office will be reviewed and its work scrutinized. This should discourage, on the one hand, the overreaching of an arbitrary or overzealous special prosecutor and, on the other hand, the overcaution of a timid special prosecutor."[82] The best reading of the legislative history of the original act, in other words, is that Congress meant to authorize criminal investigations, which would be both thorough and loosely controlled and in which the prosecutors would, at day's end, explain themselves.

The subsequent reauthorization debates — which took place because of the five-year sunset provision embedded

within the law — resolved any ambiguity about Congress's intentions. In both 1983 and 1994, Congress altered the statute
to push independent counsels toward prosecutorial normalcy.
The relevant changes in 1983 responded to criticisms of the
law generated by the investigations of Hamilton Jordan and
Timothy Kraft, both officials of Jimmy Carter's administration. Jordan and Kraft had been subjected to special-
prosecutor probes related to allegations of possession of small
quantities of cocaine. Both were eventually cleared, but they
suffered serious financial and reputational harm in the process.
There was a widespread sense following these investigations
that such matters — which federal prosecutors would normally
avoid even investigating — were not what the special prosecutor mechanism had been created to handle. Congress, in response, clarified that the attorney general had the authority to
decline to request an independent counsel where a clear Justice Department policy would preclude an indictment.[83] It
also clarified, as noted above, that an independent counsel
could dismiss an allegation without investigating it if doing
so would be consistent with departmental policies.[84] These
changes make little sense if Congress had a truth commission
in mind. The latter change, in particular, clearly contemplates
that independent counsels themselves might close matters
without taking any steps whatsoever to discern the truth. Congress here was insisting that independent counsels should treat
allegations as would any other federal prosecutor.

This understanding is also evident in the legislature's decision that year to tighten the obligation of independent
counsels to follow Justice Department policies. Whereas the
original law left compliance to independent counsels' discretion, the 1983 law required that they follow Justice Department policies "except where not possible."[85] The Senate
Governmental Affairs Committee explained this change by

noting, "The goal of the special prosecutor should be to conduct an impartial investigation while assuring that treatment of officials is equal to that given to ordinary citizens under similar circumstances. If he does deviate from established practices of the Department, the special prosecutor should thoroughly explain his reasons for doing so in his report to the court at the conclusion of his investigation."[86] To further harmonize independent counsel investigations with those of Justice Department prosecutors, the amendments also permitted independent counsels to consult with the U.S. attorney for the district in which the offense allegedly took place.[87] Starr sees these changes in the law as merely demanding that subjects of independent counsel investigations not be *prosecuted* for crimes that the Justice Department would likely have ignored. But read together, the amendments amount to far more than that; they constitute a statement by Congress that it wanted independent counsels to behave as much like the Justice Department as possible, not only at the indictment stage but in the conduct of the investigation itself.

One last piece of evidence that Congress imagined that independent counsels would mimic Justice Department investigations was its decision to authorize the Special Division to reimburse the attorneys' fees of subjects of independent counsel probes who were not ultimately indicted.[88] The statute authorized such reimbursements only if "the attorney's fees would not have been incurred" by an ordinary citizen facing an ordinary federal investigation. This provision serves, at one level, as an acknowledgment on the part of Congress that the particularly vigorous investigations the law authorized could produce especially costly defense lawyering for innocent people. It also, however, reflects the understanding that such eventualities might happen in spite of Congress's will, not because of it. The Senate committee report stresses that the committee did not anticipate that such situations would arise frequently, an indication that members did not expect independent counsels generally to behave differently from other prosecutors. The other changes to the law, the committee expected, would serve to "ensure that covered officials will not be subjected to a more rigorous application of the criminal law than is applied to other citizens. Thus, the Committee believes that reimbursement of attorneys' fees would be warranted, if at all, in only rare instances. This amendment is included, however, as a safeguard to compensate officials in the event that they do incur extraordinary expenses during a special prosecutor investigation which eventually absolves them of any wrongdoing. Reimbursement may be warranted, for example, in instances where the special prosecutor duplicates actions which have been taken by the Attorney General during the preliminary investigation. *The committee stresses, however, that the court should award attorneys' fees sparingly, and that reimbursement should not become a routine event*" (emphasis added).[89] Congress intended the reimbursement provision, in other words, not to compensate people for the truth commission nature of the law but to permit compensation in what it believed would be rare instances in which the law was deployed, in spite of Congress's admonitions, in ways that caused extraordinarily burdensome costs. In short, Congress in 1983 all but directly commanded independent counsels to behave like Justice Department prosecutors, and provided both specific mechanisms to facilitate compliance with this instruction and a stopgap financial reimbursement scheme in case they failed to comply. In light of these amendments, the truth commission vision seems difficult to sustain.

In the 1994 amendments, Congress sought further to bind independent counsels to the norms of federal prosecutors.[90] Most significantly, it changed the final report require-

ment, by removing the requirement that independent counsels explain the reasons for their decisions not to bring cases,
instead leaving such explanations to their discretion.[91] The
impetus for the change was the required inclusion in some
prior final reports, particularly Walsh's, of conclusory statements about the conduct of unindicted individuals. The conferees, in explaining the change, noted that the final report
requirement "is unique to the independent counsel process"
and "must be understood to be an exception to the norm."
The exception is justified, according to the conference report,
"by the unique environment in which an independent counsel
must operate — without direct and ongoing supervision by
senior Justice Department officials. It serves as an important
check on independent counsel investigative and prosecutorial
activities by requiring them to identify and explain their actions." Consequently, "the conference agreement reaffirms
the duty of independent counsels to provide a full and complete description of their work," and the conferees noted as
well that they "consider to be crucial a discussion of the conduct of the person for whom the independent counsel was
appointed to office." They also stated:

> Congress also wants to clarify, however, that indepen-
> dent counsels are not expected to and should not take addi-
> tional investigative steps, such as additional interviews or
> document requests, in order to produce a detailed report.
> *No investigation by an independent counsel should be lengthened
> or deepened simply because of the final report requirement. The
> report should instead reflect only the work required for a prosecu-
> tor to execute his or her normal investigative and prosecutorial
> responsibilities.*
> The conference agreement eliminates the requirement
> that independent counsels explain, in every instance, their
> reasons for not prosecuting any matter within their juris-
> diction. Other federal prosecutors do not normally provide

public explanations of decisions not to indict and, in deviat-
ing from this norm, independent counsels must exercise
restraint. The power to damage reputations in the final
report is significant, and the conferees want to make it clear
that the final report requirement is not intended in any way
to authorize independent counsels to make public findings
or conclusions that violate normal standards of due process,
privacy, or simple fairness. (emphasis added)[92]

This language simply cannot be reconciled with Starr's idea
that the final report requirement binds together a cohesive
vision of the independent counsel as an agent of truth. By
stating explicitly both that independent counsels are to avoid
taking investigative steps in order to write more thorough
reports and that they are to avoid conclusory findings that
might be unfair, Congress left little space for truth commissioners to ply their trade. How, after all, can one report the
truth without making findings that some might deem unfair?
More importantly, how can independent counsels "get to the
bottom" of the matters within their jurisdiction, as Starr con-
tends the reporting requirement compels them uniquely to
do, without taking any investigative steps beyond what a normal prosecutor would take?

In the 1994 reauthorization, Congress also tinkered further with the requirement that independent counsels follow
Justice Department policies, changing the insistence that they
do so "except where not possible" to a requirement that they
follow Justice Department policies "except to the extent that
to do so would be inconsistent with the purposes" of the statute.[93] Under the new language, in other words, an independent counsel could waive departmental policies only when
complying with them would be inconsistent with the prosecutor's independence. Congress also added a requirement that
independent counsels consult on law enforcement policies

with the department unless to do so would undermine their independence.[94] Once again, the purpose of the changes was to ensure that subjects of independent counsel probes were not treated more harshly than other citizens. The conference report explains them by noting that the new law "signals the need for independent counsels to balance the goal of handling matters in the same way as other federal prosecutors with the goal of retaining appropriate independence."[95] The Senate committee report stresses that "the Committee intends independent counsels to follow established Justice Department policies on criminal law enforcement to the maximum extent possible," but "does not intend that independent counsels comply with Department policies which would undermine their independence or hinder their mission."[96]

If members thought the change would make independent counsels more accountable, it turned out to be laughably ineffectual. It may even have made the accountability of special prosecutors to Justice Department policies more ambiguous than it already was. There exist, after all, hypothetical situations in which it would be technically possible for an independent counsel to follow a Justice Department policy but nonetheless inconsistent with his independence to do so. Following the policy in such situations would seem to be required by the earlier language but not by the 1994 law. The House Judiciary Committee suggested that the change was a kind of clarification designed to make the law reflect more accurately when Congress expected independent counsels to waive Justice Department policies. The committee explained that "the existing exception clause does not accurately describe circumstances where it may be literally possible, but nonetheless undesirable for an independent counsel to follow the rules that generally guide the conduct of attorneys for the Department of Justice."[97] For our purposes, however, what Congress meant to do is more important than how effectively legislators actually did it, and the committees were clear that they meant for independent counsels to be bound generally by the conduct of traditional federal prosecutors. The House Judiciary Committee, for example, described the change as intended to maintain "the policy that independent counsel are expected to follow the same rules as the Department of Justice in their investigations and in making decisions on whether or not to seek indictments."[98] The 1994 reauthorization, which precipitated Starr's own appointment, should have put Starr on notice that after the Iran-Contra experience, Congress had no appetite for a repeat of the perceived excesses of Walsh's investigation.

The full legislative history of the statute, in short, lends little support to Starr's vision of the law. In its consideration of the early versions of the statute, Congress did not express directly its intent to create a traditional prosecutor, largely because the underlying nature of the office was never seriously discussed at all. The purpose of the law was to codify in statute a mechanism to replicate, when necessary, the Watergate Special Prosecution Force, which was, after all, a fairly traditional criminal investigation that examined and prosecuted a series of very serious crimes. Nobody was selling the special prosecutor law as a potential truth commission. Only as it became clear in the law's implementation that the structure of the 1978 act encouraged investigators to examine matters with an uncommon intensity did the question of the nature of the office appear to have arisen in the minds of legislators. In response, Congress insisted with increasing explicitness that it wanted independent counsels to perform traditional criminal investigations. The 1983 amendments were a lame step in that direction. The 1994 amendments were, as actual change, likewise minimal. As a general statement of Congress's instructions to independent counsels, however, the 1994 conference report could hardly have been clearer. The healthiest and most faithful way to read the statute's history is that Congress was telling independent counsels to conduct criminal investigations that closely mimic the way the Justice Department would handle a similar matter involving a person not covered by the statute. Having done so, the independent counsel is then to write a report on the probe that offers an account of the underlying conduct only insofar as the course of the normal criminal investigation yielded it up and only insofar as telling the story is necessary to assure the public that the special prosecutor conducted a reasonable investigation.

I do not intend the preceding argument to sound unsympathetic to Starr's predicament. The independent counsel structure presents unique challenges, and Congress clearly envisioned certain differences between independent counsel probes and Justice Department probes. The final reporting requirement is highly unusual; normal prosecutors, after all, do not write reports. Even more unusual is the requirement that independent counsels refer potential impeachment information to Congress. As a practical matter, such provisions create the need in the minds of special prosecutors to justify themselves — a result Congress clearly desired. The impeachment referral provision creates an analytical anomaly as well. If one believes, as some observers do, that presidents cannot be indicted while they remain in office, the provision suddenly takes on a great deal of weight when a president becomes the principal, immediate target of a probe.[99] If the president cannot be prosecuted, one can fairly ask, what is the point of conducting an investigation other than to file an impeachment report? Potential answers to this question exist. The independent counsel could conduct the investigation for a possible indictment after the president's term of office ends, or could use the possible misbehavior of other people as a cover. Neither of these approaches, however, presents a particularly satisfying justification for the type of disruption a major investigation of the president would necessarily entail. Starr can reasonably hypothesize that Congress must have envisioned at some level that an investigation of the president involving possibly impeachable offenses would be a search for the truth about those allegations.

Even allowing this point, however, Starr's reading is unnecessary. Congress had clarified repeatedly that it wanted mainstream prosecutions. Independent counsels, therefore, faced at most a problem of mixed messages from Congress. Every prudential factor weighed in favor of resolving the conflict by adopting a modest reading of the law. At the level of statutory construction, the most explicit, and the most recent, congressional statements sought to limit the impact of the more grandiose earlier language. At the level of basic fairness, it seems wrong to loose a truth commission on a public figure — with all the potential for privacy violations and intrusiveness using a grand jury to report history may entail — in the absence of the clearest of congressional commands. At the level of the constitutional hygiene to which Starr was so deeply committed, it is hard to justify hanging a heavier albatross around the executive branch's neck when a lighter one would satisfy the terms of the law no less, and perhaps more, faithfully. Most important, Starr's reading ignores the fact that there is no need for a truth commission, which already exists in Congress's impeachment and oversight powers to whatever extent members of Congress — who, unlike independent counsels, are politically accountable — choose to use those powers. In the face of that reality, nothing but the most explicit congressional command could justify Starr's breaking away from the traditional role of prosecutors.

Starr's decision to read the central ambition of the statute broadly may seem like a mere academic failure. It was, in fact, far deeper and more fateful. It created an incentive structure under which the prosecutor had no reason to stop asking questions, issuing subpoenas, or litigating privileges. In his now famous dissent in *Morrison*, Justice Antonin Scalia wrote,

> The mini-Executive that is the independent counsel, . . . operating in an area where so little is law and so much is discretion, is intentionally cut off from the unifying influence of the Justice Department, and from the perspective that multiple responsibilities provide. What would normally be regarded as a technical violation (there are no rules defining such things), may in his or her small world assume the proportions of an indictable offense. What would normally be regarded as an investigation that has reached the level of pursuing such picayune matters that it should be concluded, may to him or her be an investigation that ought to go on for another year. How frightening it must be to have your own independent counsel and staff appointed, with nothing else to do but to investigate you until investigation is no longer worthwhile — with whether it is worthwhile not depending upon what such judgments usually hinge on, competing responsibilities. And to have that counsel and staff decide, with no basis for comparison, whether what you have done is bad enough, willful enough, and provable enough, to warrant an indictment.[100]

Starr's reading exacerbates all of Scalia's concerns. Even Scalia, after all, assumed that — with all the loss of perspective the statute encouraged on the part of its prosecutors — the independent counsel and his staff would still be prosecutors. In Starr's vision, however, the prosecutorial objective had itself been subjugated to a quest for the truth whose investigative demands go far beyond doing justice. Building a microcosm of the Justice Department avails a prosecutor little if he

or she asks that microcosm to work toward a goal to which the
Justice Department itself would never aspire.

The following chapters attempt to trace the impact of
Starr's vision of the law on the conduct of his investigation. At
the margins, of course, it is an impossible task. Individual
investigative steps seldom have single causes or flow directly
out of a particular statutory vision. We will never know precisely which subpoenas represented the truth commission vision in action and which were merely the work of aggressive
law enforcement. In more general terms, however, the impact
of Starr's understanding of the law is both admitted by Starr
and, with respect to certain important steps he took, painfully
obvious based on the public record. Broadly speaking, its effect
was twofold. It caused Starr to examine the matters within his
mandate with an intensity and a depth a traditional prosecutor
would have eschewed and to resist closing matters until every
lawful and ethical step to garner the truth had been exhausted.
Second, it made him less willing to overlook the sort of self-
protective, petty lies that many witnesses tell during investigations and that prosecutors typically waste little time investigating. At key junctures in his investigation, Starr took actions
that an independent counsel pursuing narrowly prosecutorial
objectives would have avoided, and he justified these steps with
reference to the need to get to the truth. Many of these are the
very steps — the second indictment of Susan McDougal or the
intensive investigation of the Lewinsky affair, for example —
that come to mind when we imagine Starr's excesses. Compounded by his other idiosyncratic readings of the independent counsel law's provisions, the truth commission vision
clearly played a profound role in the direction Starr's probe
took. A president with a pathological allergy to telling the truth
thus found himself confronted by a prosecutor who had refor-
mulated the prosecutorial process into a search for it.

CHAPTER 3

The Truth Commission and Whitewater

"It is not normal for a prosecutor to keep indicting the same person
over and over again."

JOHN NIELDS JR., RESPONDING TO KENNETH STARR'S
THIRD INDICTMENT OF HIS CLIENT, WEBSTER HUBBELL

Kenneth Starr's truth commission understanding of the
independent counsel statute manifested itself subtly during
the early portions of his investigation. That subtlety, to some
extent, resulted from the density of the probe's often mind-
numbing subject matter. Few members of the public understood even the parameters of the questions at issue in Whitewater, much less how Whitewater intersected with Madison
Guaranty Savings and Loan, the Castle Grande real estate
deal, the death of White House aide Vincent Foster Jr., or —
more tenuously — to the White House Travel Office or the
FBI files scandal. Especially before the Monica Lewinsky
scandal erupted in 1998, the incidents that gave rise to the
constituent parts of Starr's investigation tended to embroil the
press and Washington's political culture far more than they
did the public at large. Even among that segment of the public
that was actually engaged by the issues Starr was investigating,
most people had no intuitive sense of how a prosecutor would
conduct such a far-flung investigation or where one would

appropriately stop. The difference, therefore, between the way a prosecutor would handle it and the way a truth commissioner would proceed was, at least initially, difficult to discern.

Also obscuring Starr's approach was the fact that those differences were minimal in the early stages of the probe. As a general matter, after all, the truth commissioner and the prosecutor start out their inquiries by asking similar questions. The truth commissioner's probe separates itself from the prosecutor's only later, when the prosecutor decides he knows enough to make indictment decisions and begin closing matters, while the truth commissioner feels the need to address the demands of history as well as those of justice. By its nature, a truth-oriented approach to a criminal investigation becomes increasingly pronounced as time goes on.

In retrospect, however, it seems obvious that Starr's vision of the statute and his conception of his role under it affected the investigation deeply from the outset. From the time Starr took over the investigation from Robert Fiske Jr. in August 1994, as this chapter details, he made clear that he did not share Fiske's concern with speed, but, instead, intended to be exhaustively thorough, however long that might take. Toward that end, he reopened the Foster suicide investigation, which Fiske had completed in June. He also came to rely upon attorneys and investigators who shared a taste for relatively sprawling, unfocused probes. As the investigation wore on, Starr also demonstrated extraordinary reluctance to bring issues to a close, even long after the line prosecutors who conducted the investigations thought they had resolved the issues the cases presented. In one instance, Starr held an investigation open while he pursued litigation he was unlikely to win and that had only hypothetical bearing on his case. In others, he brought indictments in efforts, at least in part, to encourage recalcitrant witnesses to tell the truth — even though their eventual cooperation seemed entirely improbable. Such actions have been cast as the fruits of excessive prosecutorial zeal on Starr's part. They are, however, better understood as logical extensions of the philosophy he brought with him to the job.

By the time Starr took over the investigation, Fiske had already made considerable headway. In less than seven months on the job, he had garnered pleas from three Whitewater-related targets in Arkansas, including the man who would become the central witness in the case: David Hale.[1] Fiske was also preparing to indict former Associate Attorney General Webster Hubbell for an overbilling scheme at the Rose Law Firm, and he had examined and closed the Foster suicide matter and allegations that the White House had sought illegally to influence the Treasury Department's handling of criminal referrals related to Madison Guaranty. Starr went down to Little Rock expecting the investigation to be "fairly quick — several months, a year at most."[2] He had a hard time initially believing that the Clintons were guilty of any serious misconduct. "The president is not a wealthy person," he recalled. "I grew up in Texas. I saw the [Lyndon Johnson] phenomenon of growing vastly wealthy while being in public office. President Clinton wasn't that way. He didn't seem by his life to be avaricious." Starr asked rhetorically, "How could he be in the middle of some huge fraud? And I had friends who had prosecuted fraud cases. . . . And the people who were taking advantage of these [savings and loans] were really living these unbelievable lifestyles, and he didn't strike me as leading the lifestyle of the rich and famous."[3] Somewhat to his surprise, however, Fiske had taken the investigation far afield of the original Whitewater land deal, and as Starr later wrote, he quickly realized that the scope of the investigation eclipsed his prior imagination. "When I got to Little Rock . . . I found that the work went far beyond a real-estate transaction once upon a time.

Mr. Fiske and his staff had been investigating cases of bankruptcy fraud, various tax matters and apparent irregularities in a gubernatorial campaign."[4] In a speech, he noted that by the time he "inherited the office from Bob Fiske, there were 120 people on the ground in Little Rock. It was the largest FBI contingent on the ground. There were a number of lawyers. This was a huge case."[5] Starr was also surprised to find that the Washington phase of Fiske's probe still needed more work: "It had been my sense that there had been such a very elaborate and intense effort in the Washington phase of the investigation, that the facts were sort of there and the facts needed to be assessed. But as it turned out, there was a substantial amount that still needed to be done in the Washington phase of the investigation when I arrived. I had not anticipated that."[6]

To members of Fiske's staff, Starr's appointment came as an unwelcome jolt, and the differences between his approach and Fiske's were immediately apparent. In some sense, these differences simply reflected Starr's inexperience as a prosecutor. They also, however, reflected differences of philosophy. In our conversations, Starr expressed admiration for Fiske's work, but insisted as well that his job was different from his predecessor's. "I think frankly we were on a pretty good track with Bob Fiske, who was a very aggressive federal prosecutor who was acting like a prosecutor, who wasn't acting like a truth commission. He was acting like a prosecutor — which was the way he should act. But he didn't have a reporting requirement."[7] As Julie O'Sullivan, who served in Fiske's office, recalled, Fiske "was a prosecutor; that was his entire orientation, though he was cognizant of his civil jurisdiction as well." As such, he worked full time on the probe, moved to Little Rock, and was always "down the hall" and "very involved." Starr, by contrast, was "very uncomfortable with the role" of a prosecutor, O'Sullivan said, and "saw himself as the attorney general" instead. Fiske, she added, "had the view that it was in the public interest to have a thorough investigation but also a quick one, that a protracted investigation was a distraction for every branch of government, and that time was of the essence. And Ken clearly didn't share that." O'Sullivan also noted that Fiske had staffed his investigation with prosecutors whom he knew well and who had "personal loyalty to Bob or [were] recommended by people he really trusted." Under Fiske, she said, the office had about thirteen staff members — not including FBI agents — almost all of whom told Starr when Fiske was replaced that they too would be leaving. There was an "enormous amount of upheaval, so what Ken was faced with was hiring a whole new staff. . . . Ken took weeks to get replacements." This, O'Sullivan suggested, was partly because "he apparently did not know as many people who were prosecutors or who had experience as prosecutors." It was also, however, partly a function of the fact that Starr "was not in a hurry."[8]

When Starr did bring in his own staff, it differed profoundly from Fiske's. Starr explained the change in emphasis, saying that he "avoided what Bob did. Bob had a good system for Bob, which was [to have] some really sharp people with a fair amount — but not elaborate — experience from the [U.S. attorney's office in the Southern District of New York] and then some folks that very senior lawyers who were in the American College of Trial Lawyers recommended." Starr said that he, by contrast, sought aggressive and experienced career prosecutors. This comparison actually sells Fiske's staff short; Fiske's team had proceeded with an efficiency and prosecutorial professionalism that Starr's would never match. That said, Starr's own much-caricatured staff was a far more eclectic bunch, and a less monolithically conservative one, than was commonly imagined. Starr was certainly sincere in his efforts to assemble a staff whose range of experience could approximate that of the Justice Department, and he hired many respected career prosecutors who could reasonably be expected to advance that goal. Indeed, the Justice Department itself would have been proud to have done much of their work, particularly the prosecution of Arkansas Governor Jim Guy Tucker and the Clintons' former business partners, James and Susan McDougal. Unlike Fiske, however, Starr also brought in people who pushed the investigation toward a more open-ended inquest. The most important of these hires was W. Hickman Ewing Jr.

Ewing became, over the course of the Starr investigation, a particular target of Starr's critics. This was partly because he was a central-casting stereotype of a prosecutor working for Starr: born-again Christian, conservative, and displaying a charming — if somewhat alarming — candor in acknowledging that he was not approaching the investigation with a presumption that the Clintons were innocent of wrongdoing. "After you've been doing this kind of work for ten, fifteen, twenty years," writer Jeffrey Toobin quotes him as saying, "it doesn't take too long to determine whether somebody has committed a crime. You draw your preliminary conclusions, and then you shut this down or you proceed. We proceeded."[9] For Clinton's defenders, Ewing came to embody the culture-war dimension of the fight the White House was waging against Starr's office. White House aide Sidney Blumenthal once called him a "religious fanatic" — a remark for which he later had to apologize.[10] For many of Starr's foes, Ewing symbolized Starr's inner redneck; appropriately nicknamed "Hick," he was the unpolished zealot beneath Starr's own presentable exterior.

More interesting than the fire it drew from Clinton's defenders, Ewing's approach as Starr's deputy in Little Rock was highly controversial within Starr's office itself. Ex-staffers described him to me with radically differing levels of sympathy, and some even suspected him of political motivation. Several of Starr's staff reported feeling anxious about the scope and aggressiveness of his approach. Still others defended him strongly. In almost all of the descriptions, however, certain common themes emerged. Ewing, his former colleagues said, did not believe in focusing investigations narrowly on specific criminal allegations but in casting a wide net and keeping investigations open. As former Starr prosecutor Brett Kavanaugh described it, Ewing had learned "from long experience that you had cases where things just turn up if you keep at it long enough."[11] John Bates, who served as Starr's Washington deputy, added that Ewing's approach was to "look broadly, to keep things open, to look for the interconnected aspects, to keep one thing open beyond what the facts would warrant because of the possibility that it might interconnect" with another allegation.[12] Another former Starr prosecutor summarized Ewing's philosophy a touch less generously: "Everyone's guilty until proven innocent. In order to maintain pressure, never close anything until the last day" on which a case could be brought. Noted this source with evident disgust, Ewing—who played football in high school and had planned to be a coach like his father—"used to draw football diagrams on the wall with everyone close to the Clintons as layers of defenses."[13]

Simply dismissing Ewing as a Clinton hater is probably too simplistic. Both Bates and Kavanaugh, for example, disputed the contention that Ewing's approach flowed out of hatred of the president. Bates described Ewing's hard-charging style as "his fundamental perspective as a prosecutor."[14] Ewing, unsurprisingly, denied that he began the probe with animus toward the president, though he acknowledged that

"nothing he did or said [during the probe] changed my opinion of him for the better." Ewing told me his aggressive approach as a prosecutor was forged in the U.S. attorney's office
in Memphis, where he served both as an assistant U.S. attorney and, for the last ten years of his service there, as the
office's chief. Ewing was the third in a line of crusading anti-
corruption U.S. attorneys in Memphis, who had collectively
prosecuted much of the state's political elite. Despite his reputation as a right-winger, he described himself in apolitical
terms, saying that both political parties had tried to recruit
him to run for elected office when he was finally forced out of
the U.S. attorney's job by the elder President George Bush.
Ewing said his prosecutorial philosophy was rooted in his
experience in Memphis, where he had seen public corruption
investigations finally pan out after lying dormant for long
periods of time. While he denied operating with a presumption of his target's guilt, he paid little lip service to the notion
that a prosecutor ought to keep an open mind about his targets, and he frankly sang the praises of sprawling, unfocused
investigations perpetuated on the basis of hunches, rather
than evidence. "Sometimes a crime has been committed but
you don't know how many participants there are," he explained. "You know that A and B did it, because you found
them with the dope. But what about others? Take corruption
investigations in Tennessee — like a road built to nowhere.
Everyone says it's okay, but you keep it open, and two years
later, you get the contractor on a totally unrelated crime, and
his lawyer says, 'Go easy on him and he'll give you the kick-
back scheme.'" Ewing added, "There are lots of prosecutors
in this country who have never seen a crime by a public official
because they don't want to. So they don't take the necessary
steps to find out. . . . I don't think I presume guilt, but I do at
some point presume a crime has been committed and have a

pretty good reason to assume the person is involved. It's an optimistic attitude in the sense that I've seen too many times when prosecutors come in and say, 'There's nothing here. There's no reason to pursue it.' It's willful blindness. I'm looking in my mind to prove that there *is* a case." In football, he said, "you call it having a nose for the ball. There are people who always get through to the end zone."[15]

Even assuming that Ewing's approach was not politically driven, his elevation to deputy independent counsel in Arkansas says a lot about Starr.[16] Because Starr also hired a group of people who disagreed — in some cases vehemently — with Ewing's approach, it would be wrong to assume that Ewing's hire constituted an unequivocal endorsement of his style or an adoption of it. It certainly suggested, however, comfort on Starr's part with an open-ended approach to the probe. Ewing, to be sure, was not a truth commissioner at heart. "This whole thing about finding the truth, that's not what I was over there for," he told me. "Ken would say 'We're trying to get the truth.' But I always thought what we were doing was getting the truth so we could make charging decisions."[17] In the end, however, Starr's truth commission instincts and Ewing's prosecutorial sensibilities proved highly compatible. Given what Starr believed he was obligated to accomplish, a sprawling, aggressive, and unfocused probe was more congenial than one that tackled a narrow question in isolation from all other questions. One striking fact testifies to the particular compatibility of Ewing's and Starr's approaches: Ewing ultimately outlasted within the office all of the prosecutors whom he discomforted. Among the several generations of prosecutors who drifted through that office, Ewing alone both worked for Starr in 1994 and was still in the employ of the Office of Independent Counsel throughout the year 2000.[18]

Starr's office has sometimes been portrayed, particularly

by Toobin, as riven into two camps — one composed of traditional, apolitical federal prosecutors, and the other composed
of anti-Clinton zealots.[19] This greatly overstates the matter,
and it probably misidentifies the central motivations of the
office's hawks as well. It does, however, correctly identify a
tension within the office between the different approaches
brought by the various prosecutors. The division was too subtle to split the office neatly into clear camps; the prosecutors
I interviewed disagreed, for example, about who belonged in
which group and what the fundamental fault lines really were.
In general terms, however, it is fair to talk about different
centers of gravity within the office, groups that had different sensibilities and approached questions with different ideas
about the relative benefits of exhaustiveness and speed. Given
Starr's own beliefs, it is not surprising that the more aggressive
side of his office often tended to prevail in disputes that arose
within the independent counsel's shop. As one Starr prosecutor put it, "Time after time, [Starr] sided with people who had
the aggressive prosecutorial philosophy he most admired, because that fit his approach to turn over every rock."[20]

Nowhere in the early phases of Starr's probe was the turn-
every-rock agenda more apparent than in his decision to re-
open the investigation of Foster's death. The decision, in fact,
presents a relatively tight analogue to a controlled scientific
experiment, an analogue of a sort history seldom offers. Fiske,
who understood his role as a narrow one, and Starr, who embraced a far more wide-ranging vision, both examined the
same subject matter, and both issued reports focusing only on
Foster's death. The back-to-back investigations thus offer an
opportunity to examine the impacts of the two prosecutors'
respective visions. The differences are instructive.

To be precise, an element of the truth commission instinct
infected Fiske's own decision to issue a report on the Foster

matter in the first place. Foster had been found dead in Fort Marcy Park on July 20, 1993. Nothing about the crime scene suggested foul play: there was no sign of a struggle; Foster was holding a gun; he had been shot in the mouth; he had been depressed in the weeks preceding his death. The United States Park Police, who initially investigated the death, ruled it a suicide, a finding that seemed entirely persuasive given the paucity of evidence suggesting any other scenario. Despite the fracas that developed, in fact, suicide was the only reasonable conclusion. Yet in the months that followed the Park Police's determination, a cottage industry devoted to attacking the integrity of the investigation sprang up.[21] Though largely confined to the political right, skepticism regarding the place and manner of Foster's death was not especially marginal. To cite one example, Martin Anderson, who had served as a domestic policy advisor to President Reagan, wrote shortly after Fiske's appointment that he had anxieties about the suicide finding. Citing articles by *New York Post* reporter Christopher Ruddy, Anderson declared that

> the murder of a White House senior advisor is monstrous even to contemplate. As the horror of that possibility began to sink in, most people, quite understandably, shied away from it.
>
> Facts and clues that did not point toward suicide were shunted aside. Questions that should have been asked were not asked.

The crime scene, Anderson claimed, did not seem like a suicide:

> Virtually no blood. A clean white shirt. No evidence of an exit wound. The body lying perfectly straight. All witnessed by three credible professionals.
>
> This may not prove murder. Such circumstances could have resulted from a suicide.

But questions surrounding Mr. Foster's death do remain in the minds of some.[22]

Fiske did not take up Foster's death to settle questions
remaining in the minds of "some." He initially looked at the
Foster case, rather, because "there had been a lot of allegations that Vince Foster had committed suicide because of revelations to him about Whitewater," a matter on which he had
done legal work for the Clintons. The possibility that Whitewater concerns had triggered the suicide, Fiske said, "bore
directly on whether the president and Hillary Clinton had
been engaged in criminal conduct." Fiske, however, acknowledged that his Foster report was designed to quiet the conspiracy theories and clarify the accuracy of the Park Police finding: "Once we started looking at that issue and allegations
[of murder] arose, it became a huge cloud that we had to
clear up."[23]

Though he adopted some measure of the truth-seeking
role with respect to Foster, Fiske's approach was still a far cry
from Starr's. For one thing, he was greatly concerned with
resolving the Foster matter quickly, which he did. "When
an allegation like this is made about the president," he said,
"there is a cloud over his head, and it's very important to
evaluate it as quickly as possible and clear it up, and if there's a
crime to say so, but if there is no crime, to say that quickly too.
That doesn't mean speed at the expense of doing the job right.
But it does mean not investigating more than is necessary." To
Fiske, that meant that "when we got to 98 percent" certainty
that Foster's death had been a suicide, which took only a few
months, the marginal returns of continued investigation diminished compared to the marginal costs. "We had a concern
that if we kept investigating for the other two percent, people
would think maybe it *was* a homicide because we were inves-

tigating so long." With a panel of pathologists telling him that it was "one of the easiest cases" they had seen, Fiske stopped investigating and disclosed his findings.[24] In short, aside from his decision to release a report, Fiske treated the matter like a prosecutor. He assumed jurisdiction on January 20, 1994, and examined Foster's death because of specific allegations linking it to the issue — Whitewater — that lay at the core of his investigative mandate. On determining that those allegations were false and that the suicide was actually a suicide, he closed the matter and issued a report within six months of his office's creation. Having satisfied the law enforcement interest in the matter, in other words, Fiske left the remaining questions to historians.

To a serious person approaching the question with an open mind, Fiske's report, issued on June 30, 1994, should have been altogether conclusive. The report candidly states that it "does not purport to provide definitive answers to all questions surrounding Vincent Foster's death."[25] Fiske had set out to address three questions, which he laid out tersely in his introduction:

> 1) Were the Park Police correct that Foster committed suicide, or was he murdered?
> 2) If the death was a suicide, did it occur in Fort Marcy Park or had the body been moved?; and
> 3) If Foster committed suicide, was it motivated in any way by concerns Foster may have had about legal issues related to the Clintons' involvement with the Whitewater Development Company, Inc. ("Whitewater"), Madison Guaranty Savings & Loan ("Madison Guaranty"), or Capital Management Services, Inc. ("CMS")?[26]

On each of these questions, the report is unequivocal:

> On the afternoon of July 20, 1993, in Fort Marcy Park, Fairfax County, Virginia, Vincent W. Foster, Jr., committed

suicide by firing a bullet from a .38 caliber revolver into his mouth. As discussed below, the evidence overwhelmingly supports this conclusion, and there is no evidence to the contrary. This conclusion is endorsed by all participants in the investigation, including each member of the Pathologist Panel.

We found no evidence that issues involving Whitewater, Madison Guaranty, CMS or other personal legal matters of the President or Mrs. Clinton were a factor in Foster's suicide. While Foster did confide to family and friends in the weeks prior to his death that certain matters were troubling him, we have learned of no instance in which Whitewater, Madison Guaranty, CMS, or other possible legal matters of the Clintons were mentioned. Moreover, in the spring and summer of 1993, Whitewater and Madison Guaranty related matters were not issues of concern either within the White House or in the press.[27]

Fiske's report made an overwhelming forensic case for Foster's suicide in Fort Marcy Park. The panel of pathologists Fiske retained found that there had been gunpowder residue on Foster's soft palate, meaning the gun had been in his mouth when it was fired, and the panel also cited FBI lab evidence that Foster's DNA had been found near the gun's muzzle. The condition of Foster's body "indicat[ed] that Foster voluntarily placed the gun in his mouth. . . . No broken teeth or other trauma to Foster's body were discovered during the autopsy, and there was no sign of a struggle." The panel also noted "a mark on Foster's right thumb consistent with the recoil of the trigger after firing," and "gunpowder on the portion of Foster's right index finger facing his thumb and in the web area between the index finger and the thumb." Moreover, "the condition of Foster's body and clothing at the time he was found precludes his having been moved to Fort Marcy Park from another location following his death." The very cleanliness of the body, Fiske's panel determined, was consistent only with Foster's body remaining where it fell.[28]

The only point on which the report admitted of any real question was Fiske's conclusion that Whitewater concerns played no role in the suicide. Fiske reports that "each of Foster's co-workers, friends and family whom we questioned was explicitly asked whether Foster had ever mentioned Whitewater or Madison Guaranty related matters as a cause of concern or distress. According to each of these people, Foster had never expressed any concern about these matters," though he had repeatedly expressed concern about the White House Travel Office conflagration and criticism he had received over it. "Obviously," Fiske wrote, "the fact that Foster never expressed a concern about Whitewater or Madison to anyone does not mean that he did not, in fact, have such a concern. Thus, we cannot conclusively rule out such a concern as a possible contributing factor to his depression. What we can conclude is that there is no evidence that he did have such a concern against a background in which Whitewater/Madison issues were neither a matter of expressed concern in the White House, nor the subject of media attention."[29]

The confidence of this conclusion eventually came back to haunt Fiske, when Foster's notes on the Clintons' 1992 tax return became public in 1995. Those notes showed that Foster had clearly been anxious about whether or not the Clintons should report a loss on the sale of their Whitewater investment. On the one hand, failing to declare a loss could undermine their public claims that they had lost money on Whitewater. On the other hand, claiming a loss was risky, since the Clintons were unable to document their actual losses on their investment — a fact that could lead to further scrutiny. One Foster note described the possibility of an audit as a "can of worms you shouldn't open."[30] The notes can reasonably be read to indicate that Whitewater was possibly a greater source of concern in Foster's final months than Fiske had realized. Yet despite this possibility, Fiske's conclusion was a powerful one. However concerned about Whitewater Foster may have been, it wasn't the specific stress about which he was complaining to his friends and family. Indeed, the notes may represent nothing more than a cautious lawyer preparing conservative advice for his clients. In fact, other material withheld from Fiske indicated, even more strongly than Fiske had reported, that Travel Office concerns were foremost in Foster's mind.[31] On the big picture, in other words, Fiske's report was perfectly correct: a fair-minded person reading it should have concluded without question that Foster's tragic death did not implicate the Clintons, directly or indirectly, in criminal misconduct of any kind, and that he did not kill himself either to help them cover up Whitewater wrongdoing or because he had discovered some grave threat to Clinton's presidency.

Fair-mindedness, alas, is a commodity in short supply in politics, and Fiske's report was swiftly attacked on all three of its major conclusions. Elements on the right refused to accept the conclusion that Foster had killed himself, much less that he had done so in Fort Marcy Park. Fiske, critics said, ignored physical evidence that the body had been moved, specifically a bloodstain on his shirt that had apparently been caused by head movement.[32] Fiske also reported that the FBI lab found no "coherent soil" on Foster's shoes, which critics saw as proof he had not walked to the spot in the park where he was found.[33] The Park Police had found some carpet fibers and some blond hairs on the body for which Fiske had not attempted to account. Fiske was unable to definitively link the gun to Foster, and there were no fingerprints on a torn note that had been found in a briefcase in Foster's White House office several days after his death. Against the power of Fiske's findings, such loose ends were, in reality, trivial. Yet they provided good grist for conspiracy theorists — some quite prominent — for whom the death had to be sinister. Representative Dan Burton, for example, made a series of speeches on the floor of the House in which he attacked the Fiske investigation as having "so many holes in it you could drive a truck through it," and as "not worth much of the paper that it is written on."[34] To highlight what he deemed the inadequacies in Fiske's work, Burton actually reenacted the death outside his home using something "similar to a head."[35] The bottom line, he said, is that

> there just is no question about the major question about the death of Vince Foster. The man who found the body said the hands were moved. He swears before God that the hands were moved in a court report. He swears the head was moved. There were no fingerprints on the gun. There were no fingerprints on the suicide note.
>
> The counsel, Mr. Fiske, never checked the carpet samples from his office to see if those were the same ones on his clothes. At least, he did not say so in the report. He did not check his house to see if the carpet samples were off his home. Where did those carpet samples come from? There is just a ton of questions that need to be answered.
>
> For any intelligent person to hear what I have said tonight and to read this report and to conclude that this is accurate, they just must have their eyes closed. I just do not know how they can believe that. . . .
>
> He may have committed suicide, I do not know, but I do know this: That body was moved, and if the body was moved, the report is wrong, and if the report is wrong, we need to ask Mr. Fiske why.[36]

Burton was not the only prominent public official to doubt Fiske's conclusions. As late as July 1995, long after Fiske had departed the scene and Starr was on the case, House Speaker

Newt Gingrich said he doubted the official finding of suicide. "I just don't accept it," Gingrich said, noting that there "are plausible grounds to wonder what happened and very real grounds to wonder why it was investigated so badly." There's something, Gingrich declared, "that doesn't fit about this whole case and the way it's been handled. . . . I'm not convinced he didn't [kill himself]. I'm just not convinced he did."[37] A July 1995 poll published in *Time* magazine showed that only 35 percent of Americans surveyed believed Foster had committed suicide, while 20 percent believed he had been murdered and 45 percent were unsure.[38]

More widespread than the doubts about the suicide finding was skepticism of Fiske's conclusion that the suicide had been unrelated to Whitewater. Shortly after Fiske's report came out, *The Wall Street Journal* editorialized that his "forensic evidence on the events surrounding Vincent Foster's death" is "extensive and persuasive."[39] A month later, however, the *Journal* questioned Fiske's conclusion that Whitewater played no role in the suicide, citing the suspicious handling by White House officials of Foster's files after his death.[40] "Of course he didn't fret aloud over Whitewater with his wife or friends; the whole reason for suspecting he might have worried about it is that his closest associates worried enough to want control of the Whitewater papers in his office," the *Journal* wrote. "But Mr. Fiske can tell us Whitewater worries were not a factor in the suicide without telling us what he's learned about what happened to the papers."[41] Republican Senator Christopher Bond of Missouri raised similar questions more directly in an op-ed around the same time. "In my mind, the issue is not, nor has it ever been, that Mr. Foster committed suicide. That is what I believed happened. Rather, it is whether Whitewater issues played a part in his death and whether the White House made a conscious effort to withhold information relevant to Mr. Foster's state of mind," Bond wrote. "If we are to believe Special Counsel Fiske, Whitewater issues were not a significant factor in Mr. Foster's suicide. The special counsel's report, however, raises significant questions regarding this issue."[42]

To Starr, who took over the probe as the debate over the Fiske report was raging, that questions had arisen about the suicide was alone enough to justify reopening the matter. Starr took up the Foster death both because he felt obliged to address every issue Fiske had examined and because, in his judgment, the attacks on the Fiske report demanded a response. Starr described the Fiske report respectfully, saying that it "well stated a conclusion and a process."[43] On reading the report, he said, "I talked to Rod[erick] Lankler, the principal author of the report, . . . and I was satisfied that it had been done in a professional way."[44] Starr also noted, however, that Fiske's report "did not go through an elaborate, deeply detailed, fact-based, rigorous analysis."[45] Criticisms of the report, consequently, "were cascading in, . . . extraordinarily direct assaults on it." It is worth stressing that Starr himself was never conspiracy-minded about Foster's death. He said he had "no reason to doubt [Fiske's] ultimate conclusion."[46] He described the furor that followed its release, moreover, as composed of "all kinds of outlandish, unfounded allegations."[47] Kavanaugh, the prosecutor responsible for actually conducting much of the Foster investigation under Starr, said he "tried to keep an open mind" about how Foster died, but he saw the probe's purpose as "ruling out a crime." The bottom line, he said, is that "you have a dead person with a gun in his hand and a wound in his head. You have a presumption that it is a suicide but you're looking at it as though it could be something else."[48] Ewing, who also participated in the investigation, likewise said he was convinced "pretty early on" that Foster killed himself.[49] Had Starr been trying to prove a murder, he presumably would have shown more tolerance for the work of Miquel Rodriguez, a civil rights prosecutor in the office who, as Starr put it, "just was convinced that something had, in fact, happened." Rodriguez, whose hiring Starr described as "an unfortunate start" to the Foster investigation, found no sympathy, however. After he insinuated to a grand jury that one of the Park Police officers may have been involved in Foster's death, then–Washington deputy Mark Tuohey III quickly reined him in and Rodriguez left the office shortly thereafter.[50]

But if conspiracy-mongering was not driving the Foster death investigation, neither was any prosecutorial instinct. Starr believed he had to settle the outstanding historical questions for the sake of posterity, however unlikely those questions were to result in criminal prosecutions. In his view, public doubts about the suicide were "corrosive" in the face of "the potential historical significance of the death of an individual so close to the president and first lady," an event he saw as the "most significant death in office since that of [Truman administration Defense] Secretary James Forrestal."[51] Because of the seriousness of the matter and the "withering scrutiny" he knew his own work would face, Starr believed that he "had to have this absolutely air-tight." His role, he believed, "was [to] put this to rest to the fullest extent possible." He regarded this role, which he likened to that of the Warren Commission's investigation of John F. Kennedy's assassination, as "very important for the well-being of the country" and flowing out of "the uniqueness of the independent counsel, who is sort of a blue-ribbon grand jury kind of person who issues reports on issues of public moment."[52]

John Bates, the Washington deputy who oversaw the latter part of the Foster death probe, acknowledged that the decision to use the inquiry to settle historical questions made it exceptionally difficult to close. "A reasonable decision was made that it had to be reexplored. There were some forensic questions that really required some independent examination by this independent counsel," Bates told me. The persistence of conspiracy theorizing among "the fringe elements convinced [Starr] that he had to issue a thorough, exhaustive report that would settle the questions." Starr, he said, "realized that this was not the traditional role of a prosecutor, as did some of us in the office, and we were frustrated that the case put us in that position." Starr, however, "felt that it was incumbent upon him to come out with a thorough and dispositive report."[53] As such, said Kavanaugh, speed was not the priority that it had been for Fiske. Starr's "goals in the investigation were to not worry about carping that this was taking too long but to produce something we could be proud of ten, twenty years later. To do that, he felt we had to take all steps within reason."[54]

"All steps within reason" took nearly three years. By the autumn of 1995, Kavanaugh said, the office had conducted a much broader set of interviews than Fiske had done, including interviews with Foster's children and his mother. At that point, he and Tuohey assessed their progress and gave Starr a status report. Starr, however, "was still not satisfied in terms of going the extra mile," Kavanaugh recalled. In response, they went back and conducted an ultra-thorough search of Fort Marcy Park for the bullet that killed Foster (which they never found). They did carpet-fiber tests, and the office brought in its own outside forensic specialist.[55] Ewing recounted that Starr even went so far as to suggest, on the advice of the late Republican Representative Steve Schiff, that he interview Foster conspiracy theorists Christopher Ruddy, Ambrose Evans-Pritchard, and Reed Irvine.[56] This led to what Ewing described as a "two-day kamikaze run" of meetings with the conspiracy theorists.[57] The office also brought in a Memphis prosecutor named Steve Parker, a Ewing protégé who had significant experience in homicide cases, to help finish up. Yet even after bringing Parker on, Starr took more than a year before issuing a report that, once again, declared Foster's death a suicide.

Assessing the marginal costs and benefits of Starr's Foster investigation is an interesting exercise. Starr's major accomplishment was closing — as he intended — many of the niggling questions that had permitted skepticism about Fiske's findings. Starr's report contained far more extensive forensic analyses than Fiske's did and, in spots, corrected omissions and oversights in the prior report. Starr found, for example, that Foster's shoes had soil on them after all; an expert who examined the matter for him concluded that "microscopic and macroscopic examination showed this material to contain mineral particles, including mica, other soil materials, and vegetative matter" that were consistent with his having walked through Fort Marcy Park.[58] Starr also reported the results of tests on sunflower seed husks found in Foster's pants pocket and in an oven mitt discovered in his car. The husks, along with traces of lead found in both locations, suggested that Foster had carried the gun in the oven mitt and then transferred it to his pocket on reaching Fort Marcy Park.[59] Starr had the FBI lab test the thirty-five carpet fibers found on Foster's clothing — which had been grist for much speculation that Foster's body had been wrapped in a carpet and moved — and found, unsurprisingly, that twenty-three of them were consistent with those in Foster's home, four others were consistent with those in the White House or Foster's car, and eight could not be identified, a finding that "does not support speculation that Mr. Foster was wrapped and moved in a carpet on July 20."[60]

On the whole, however, Starr's report read as a ringing endorsement of Fiske's earlier work; his report contradicted Fiske's on no significant points and served largely to answer specific questions people had posed in light of the Fiske report, three years earlier. The only one of Fiske's Foster findings that Starr did not explicitly endorse was Fiske's contention that Whitewater concerns had not been a factor bearing on Foster's state of mind. Starr, as he explained in a footnote, was loath to provide "an exposition of substantive events under investigation by the OIC — including Whitewater, Madison, and Travel Office issues — and Mr. Foster's possible relationship to those events."[61] His staff, however, clearly believed that Fiske had overstated the disconnect between the suicide and Whitewater. Ewing, for example, said that he remains unconvinced that Whitewater did not weigh on Foster, noting that "Fiske didn't know what we know now about what may have been on [Foster's] mind."[62] Such comments aside, nothing in Starr's discussion of Foster's state of mind contradicted Fiske's report on this point. Starr reported that he "is not aware of a single, obvious triggering event that might have motivated Mr. Foster to commit suicide." Starr noted that Foster had been involved in "a number of important and difficult issues" in the White House, including a Supreme Court appointment, naming an attorney general, litigation over the first lady's Health Care Task Force, and the Clintons' tax return, "which involved an issue regarding treatment of the Clintons' 1992 sale of their interest in Whitewater." Foster had been upset about a controversy over his membership in the unintegrated Country Club of Little Rock and by press criticism, particularly on *The Wall Street Journal* editorial page. He had been particularly troubled by the flap following the firing of the White House Travel Office employees.[63] "In short," Starr wrote, "the OIC cannot set forth a particular reason or set of reasons *why* Mr. Foster committed suicide. The important issue, from the standpoint of the death investigation, is whether Mr. Foster committed suicide. On that issue, the state-of-mind evidence is compelling, and it demonstrates that Mr. Foster was, in fact, distressed or depressed in a manner consistent with suicide."[64] Three years after the release of Fiske's report, Starr's 114-page tome concluded: "In sum, based on all of the available evidence, which is considerable, the OIC agrees with the conclusion reached by every official entity that has examined the issue: Mr. Foster committed suicide by gunshot in Fort Marcy Park on July 20, 1993."[65]

The detail in Starr's Foster report certainly accomplished the prosecutor's goal of marginalizing doubts about Foster's death. Members of Congress stopped speculating — at least publicly — about whether Foster had been murdered. The report also prompted something of a flight on the part of much of the conservative movement from the conspiracy theorists with whom prominent conservatives had previously been flirting.[66] To the extent that Starr had set out to settle the historical questions about Foster's death so authoritatively that conspiracy theories could only continue through leaps of faith, he certainly succeeded. The belief that Foster did not kill himself is today almost entirely confined to those on the political fringe.

One is entitled to ask, however, whether the costs of this public good were too high. The three years Starr spent on the project constituted an enormous investment of time, during which — as Fiske had worried — a cloud was permitted to hang over the Clintons on a matter in which they deserved no censure or taint of investigation. The Foster probe also diverted

human resources from other matters in which live prosecutorial questions did exist and put them on an issue that nobody
expected would ever lead to indictments. This extraordinary
investment in a nonprosecutorial matter served, at the end of
the day, to generate a report that, predictably enough, essentially reiterated the conclusions of an earlier investigation —
the soundness of which there had never been any particular
reason to doubt. One has to sympathize, to some degree, with
Foster's sister Sheila Foster Anthony, who complained in a
statement following the report's release that "a more expe-
ditious handling of this matter by the independent counsel
would have spared the family further anguish and the public
further uncertainty caused by the ridiculous conspiracy theories proffered by those with a profit or political motive. In my
view, it was unconscionable for Mr. Starr for so long to allow
the American people to entertain any thought that the president of the United States somehow had complicity in Vince's
death."[67] Starr's handling of the matter, to a great extent, validated Fiske's fear that a lengthy investigation would stoke, at
least while the investigation remained pending, the belief that
the death had been a homicide after all.

The Foster investigation was, perhaps, a marginal example of Starr's attitude in action. It was something of a side
project, after all, one that differed greatly from everything else
Starr was looking at. Because the ultimate outcome of the
investigation was so obvious from the beginning, nobody ever
faced the serious possibility of criminal charges as a result of
it. While it took a long time, moreover, the Foster investigation was not an especially costly component of the investigation overall.[68] In some respects, however, its very marginality
only increases its poignancy as an illustration of Starr's philosophy. That Starr was willing to spend three years of his office's

energy in order to prove a historical point that had already been proven and was, in any event, somewhat removed from the core of his prosecutorial mandate demonstrates just how broad he understood the truth-finding function of his office to be. The pattern evident in the Foster inquiry also proves, though more subtly so, a generalizable one in Starr's Whitewater investigation. In matter after matter throughout his tenure, issues lingered long after the genuine law enforcement interests had been exhausted. The typical pattern saw the office's more traditional prosecutors dispose relatively quickly of the actual law enforcement questions a given issue presented. These prosecutors would then leave the office, having accomplished what they came there to do, and the matter would then get picked up by more aggressive investigators less inclined to close the matter quickly. Their inclination to follow additional leads would feed upon Starr's own insistence that the office address every question authoritatively, and as a consequence, huge blocks of time would elapse before the office finally closed the matter. The core of the Whitewater mandate presents an excellent illustration of this pattern.

By the time Starr received jurisdiction over Whitewater, the term had come to encompass a raft of allegations that went well beyond the land deal that gave the scandal its name.[69] The Whitewater scandal began during the 1992 campaign, when *The New York Times* published a story outlining a land deal between the Clintons and the McDougals. The *Times* story raised questions about whether Jim McDougal's savings and loan — Madison Guaranty — had improperly subsidized the Clintons' real estate investment and received favorable treatment from Arkansas state regulators as a result of McDougal's relationship with the governor and his wife. The story disclosed that the Clintons had bought land in the Ozarks as part of a 50 percent partnership with the McDougals dubbed the Whitewater Development Corp. The McDougals heavily subsidized the Clintons' investment, and Madison Guaranty apparently did as well, the *Times* claimed. The Clintons also appeared to have misreported aspects of the investment on their tax returns, by deducting interest payments that had been made, in fact, by the corporation. To make matters still cozier, Bill Clinton appointed as Arkansas state securities commissioner a woman who had previously worked as a private lawyer at a firm that represented Madison, and the appointment came at a time when Madison was in trouble as a result of McDougal's tangled lending practices. Hillary Clinton, meanwhile, who also represented Madison as an attorney at the Rose Law Firm, later wrote to that commissioner, Beverly Bassett Schaffer, with novel plans for a stock issue by the savings and loan — an idea Schaffer approved but that was never implemented.[70]

The story made few waves during the campaign, chiefly because of its turgid complexity and because the *Times*'s initial reporting — notwithstanding much subsequent media criticism — had been scrupulously fair to a degree that actually obfuscated somewhat the issues the paper was raising.[71] Whitewater only exploded onto the national scene in the fall of 1993, when *The Washington Post* reported that the Resolution Trust Corporation (RTC) — the federal agency in charge of cleaning up the S&L mess — had made a series of referrals to the U.S. attorney's office in Arkansas for possible criminal investigation of Madison.[72] Whitewater further snowballed when David Hale, a municipal judge in Little Rock, alleged that Governor Clinton had pressured him to make a $300,000 loan to Susan McDougal as part of an effort to cover Madison's debts.[73] The matter became a national scandal when the public learned that Foster had been working on Whitewater-related tax questions, and that Whitewater materials had been turned over to the Clintons' personal lawyers following his death. That revelation focused attention on the way White House officials had impaired Park Police investigators and Justice Department officials who were attempting to search Foster's office following his death, and how they had, more generally, handled his papers.

Even after Fiske began as special prosecutor early in 1994, the scandal continued to expand. White House and Treasury Department officials acknowledged contacts between them concerning the Madison Guaranty criminal referrals — contacts that turned out to be broader than the administration initially admitted and which some construed as White House attempts to influence supposedly apolitical law enforcement matters. Questions also arose as to how Hillary Clinton had come to represent Madison — specifically, whether Jim McDougal's claim that Bill Clinton had encouraged him to give her business was accurate. Regulators likewise examined whether the Rose Law Firm had conflicts of interest when it later represented the RTC in a civil suit against Madison's accountants. As part of his mandate to prosecute any crimes related in any way to the relationship between the McDougals, Hale, and the Clintons, Fiske began looking into a cable television deal involving Arkansas Governor Jim Guy Tucker, and he also examined the relationship between Clinton's 1990 campaign for governor and a small Arkansas bank in Perry County. By the time he left office, Fiske was also nearly ready to indict Webster Hubbell, a former Rose partner who had served as Clinton's associate attorney general, for an overbilling scheme at the Rose firm that had defrauded clients and firm partners alike.[74] The investigation Starr inherited when he took over from Fiske was already a broad-based one that presented several distinct questions.

These questions varied significantly in gravity, particularly with respect to the Clintons themselves. The criminal allegations surrounding Madison were, as subsequent events showed, quite serious, suggesting both widespread and exceptionally high-level misbehavior in Arkansas state government. For all that Whitewater was disparaged as involving unintelligible pre-presidential conduct, the questions it raised specifically about the Clintons were far from trivial. They amounted to allegations — however credible they ultimately proved — that the president and first lady were S&L criminals who had abused Clinton's governorship in a corrupt, if ineffectual, effort to enrich themselves at the expense of both federal taxpayers and Madison depositors. At the same time, many of the allegations that larded the periphery of Whitewater seemed highly implausible as criminal matters. However suspicious the handling of Foster's papers or the contacts between the White House and the Treasury Department over the Madison referrals may have been, these hardly seemed like promising criminal cases. The job of the Whitewater independent counsel was, to some extent, one of winnowing — finding a way to focus on and resolve the genuine public integrity issues that lay beneath a giant, and very public, conflagration largely focused on matters that were objectively less troubling, if somewhat easier for the public to understand. Unlike Fiske, who had worked aggressively and quickly to separate the wheat from the chaff, Starr made little public effort to narrow his field of inquiry.[75] Matters that lay at Whitewater's periphery and which surely could have been resolved expeditiously were left to dangle over the Clintons' heads, thereby preventing the public discussion from ever focusing narrowly on the real questions the Clintons needed to answer. By failing over many years to augment the scandal's signal-to-noise ratio, Starr subtly encouraged the public to dismiss the scandal entirely as just so much Washington political bickering.

Internally, however, the office did focus relatively quickly on the matters at Whitewater's heart. Indeed, other than its slowness, there was nothing especially peculiar about the trajectory of the initial phases of the Whitewater investigation. Building on the groundwork Fiske had laid, Starr proceeded fairly systematically against Fiske's targets, indicting or reaching plea agreements with those who both had information about Madison Guaranty's business dealings and had stepped over legal lines. Within a year and a half of taking office, he had brought cases against thirteen additional figures.[76] There were, to be sure, some unnecessary detours. Some of these prosecutions involved the Perry County Bank issue, a matter somewhat marginal to Starr's broader project and one that was arguably worth ignoring.[77] Starr also faced significant delays that were beyond his realistic control. Conspicuous among these delays was that caused by the mysterious disappearance of Hillary Clinton's Rose Law Firm billing records, which finally showed up in the White House in 1996 and which seemed to show that the first lady's work on a fraud-riddled land deal called Castle Grande had been more extensive than she had earlier acknowledged. That same year, investigators learned of large payments supporters of the president made to Webster Hubbell in the months between his departure from the Justice Department and his guilty plea, payments that — in light of the unsatisfactory cooperation the office believed he had offered — raised potential obstruction of justice questions. Such complications made headlines. They did not, however, prove to be the rate-limiting factors in Starr's efforts to resolve the Whitewater controversy. Rather, the first two years of Starr's Arkansas investigation were organized, as they should have been, around securing the cooperation of those witnesses who could answer the key questions about the Clintons. That endeavor became possible only after a jury in 1996 convicted Governor Tucker and both McDougals.

For all the criticism Starr has received, the prosecution of Governor Tucker and the McDougals in relation to a scheme to defraud the Small Business Administration (SBA) using both Madison Guaranty and Hale's SBA-backed lending company, Capital Management Services Inc. (CMS), remains a significant prosecutorial accomplishment that was entirely justified and has, in retrospect, been significantly underappreciated.[78] The indictment, handed down on August 17, 1995, alleged a complex fraud designed to increase the on-paper capital of CMS, so that it would receive — and could lend out — more federal money and could provide a financial infusion into the overextended Madison Guaranty and, as Jim McDougal was alleged to have said, "clean up some members of the political family." The SBA program under which CMS operated was designed to provide capital to disadvantaged businesses that were normally unable to borrow. Under its terms, private lenders who raised capital were offered, in effect, three dollars in federal matching money for every dollar in private capital they raised. The federal rules restricted the lending organization to making loans equivalent to 30 percent of the company's capital. As a consequence, Hale's lending limit at the time the scheme was hatched was $150,000. The scheme's purpose was to jack up Hale's lending limit. In order to accomplish this, Hale, Tucker, and McDougal arranged for Hale to sell a restaurant at an inflated price to a straw buyer, who received the money for the purchase in a loan from Madison Guaranty. Hale then invested the windfall in CMS, creating through this fraud significant new lending capacity. Once the new funds were available, Jim McDougal called

Hale to meet with him and Governor Clinton, the independent counsel claimed. At this meeting, Clinton and Mc-Dougal requested that Hale make a $300,000 loan to Susan McDougal in the name of a fictitious advertising company called Master Marketing, the prosecutors further claimed. While the loan was ostensibly intended as working capital for the advertising agency, it was, in reality, deposited into the McDougals' personal checking account. About half of it was used to service existing loans as part of Madison's and the McDougals' endless circles of debt. Some was used for renovations on the McDougals' house. Most interestingly, $45,000 was used to acquire seven hundred acres of property in the name of the Whitewater Development Corporation.[79] The conviction of Tucker and the McDougals, which took place on May 28, 1996, offered a significant validation of important premises of the Whitewater investigation.

It also offered Starr, as Ewing later pointed out, his first opportunity to address the core questions before him, which related to the extent of the Clintons' involvement in the schemes that led to Madison's collapse.[80] As such, it represented a pivotal moment for the Whitewater investigation. The evidence Starr had amassed against the Clintons, so far, was highly suggestive but both inconclusive and largely based on the testimony of Hale, a disreputable felon. The Mc-Dougals, though now felons too, were in a position to clarify either that there was or was not a case to be made against Clinton. Starr's investigation would ultimately stand or fall on whether their cooperation could be secured and what, if anything, they said.

The office proceeded in this project half successfully. Though previously belligerent in his attacks on the independent counsel, Jim McDougal, now in bad health and facing a potentially lengthy jail term, agreed to cooperate and backed up Hale's account of Bill Clinton's involvement in Susan McDougal's Master Marketing loan. McDougal's new account — in his memoirs, anyway — differed somewhat from Hale's, including with respect to Clinton's precise role, and he played down somewhat his own part in the scheme for which he was prosecuted.[81] But McDougal was clear that then-Governor Clinton showed up at a meeting between Hale and McDougal at Castle Grande, mentioned the loan, and offered to put up "some land up in Marion County" as collateral.[82] McDougal also implicated Clinton in other ways. He claimed that the president had, in contrast to Clinton's testimony at the McDougal-Tucker trial, borrowed money from Madison Guaranty.[83] He described a scheme to route $2,000 a month in illegal money from Madison Guaranty to Clinton during the 1980s.[84] He also reiterated an earlier allegation that the governor had arranged with McDougal for Madison to send business to Hillary Clinton in 1984. According to McDougal, the arrangement was hatched at a meeting at Madison and resulted in a $2,000 per month retainer for the Rose Law Firm. McDougal wrote that he saw the retainer as a way of making his payments to Clinton "take place over the table."[85]

Having secured Jim McDougal's cooperation, Starr had two convicted felons and a developing paper trail that collectively sketched out a case against the Clintons. It was not enough. It was not enough to file charges, as the office ultimately admitted years later when Robert Ray finally closed the Whitewater investigation without bringing a case.[86] It also was not enough for an impeachment referral to Congress, though Starr had a lawyer on his staff named Stephen Bates draft an impeachment referral that he eventually declined to send to Congress. "I had documentary information and I had witnesses who suggested that the president committed perjury [at the McDougal-Tucker trial], or, at least, the testimony was untruthful," Starr told me. The draft referral "sits in our archives right now. It has never seen the light of day. It is one hundred pages long. . . . There were offenses; we prosecuted those. There were some guilty pleas. But we evaluated this, and I felt that it did not pass muster."[87] Without Susan McDougal's help, the prosecutors could envision the case they would bring against the president and his wife, but the evidence would not adequately support it.[88]

Susan McDougal, however, was unappeasable. In the days before her sentencing, she publicly flirted on national television with the notion of cooperating with Starr, saying she found the prospect "tempting."[89] By the time she appeared before the grand jury on September 4, 1996, however, she had decided against it. For reasons that are still obscure, she refused to answer questions before Starr's grand jury, even under a grant of court-ordered immunity. Claiming that Starr wanted her to lie and would prosecute her for perjury if she didn't say what he wanted to hear, she chose to face a civil contempt citation instead of answering questions, and remained jailed until the grand jury's term expired eighteen months later. By so doing — and particularly when she appeared in chains on television in a display of what is actually standard U.S. Marshal Service procedure for moving prisoners — Susan McDougal handed Starr a major public relations problem, one that President Clinton capitalized upon in his mounting verbal war against Starr. "They wanted her to say something bad about us, whether it was the truth or not," Clinton said in a television interview. "And if it was false, it would still be perfectly all right. And if she told the truth and it wasn't bad about us she simply would be punished for it. That's what her lawyer said." Asked whether he personally believed that Starr was out to get him and his wife, the president responded, "Isn't it obvious?"[90]

The reality, however, was that Starr was only doing what any serious prosecutor would have done in that situation. McDougal's testimony was critical to determining whether Clinton had, as her ex-husband indicated, lied both about his role in the Master Marketing loan and about whether Madison had ever lent him money, and Starr was employing an instrument—civil contempt—intended for precisely the circumstance in which a recalcitrant witness refuses to provide key information. Indeed, up through Susan McDougal's jailing, Starr's entire Whitewater investigation looked traditional enough, if occasionally quirky. It had been, to be sure, thorough in the extreme, and thus had infuriated much of the Arkansas political and economic elite. It had also been slow, a result simultaneously of the wide scope of Starr's inquiry, its exhaustiveness, Starr's inexperience as a prosecutor, the methodical pace of deliberations within the office, and a certain amount of non-cooperation by key witnesses. Nevertheless, Starr's probe, at that point anyway, had not been especially lengthy by the standards of independent counsel investigations. Had Starr, at some point during Susan McDougal's contempt, accepted the increasingly obvious fact that no amount of coercion would make her talk, made his final prosecutorial decisions, and brought Whitewater to a close, people would today see his investigation very differently. Starr would be remembered as a man who investigated the key matter within his jurisdiction thoroughly but reasonably and shut the investigation down when it reached the point of diminishing returns. Indeed, as late as 1997, thoughtful commentators who later became critics were still writing sympathetically. Jeffrey Rosen, for example, bemoaned that the end of Starr's probe "seems always just out of reach," but he portrayed Starr as fundamentally reasonable and making serious efforts to mute the havoc latent in the independent counsel law. "Although Starr has faced charges of partisanship from the beginning of his tenure, the criticisms are largely unfair," he wrote. "Rather than calling into question Starr's own integrity or professionalism, much of the controversy reflects structural flaws in the independent-counsel statute, which creates a free-floating prosecutor with an ever-expanding mandate, unconstrained by time, money or political accountability."[91] Within the office, the year following the McDougals' conviction saw many of the office's key prosecutors leave, and they left, as one put it, "very comfortable with what they had accomplished."[92]

The prosecutors who stayed were, generally speaking, far less comfortable, and Starr himself was hardly a disciplining exception. Having done the work that a normal prosecutor would have done, Starr had deep trouble accepting that he would not learn the truth about the issues at the core of his jurisdiction. This realization was compounded by his having become personally unseverable from the investigation. When he tried to resign in 1997 to take a position at Pepperdine University, the result was an uproar both in the political culture at large and — more important to Starr — among his own staff.[93] Unlike the Watergate Special Prosecution Force, which had seen a few different leaders over a relatively short period of time, the Starr investigation had become so personally identified with Starr that both inside and outside the office, he was universally expected to finish the job he had started. This represented a deeply ironic twist of fate that to some extent was evidence in and of itself that Starr's vision of a microcosm of the Justice Department had failed. Starr's approach to the office, after all, had been to depersonalize the investigation, to prevent a single prosecutor from becoming monomaniacally focused on a single target, and to create instead in the independent counsel's office an institution, not an individual. The reaction to his attempted resignation, however, showed that this effort had done nothing to blunt the public's perception that bringing the case against Clinton — or deciding not to bring it — was Starr's personal role that he could not slough off on anyone else. In retrospect, ironically, Starr was exactly the wrong man to serve as independent counsel in the wake of the Pepperdine incident. The reason was his truth commission understanding of the statute, which at that point in the probe was pulling him in a profoundly different direction from the instincts of a prosecutor. A prosecutor would have seen late 1997 as a natural endpoint for the investigation. For Starr, however, the salient fact was that witnesses were still holding out on him and preventing him from fulfilling the central command of the statute as he understood it. He still felt obligated to get the truth from them.

The most poignant example of this urge was Starr's reindictment of Susan McDougal in May 1998 — while the Lewinsky investigation was proceeding full throttle — for obstruction of justice and criminal contempt of court in connection with her refusal to answer questions before the grand jury. Starr had, of course, already prosecuted her successfully once before, and she had already been jailed for civil contempt on the same matter for more than a year. Formally, the civil and criminal contempt questions are different from each other and properly addressed through different cases. When McDougal was locked up for civil contempt in an effort to force her to testify, she could have gotten out at any time merely by complying with the court order that she testify. The indictment, by contrast, was an attempt to punish her for her refusal to comply. In practice, however, the coercive and punitive dimensions of contempt bleed into one another.

Spending many months in jail is innately punitive, and an indictment from a prosecutor who wants his target's cooperation more than he wants to punish her is innately coercive. In this case, Starr made no effort to hide that the second indictment was chiefly motivated by the desire to get McDougal to talk. "Here I was absolutely determined to do everything that I could to get the truth about the core of this investigation," he said. "We knew from documents . . . that she was a veritable treasure trove of information that directly related to the president himself."[94] Starr, to be sure, also saw the indictment as an effort to "vindicate the interests of the justice system" from the misconduct of a woman who "flouted that grand jury."[95] That concern, however, appears to have been secondary. When initially asked to explain the indictment, Starr said that he "honestly felt the obligation to do everything that I could that was right and just to do . . . in order to get that information which involved the president of the United States and whether the president of the United States had committed crimes."[96]

Starr's decision to file the case — and, for that matter, his justification of it — offers a remarkably stark vision of the full implications of the truth commission vision. Even in the peculiar absence of competing priorities that always prevails under the independent counsel law, a prosecutor considering such a matter with any interest in the balance between the costs and benefits of the case would likely have refrained from going forward. Criminal contempt indictments in the wake of civil contempts are not unheard of in dealing with organized crime or major drug trafficking cases, or other situations in which prosecutors are pursuing the more dangerous and powerful of society's miscreants.[97] But whatever she may have been, Susan McDougal was no mobster. Moreover, while her motives remain unclear, she had emphasized for the better part of two years that she would never cooperate with Starr's team. She had, indeed, been willing to spend time behind bars to avoid doing so, deferring the start of her sentence for the fraud conviction in the process. For the traditional prosecutor, the likelihood of any real payoff from an indictment was so small that the case was simply not worth the trouble — particularly given the possibility of an acquittal. Starr, however, had never planned to step back at the point of diminishing returns. For him, the salient calculation was that McDougal had stuck her thumb in the eye of the truth-seeking process and that a lawful and ethical step remained open to him that would both punish her and hold out some small chance of his garnering facts both relevant and previously elusive. As he read his role, he could not responsibly evade such a step. This understanding led him to greatly overestimate his chances of prevailing upon McDougal to change her mind, and consequently to prosecute her in the face of an overwhelming likelihood that it would avail him nothing. "I had great hopes that . . . even with impeachment, . . . in the courtroom we would be able to set aside all of those predilections and that the jury would do its duty. . . . And that if that had happened, if she were convicted on one or more counts," he would have the leverage he needed. "I have said this time and time again to defense lawyers: 'I do not have any interest in your client serving one day in jail. I have a fundamental obligation, and that is to get all of the facts and to have some kind of appropriate disposition.' "[98]

A federal jury in Arkansas, however, balked at Starr's second case against Susan McDougal. This happened even though much of the evidence was not in dispute: nobody denied, after all, that McDougal had defied court orders or impaired the grand jury's work. Yet the jury, on April 12, 1999, acquitted her of obstruction of justice and deadlocked on two contempt charges.[99] Starr blamed his failure to gain a conviction in the case on the pollution of the jury pool as a result of the impeachment and the White House's campaign against his office. A juror whom his investigators were permitted to interview, he said, told the office that the jury had been hijacked by a trio of jurors spouting highly political rhetoric that they had managed not to betray during jury selection. What the juror described, he said, "was an act of commandeering by three jurors who asserted control over the process, including physical control over the jury instructions. They would not permit their fellow jurors to review the instructions. One of these jurors gave very inflammatory statements. Never before in the course of the trial, at any break, at any adjournment, had such sentiments been expressed: that this was all political, that Starr was out to get the Clintons, and that he was going to do nothing to assist Starr in getting the Clintons. When specific issues would be discussed, questions would arise about the law, and one of these three commandeering jurors said, 'We are the judges now. It doesn't matter what the judge said. We are the judges.' It became very clear that those three jurors were going to acquit on all counts." The other jurors, Starr said, hoped that by agreeing to acquit on the obstruction charge, they might induce moderation on the contempt charges. This, however, did not work, and the result was the hung jury.[100]

Starr's belief that the three jurors were acting in bad faith and had lied during jury selection is certainly plausible. It also seems possible, however, that jurors were merely responding viscerally to the genuine oddity of the case and framing their objections in terms of the pervasive political vocabulary of the day. Starr was, after all, bringing the full force of the law against McDougal in a fashion wholly out of proportion to the importance of the offense. That he was doing so to fulfill his understanding of his mission under the statute — not because he was on a political crusade against Bill Clinton—would hardly seem salient to a skeptical juror who had just watched McDougal's very vigorous defense. The jury's reaction to the case seems to reflect an instinctive understanding that the Starr investigation was no longer chiefly pursuing justice.

A similar problem was evident in Starr's treatment of Webster Hubbell, specifically in his two decisions during 1998 to bring additional charges against the former associate attorney general. In contrast to his very direct admission that the second McDougal indictment was primarily coercive, Starr's discussion of Hubbell's case reveals principally his deep offense at Hubbell's underlying behavior, not any great illusions that Hubbell was about to turn on his friends. "Loyalty ranked very high in his constellation of values," Starr recalled of Hubbell. "I do not believe that people reasonably anticipated that we were simply an indictment away or another conviction away from Webb's full cooperation." Still, though he stressed the punitive dimensions of the cases, Starr did not deny that the indictments had a coercive component as well. Asked whether he was concerned primarily with encouraging Hubbell to tell the truth or with punishing crimes, Starr said the decisions to prosecute him again were "based on the totality of the circumstances."[101] The indictments themselves were quite different from each other. The first of the cases alleged tax offenses far removed from Whitewater or Madison, while the other involved allegations that Hubbell had defrauded the Resolution Trust Corporation and the Federal Deposit Insurance Corporation by concealing his own conflicts of interest and the true nature of Hillary Clinton's legal work on the Castle Grande deal—a matter close to the molten core of Starr's mandate.

As with Susan McDougal, however, it is difficult to imagine that the subsequent indictments of Hubbell would have gone forward had Starr been satisfied with his cooperation following the plea agreement on the billing scheme in 1994. The indictments in 1998 surely reflected both the office's frustration at Hubbell's previous unsatisfying assistance to investigators and an effort to punish conduct that might have been overlooked had that assistance proven more valuable. It is worth emphasizing, however, that federal prosecutors run into such problems and frustrations all the time without resorting to serial indictments of the same person. Hubbell's lawyer, John Nields Jr., was convinced that "the prosecution of Mr. Hubbell had to do with the fact that it was an independent counsel case; that the ultimate targets were the president and the first lady; and that the prosecutors hoped to use the tax case to induce Mr. Hubbell to reveal incriminating information against them — information he actually did not have."[102]

To whatever extent Starr's office still hoped to flip Hubbell, the hope was a vain one — even assuming Nields was wrong and his client had held out on the prosecutors. Hubbell had, after all, said from the time of the initial plea agreement that he could offer no evidence of criminality on the part of the president or first lady. According to Ewing, Hubbell was sufficiently insistent on this point that he did not even proffer testimony in advance of the deal, and the office did not bother seeking a proffer either. Hubbell agreed to answer whatever questions the office had and help out as he could, but he never held out the prospect of delivering the bigger fish.[103] Despite this, however, Starr evidently had expectations of Hubbell's cooperation that went unfulfilled, and his offense at Hubbell's failure to deliver was compounded both by Hubbell's high law enforcement position and what seemed, in our conversations, like personal pique at having been burned. "He was a person, who — my word — was not only a lawyer but a senior government official in the Justice Department and who had, in our judgment, not been forthcoming with us. I know he has a different take on that. But there were a total of eight different prosecutors [on Starr's staff] who felt that he was simply not being fully forthcoming. I don't mean entirely unforthcoming, but he was not being forthcoming — so much so that there was a unanimous recommendation" that the office not recommend leniency to the sentencing judge on the basis of Hubbell's cooperation. Despite this, Starr said, he did not speak at Hubbell's sentencing hearing in opposition to Hubbell's motion for leniency based on his record of community service, but stood aside, saying that the court was better positioned than he to make that judgment.[104] Starr clearly felt he had played more than fairly with Hubbell.

It was only after Hubbell was in jail that investigators learned that he had received hundreds of thousands of dollars in consulting payments from Clinton's allies in the period between his departure from the Justice Department and his plea. These payments, quite naturally, cast his perceived noncooperation in a different light, particularly because presidential aides had assisted him in getting his consulting contracts and, as the second indictment alleged, Starr's office could find no evidence that Hubbell had done much work for his clients. Exacerbating the problem were comments Hubbell made in prison phone conversations in which he seemed to suggest he was protecting the White House — though his remarks were, in context, amenable to differing interpretations.[105] These factors raised the question of whether Hubbell's failure to be more forthcoming had been the result of hush money payments organized by the Clinton White House.

The hush money case never materialized, but Hubbell had, in any event, not used the money to pay any of a giant tax debt he had been carrying for years. Though he owed the federal government, the state of Arkansas, and the District of Columbia collectively $895,000 and had earned more than $1 million between 1994 and 1997, he had paid only $30,000 toward retiring his tax liability during that period, Starr alleged. By contrast, he spent more than $750,000 on extravagant living expenses.[106] This pattern enraged Starr. "Here was a high official who wielded extraordinary power in the Justice Department in the very early days of the administration, who then entered into this . . . moral undertaking" at his sentencing, "when he said, in effect, 'I am sorry,'" and "repent[ed], in the secular sense, of what he had done." At that hearing, Starr recalled, "Mr. Hubbell mustered all of these statements with respect to the kind of person he was, his numerous manifold contributions to his own community — and with me standing aside" and not objecting to leniency on this basis. Even as Hubbell was making a public break with his criminality, however, he proceeded "with what we viewed as really egregious careful planning to spend down very substantial sums of money and to leave the IRS completely out. It was a very clever, elaborate scheme, done with lots of forethought and planning."

Starr bristled at the notion that the Hubbell tax case was one the Justice Department would not have brought under normal circumstances. He brought in department tax prosecutors to look at the case, he said, and they urged him to proceed. He consulted extensively with the IRS. Everyone who examined the case, he said, concluded that the conduct was serious and constituted the sort of case the department would file.[107] On April 30, 1998, Hubbell was charged, along with his wife, Suzanna Hubbell; his accountant, Michael Schaufele; and his Little Rock lawyer, Charles Owens, with conspiracy to violate the internal revenue laws, tax evasion, impairing and impeding the IRS, and mail and wire fraud. Starr also charged Hubbell and Schaufele with assisting in the preparation of false tax returns.[108]

Starr's suggestion that the Justice Department typically pursues cases comparable to Hubbell's is, at the very least, an overstatement. Though framed as a tax evasion and fraud case, the weight of the allegations against Hubbell was less that he had taken illegal steps to avoid paying taxes than that he had simply failed to pay them. The difference is a significant one. Criminal tax cases normally require both proof of criminal intent and proof the defendant took steps to hide money or defraud the government—not merely that he did not pay money that he owed. Nonpayment alone, which is a misdemeanor, is generally handled through the IRS's administrative collection process, not through criminal prosecution at all. To be sure, the indictment against Hubbell did allege acts of evasion, specifically that Hubbell had failed to report some income on his tax returns, that he had set up a company to conceal money from the tax collectors, and that he had concealed the existence of bank accounts in order to impede collection. The Hubbell case, however, did not present a classic scheme to bilk the federal government out of its money. The indictment itself conceded that the bulk of Hubbell's consulting income was, in fact, reported to the government. At the end of the day, the indictment's weight was simply — as its conclusion makes clear — that the Hubbells did not pay the government money they owed:

> In January 1994, Webster L. Hubbell and Suzanna W. Hubbell had approximately $223,000 in an IRA and pension plan, a coin and art collection, and equity in a house and warehouse. Between 1994 and 1996, they earned over

> a million dollars. By the end of 1997, the Hubbells had liquidated all of those assets and spent virtually all their money. . . .
>
> As of December 31, 1997, the Hubbells owed the IRS . . . , the state of Arkansas . . . , and the District of Columbia . . . over $895,000 and had not made any further payments to reduce those years' liabilities.[109]

Assuming these charges, which were never tried, could have been proven, Hubbell's conduct was surely deplorable. A typical criminal tax case, however, alleges more—particularly when the defendant has already been imprisoned once before and the prosecutors are, as Starr concedes his office was doing with Hubbell, already considering indicting him again on other charges. As Nields has pointed out, Hubbell's tax case had significant mitigating factors as well:

> After Mr. Hubbell pleaded guilty in December 1994, he and his family were hopelessly insolvent. Already deeply in debt, the guilty plea added two new debts, one to the Rose law firm of about $500,000 and the other to the IRS of about $500,000. Thus, the Hubbells' debts dwarfed their assets. Their monthly expenses greatly exceeded their monthly income. And Mr. Hubbell was about to go to jail for 21 months, leaving his family without its principal breadwinner. They were in no position to pay their taxes. And the IRS knew this.
>
> The "spending down phenomenon," referred to by Mr. Starr, consisted of Mr. Hubbell paying creditors other than the IRS, so that his family could survive until he returned from jail. Mr. Hubbell even used his retirement fund, which is *exempt* from IRS levy, for this purpose. He had only negligible assets left when he went to jail in August 1995. Failing to pay taxes under these circumstances is not illegal. We abolished debtor's prison long ago.[110]

For all Starr's protestations, the case is hard to justify on entirely punitive grounds but makes perfect sense for a prosecutor determined to uncover the hush money scheme that he believed lay behind the payments.

The improbability of the case for a traditional prosecutor was highlighted by a tax lawyer retained by Hubbell's defense team as an expert witness. In a letter to Starr analyzing the case, Cono Namorato—a former deputy assistant attorney general in the Justice Department's Tax Division who had also served as chief of the division's Criminal Section—wrote that it was his "unequivocal opinion that the Tax Division would decline prosecution in this case." Namorato argued that the case would not be prosecuted "because the government's ability to prove either willfulness or an affirmative act of evasion is highly doubtful. The Hubbells made their professional advisers aware of all relevant facts and relied on their advice, and the conduct of their advisers is inconsistent with criminal intent on their part. As to proof of an affirmative act, the prosecution's case lacks anything approaching a 'smoking gun,' *i.e.*, an effort on the part of any party to conceal or falsify information or to mislead or trick the IRS. Indeed, the accounts [that Hubbell did not report to the IRS] had the Hubbells' names on them and had insignificant balances at the time [of the Hubbells' failure to report them]." Namorato concluded: "Bringing this case would push the edge of the envelope. Based on our research and experience, this would be the first criminal evasion of payment prosecution in history i) to charge taxpayers for criminal offenses where their unpaid professional advisers were aware of all relevant facts and the taxpayers relied on their advice, *and* ii) to aver as an overt act of fraud the establishment of a bank account in the very name of the taxpayers or, further yet afield, the taxpayers' failure to pay estimated taxes or live within their means. We have no hesitation in opining that the Tax Division of the Department of Justice would not break such new ground." Starr's more vigorous defenders will be tempted to brush aside Namorato's letter as the work of a hired gun. Its logic, however, resists so quick a dismissal. One can only speculate what would have happened had the case gone to trial; it would be a mistake, however, to rule out Namorato's suspicion that "while a prosecutor may infer criminal intent from the parties' conduct, we believe it reasonably likely that a jury would conclude that [the defendants] were working with good intentions under arduous circumstances."[111]

The case was especially implausible as a traditional prosecution, because of the serious problems it presented altogether independent of the gravity of the indictment's allegations. For one thing, the case was something of a jurisdictional stretch, relating only tangentially to Starr's Whitewater mandate.[112] Far more troubling, it raised a difficult constitutional question on which the office was not clearly in the right—indeed, one on which the Supreme Court eventually ruled for Hubbell in dismissing the indictment.[113] Starr's team had begun its obstruction investigation by issuing a sweeping subpoena for all of Hubbell's business records. When Hubbell refused to comply, citing his right against self-incrimination, the prosecutors produced a court order immunizing the production, and Hubbell then turned over 13,120 pages of material. The tax case ultimately grew out of these documents, so the question was whether it was consequently tainted, built on a foundation of coerced testimonial self-incrimination that violated both the Fifth Amendment and the federal immunity statute.[114] The office argued, ultimately unsuccessfully, that the documents were not protected, because under the Supreme Court's 1976 case of *Fisher v. U.S.*, the contents of documents produced under immunity are not testimony; documents are merely objects like any other. The Fifth Amendment protects only the testimonial aspects of the act of document production, which include the fact of the existence of the documents and their possession by the person who produced them.[115] Hubbell argued, by contrast, that the office had no knowledge of the existence of the documents until he produced them and was therefore relying on his testimony as to their existence in conducting the entire subsequent investigation, in violation of the Supreme Court's 1972 holding in *Kastigar v. U.S.*[116]

The Supreme Court eventually made short work of the case: "The documents did not magically appear in the prosecutor's office like 'manna from heaven.' They arrived there only after respondent asserted his constitutional privilege, received a grant of immunity, and—under the compulsion of the District Court's order—took the mental and physical steps necessary to provide the prosecutor with an accurate inventory of the many sources of potentially incriminating evidence sought by the subpoena." An eight-member majority concluded, "For these reasons, we cannot accept the Government's submission that [Hubbell's] immunity did not preclude its derivative use of the produced documents because its 'possession of the documents [was] the fruit *only* of a simple physical act—the act of producing the documents.' It was unquestionably necessary for respondent to make extensive use of 'the contents of his own mind' in identifying the hundreds of documents responsive to the requests in the subpoena."[117] The extremity of Starr's action in the Hubbell tax case, in other words, lay not just in his willingness to bring a marginal case against someone he had already prosecuted and imprisoned once and was preparing to prosecute again. It lay also in the risks he had to take in order to do so—raising a delicate constitutional question that the Justice Department had largely kept out of court for twenty-five years, and, in the process, potentially making new law that was highly unfavorable to federal law enforcement.

Starr's explanation of this second Hubbell indictment was one of his least persuasive moments. He argued not only that the indictment was one the department would have pursued, but that the department would have overlooked, as he did, the serious constitutional question the case presented. Starr noted that Nields had been a law clerk for Justice Byron White — the author of the court's opinion in *Fisher* — at the time the opinion was handed down, and claimed that Nields himself had authored the decision.[118] In his view, the *Hubbell* litigation was the result of clever strategizing by a "brilliant and . . . honorable" opponent who was "extraordinarily steeped in these areas" and who happened to be, for his particular client, the most "exquisitely qualified defense lawyer in the country, who had made the law of *Fisher*." Nields, he said, "guided us into the act of production immunity [issue], I think, full well knowing that he was bringing us into a litigation-creating arena." The Justice Department, he said, would have fallen into the same trap.[119]

Starr's contention that Nields somehow tricked the office into walking onto the turf on which he was strongest is simply incorrect. Nields first raised his claim that the documents would be off limits as evidence against Hubbell even before the office had immunized Hubbell's document production. In a 1996 letter to the office, in fact, he laid out his view that "a document or other thing produced under a grant of immunity is the fruit of the compelled act of production." He insisted further, "Since we differ as to the ability of the government to use documents produced under immunity I believe Mr. Hubbell will have to proceed under the statutory immunity route rather than by letter agreement. This will leave each of us in a position to argue later — if necessary — our positions concerning the effect of the statutory immunity."[120] Nields raised the issue again in a 1998 letter shortly before the indictment, and warned the office that "this evidence will likely be excluded. Your office would then not be able to prove Hubbell's fee income in 1994 and 1995. The part of your case that you have regarded as most appealing would be lost. You may lose your entire case."[121] If Starr was blindsided by the litigation that followed the second Hubbell indictment, it was not because Nields had been playing any cards close to his chest.

Starr's confidence that the Justice Department would have taken the same path also seems misplaced, and derives, in any event, from an entirely circular argument. Starr's faith on this point emanates from the deliberative decision-making process in his office and the depth of experience of his staff — the "microcosm of the Justice Department" on which he so relied. In other words, because Starr had set up a process that attempted to mimic the department's decision-making, because his office followed departmental policies and procedures, and because his prosecutors were career Justice Department lawyers, Starr was convinced that the department itself would have taken the same course that he did. This argument ignores the reality that federal law enforcement had not, in fact, forced this particular question in all the years since *Fisher* had come down. In addition, one cannot simply define a prosecutorial step as correct based on the integrity of the process that produced it. The step needs to be justifiable on its own terms. One of the general problems with Starr's attempts to tame the independent counsel law's dangers through the design of his office was that it relieved him to some degree of the psychological burden of justifying every step. His faith that the procedures he had designed would yield appropriate results sometimes blunted his instinct to question the appropriateness of a given decision that had emerged from these processes. That tendency is particularly evident here. From the outside, the Hubbell tax case looks like quintessential independent counsel myopia: a second prosecution on a marginal charge that risked undermining the position of federal prosecutors everywhere by clarifying a point of constitutional law in favor of investigative targets. Starr, however, failed to appreciate this big picture. He saw only that the indictment was a decision by career prosecutors acting within a deliberative framework under departmental procedures. Hence, in his view, it must have been correct.

Starr's pursuit of Hubbell lapsed into absurdity when he indicted him for a third time, on November 13, 1998. In several respects, the third indictment was more defensible than the second had been. It alleged that Hubbell had had significant conflicts of interest when he signed up the Rose Law Firm in 1989 to sue Madison Guaranty's accounting firm on behalf of the government, which had by then taken over the thrift. The conflicts emanated both from Hubbell's relationship with his father-in-law, Seth Ward, who was a Madison employee and a key figure in the Castle Grande transactions, and from the Rose firm's legal work on the Castle Grande deal. Starr alleged that Hubbell concealed from the FDIC and the RTC these conflicts and "the true nature and extent of the legal work Rose performed for Madison Guaranty" — including that performed by Hillary Clinton.[122]

This subject matter was, of course, far more germane to Starr's overall inquiry than the misconduct he took on in the tax case. The allegations, in addition, seemed more serious on their own terms. Had the third indictment preceded the tax indictment, it might well have seemed more appropriate. Being, however, the third prosecution of the same person by the same prosecutor, it carried a heavy burden that it never quite overcame. Starr told me he would have preferred to bring the conflicts case before the tax indictment, and did not do so only because of the vagaries of the grand jury process.[123] Because he brought the cases in the sequence he did, however, one cannot read the conflicts indictment in isolation from the case that preceded it by only a few short months. In the full context of the interaction between the particular prosecutor and the particular defendant, the third case, whatever its merits, read like an obtuse refusal to accept that Hubbell was not going to tell everything he knew — assuming, of course, that he had not done so already. At least in part, it was precisely that. Hubbell's purported failure to cooperate with investigators may not have been the immediate subject matter of the allegations, but it was a factor that lurked behind the office's entire interaction with him. The past crimes of witnesses whose testimony the prosecutors found unsatisfying had a way of becoming surrogates for the crimes against truth that most offended the office.

To some extent, Starr's attitude toward witnesses who held back on the office paralleled that of a traditional prosecutor. Indictments that are essentially coercive in nature are, after all, relatively common in complex cases in which the testimony of a recalcitrant witness is badly needed. Where Starr's approach diverged was both in his willingness to bring such cases even where the possibility of eventual cooperation was extremely remote and in his peculiarly warm embrace of those who eventually did come around. Starr viewed the decision to cooperate with law enforcement as a fundamental and transformative moral undertaking on the part of a defendant — one that was always possible and, in Starr's vocabulary, had almost religious overtones. Starr sometimes referred to guilty pleas as secular repentances, for example. In a speech to a law school class at George Mason University, Starr described the "complete change of heart" by William Marks Sr., a businessman whom the independent counsel had prosecuted in connection with the Jim Guy Tucker cable case, and who had fought the government tenaciously before finally coming to a deal in August 1997. As Starr recounted, at Marks's plea hearing, the defendant said to the judge, "I plead guilty. I *am* guilty, Your Honor." Starr told the students that he "saw up close and personal in the courtroom the results of someone really going through a complete change from total litigation — the culture of litigate to the hilt — to 'I'm on the government's side, and I feel much better about it.' "[124] Likewise, Starr clearly developed an affection for Jim McDougal, who was at the center of the allegations he was examining. Ewing went so far as to eulogize McDougal at his funeral, saying, "When I got a call last Sunday from the prison, it was like somebody hit me in the stomach." Ewing said, "Jim and I had become very close, too. We talked about a lot of things. We didn't just talk about stuff in investigations. We talked about life."[125]

This sort of relationship, far beyond what a prosecutor normally offers a cooperating witness, put in sharp relief the intensity of the coercive energy Starr was willing to expend against those who did not provide the assistance he believed the office was due — an intensity that also went beyond prosecutorial normalcy. A truth commission can forgive past crimes, even past lies; it cannot, however, forgive ongoing lies, which attack its essential undertaking. The full ferocity of the Starr investigation was directed not necessarily at those most culpable of the underlying misconduct but at those who Starr believed were obstructing the search for truth.

As with the Foster probe, any marginal benefit of the truth commission vision in Whitewater seems unjustified by the additional time, money, and coercion that it required. Since, as of this writing, Robert Ray's final report on Whitewater has not yet been made public, we cannot yet assess Starr's contribution to history or to our general understanding of the character and behavior of Bill and Hillary Clinton — other than to observe that any such contribution came too late. The public record on Whitewater, however, has changed only marginally since the end of 1997, and Ray's ultimate decision that there was insufficient evidence to bring charges suggests that the underlying record has not advanced dramatically either. In any event, those three years produced nothing of value from a law enforcement point of view. During that time, the independent counsel's Whitewater investigation made six sets of criminal allegations — two against Webster Hubbell and one each against Susan McDougal, Suzanna Hubbell, Michael Schaufele, and Charles Owen. These indictments resulted in a grand total of one felony plea — Hubbell's admission that he had conspired to cover up his conflicts of interest.[126] All the other charges against all of these defendants were ultimately either dropped by the prosecutors or rejected by courts or juries. This record stands in sharp contrast with that of the early years of Starr's probe, when — whatever Starr's underlying concerns and goals — substantial law enforcement interests justified the steps he took and the cases he brought, and he saw substantial success in prosecuting crimes.

That the investigation dragged out an additional three years proved unfortunate in several respects. Whitewater remained an unresolved issue for the president and his wife, over whose heads it continued to hang. For many other people who had done nothing wrong but whose names had been dragged through the mud nonetheless, the day of final vindication was deferred. By the time the final report on Whitewater becomes public, Clinton will have been out of office for many months and few will care. This failure on the part of the investigators was no small one. Part of the purpose of the independent counsel law was to clear the innocent with more credibility than the Justice Department of an incumbent administration can muster. Yet the tardiness of the Whitewater investigation's resolution grossly undermined this goal. The president surely bears blame for some of the slowness. He asserted privileges he should not have claimed, for example, and delayed in producing materials.[127] But these factors do not explain the period after 1997. For this stretch, which the office spent in the fruitless pursuit of already-prosecuted targets who would plainly never cooperate, Starr himself must take responsibility.

Starr's truth-oriented approach to the job of independent counsel also revealed itself in his handling of the two major ancillary investigations over which his office assumed jurisdiction in the years prior to the Lewinsky scandal. In both the probe of the White House Travel Office matter and the examination of the FBI files scandal, the office managed a relatively quick and thorough investigation that rapidly produced recommendations by the chief investigators that criminal charges not be brought. In both cases, however, these investigators then left the independent counsel's office, which then proved unable to close the matters in a timely fashion. Starr has said publicly that he should not have accepted jurisdiction over these questions, as doing so created the impression that he was President Clinton's personal prosecutor.[128] He has also said that assuming jurisdiction over the Lewinsky matter encumbered their completion, since he was forced to divert resources from these probes when the Lewinsky scandal broke in January 1998. This claim is surely correct, but it also tells only part of the story. Particularly in the Travel Office case, an investigation focused more on maximizing justice and less on maximizing truth would have had plenty of opportunity to finish up.

The Travel Office scandal began in the early days of the Clinton presidency when W. David Watkins, assistant to the president for management and administration, summarily fired the office's seven employees. The office was responsible for organizing White House staff travel and charter flights for the press corps that followed the president on his trips, and the staff was fired ostensibly because of allegations of mismanagement and corruption. It quickly emerged, however, that key White House personalities harbored ulterior motives. A distant cousin of the president who had done travel work for the 1992 campaign, Catherine Cornelius, wanted the job of running the office for herself and a fellow campaign aide, and an Arkansas travel outfit in which the president's close friend Harry Thomason had an interest wanted business. While the allegations against the staff were not wholly misplaced, as real mismanagement did take place and some of the irregularities were indeed fishy, many of the allegations turned out to be smears, and, in any event, not all of the employees were equally responsible for the problems in the office. Particularly after the White House involved the FBI in the matter and then disclosed publicly that a criminal investigation had been launched, the whole affair was widely seen as an effort to slime and sack long-serving officials in order to replace them with presidential cronies — and to claim credit along the way for cleaning up corruption. Ironically, nobody ever doubted that the White House was entitled to remove the staff for any reason it chose and replace them with whomever the president desired; patronage, after all, is a perk of victory. The spoils of the campaign, however, was not the spin for which the White House had hoped. Moreover, in the resulting furor and the flurry of subsequent investigations, the White House played down the role that Hillary Clinton played in the firing decision.[129] In a deposition with the independent counsel's office in 1995, the first lady denied any role in the decision, said she didn't think she'd had any input into it, and minimized her own expressions of concern about the situation to the officials who ultimately made the call.[130] In written statements in 1994 to the General Accounting Office, the White House counsel's office stated that "Mrs. Clinton was aware that Mr. Watkins was undertaking a review of the situation in the Travel Office, but she had no role in the decision to terminate the employees." The White House also claimed she did "not know the origin of the decision" and "did not direct that any action be taken by anyone in regard to the Travel Office."[131] In a 1996 statement to the House Committee on Government Reform and Oversight, Hillary Clinton said: "Although I had no decision-making role with regard to the removal of the Travel Office employees on May 19, 1993, I expressed my concern . . . that if there were fiscal mismanagement in the Travel Office or in any part of the White House, it should be addressed promptly."[132]

In January 1996, however, an unsent draft memorandum by Watkins surfaced that cast both Hillary Clinton's and Watkins's own prior statements in a different light. The memo, which had long been under subpoena yet had not been produced, was prepared in the wake of a White House internal review of the firings and the resulting reprimand of Watkins. Watkins had been upset by the reprimand, and in the drafts of the memo he stated that it was "my first attempt to be sure the record is straight, something I have not done in previous conversations with investigators — where I have been as protective and vague as possible." In the drafts, which were actually prepared by a staffer, Watkins contended that "the First Lady took interest in having the Travel Office situation resolved quickly," and that Thomason "sold the First Lady on his plan and vision of this as a good story, and he got her excited about it." Thomason and Foster "each informed me of the First Lady's attention to and interest in the Travel Office situation." When the final decision was taken, "I explained to [White House chief of staff Mack] McLarty that I had decided to terminate the Travel Office employees, and he clearly was relieved. We both knew that there would be hell to pay if . . . we failed to take swift and decisive action in conformity with the First Lady's wishes."[133] Starr assumed jurisdiction in March 1996, to examine whether either Hillary Clinton or Watkins had testified falsely or obstructed any of the various investigations in which their testimony had been given.

Unlike Whitewater, the Travel Office case did not present a sprawling mass of allegations. It involved, instead, a discrete set of questions: What precise role did Hillary Clinton play in the decision to fire the office's staff? Could that role reasonably be reconciled with her testimony and with Watkins's statements? If not, did any misstatements warrant prosecution in a reasonable exercise of prosecutorial discretion? Underlying the whole case was the fact that the firings themselves were clearly within the power of the White House and any role Hillary Clinton may have played was not itself improper. Given both the confined nature of the inquiry and that any lies were aimed at covering up legal conduct, it is amazing that the investigation took more than four years to complete. A review of Ray's final report, made public in October 2000, makes the duration of the investigation even more difficult to fathom. His footnotes reveal that the preponderance of the investigative steps were taken during a brief period in the summer of 1996, when a grand jury investigated the matter intensively. Eric Dubelier, the prosecutor who handled this phase of the investigation, produced a memorandum designed to resolve all of the issues the case presented before leaving Starr's employment near the end of 1996. According to John Bates, Dubelier's memo represented a "close-to-final" write-up of the matter.[134] Yet the office proved unable to finish the investigation for years to come.

Various factors kept the investigation alive. An entire appendix of Ray's report is devoted to White House non-cooperation with the investigation.[135] But this does not suffice to explain the additional three years. According to Bates, the Travel Office matter was kept open, in part, because other matters pending before the office related to the first lady's truthfulness under oath, matters including Whitewater, the disappearance of the billing records, and the handling of materials from Foster's office. It was, he said, "difficult for [Starr] to close out the Travel Office when these other things were still open." The issues were "to some extent interrelated [and] involv[ed] the same high-level person." The "major explanation" for the delay, Bates said, is that this reluctance on Starr's part lengthened even further the office's "thorough and lengthy process" of vetting the Dubelier memorandum. Bates suggested that the slowness was less the mark of the truth commission instinct than the result of "certain inefficiencies" combined with "a laudable care" on Starr's part for getting things right. Starr, he said, "is a very careful person in every respect, including his conduct as a prosecutor."[136]

This analysis certainly tells a significant component of the story. When Dubelier left, the work was picked up by other prosecutors — Solomon Wisenberg, in particular — who felt they had to satisfy themselves that his analysis held water. Some of the delay resulted less from the need to get at some deeper level of truth than from the need for new people to get up to speed and become sufficiently familiar with the case to make their own judgments about its merits. Given the stakes in a high-profile investigation of the first lady, the impulse to be thorough, even within a traditional prosecutorial framework, is understandable. However strong Dubelier's work may have been — and it was uniformly admired among the Starr prosecutors I spoke with — it may ask too much to expect that those prosecutors who inherited Dubelier's memorandum would simply have adopted his conclusions as their own. Particularly since the memo suggested that no cases be brought in a matter that the office had previously regarded as potentially leading to Mrs. Clinton's indictment, there was a strong impulse to reassess the evidence carefully to determine its amenability to a different reading.

The impulse to prosecutorial thoroughness, however, explains only so much, and Bates conceded that Starr's truth-seeking instinct was evident in aspects of the delay as well. During the investigation, he recalled, "substantial issues" arose as to the veracity of "some witnesses." Bates said there were different perspectives within the office regarding how serious a problem this was: "Some might feel that a prosecutor has to stand up for the prosecutorial process and that people should be prosecuted for lies to the investigation. Others say that you can't have an investigation without people lying." Starr, Bates said, "was very concerned about [lies to the investigation] and he took that very seriously."[137] Starr's view, according to Kavanaugh, was that "it was within [his] mandate and he was offended by lying and perjury. Some prosecutors might be more instrumental regarding the little fish."[138] Another prosecutor in the office put it more bluntly: "A lot of people were not telling the truth, and that drove Starr out of his mind."[139] The office, therefore, ended up spending a fair bit of energy considering whether or not to prosecute ancillary figures in the case, even though their purported misstatements had little bearing on the underlying case, or lack thereof, against Watkins or Hillary Clinton. Once again, Starr's focus on truth caused him to fixate on the interaction of witnesses with the investigation, even at the expense of resolving the big questions in a timely fashion.

The Travel Office investigation bore another, more public, signature of the truth commission: the decision to litigate all the way to the Supreme Court the question of whether the attorney-client privilege survives the death of the client. Foster had, shortly before killing himself, met with a lawyer named James Hamilton concerning the various investigations of the Travel Office firings, in which Foster had been involved. In the course of the meeting, Starr's office later learned, Hamilton had taken three pages of notes. Starr's interest in these notes originally grew not out of the Travel Office case but out of his investigation of how Foster's office and papers were handled after his death.[140] Indeed, the grand jury subpoena for the notes was issued in December 1995, weeks before the Watkins memorandum was finally delivered.[141] Yet the notes understandably acquired a certain importance once Starr had assumed jurisdiction over the Travel Office. To be sure, investigators did not know what those notes said, though they developed "several hypotheses," according to Kavanaugh, who argued the Supreme Court case.[142] Moreover, any evidence they contained would almost surely have been deemed inadmissible hearsay. The notes nonetheless presented a body of evidence, albeit a small one, that Starr believed he should not ignore. After all, if a depressed Foster were going to reveal that he had been covering up Hillary Clinton's having given a direct order to fire the Travel Office employees, his prospective lawyer was an obvious person to tell. The office was also aware that Foster had been, in his final days, deeply anxious about the Travel Office matter. The notes were, therefore, legitimately tantalizing. Making them all the more tantalizing was the fact that no settled law barred the office's getting them, and a plausible argument could be made — one with a fair degree of academic support — that unmediated by other interests, the attorney-client privilege should not survive the death of the client.[143] This combination was enough to whet the truth commission's appetite: a step was available to the office for which a strong legal argument could be made, and the step stood potentially to add to Starr's understanding of the truth. It simply had to be pursued.

From a law enforcement standpoint, though, the litigation was silly. It took two and a half years to resolve, during which time it contributed to delaying the final disposition of the Travel Office case — the investigative work for which had been largely completed within a year of the subpoena. Pursuing the notes also meant litigating a question on which, despite the academic literature, it was far from clear that the office would ultimately prevail. Indeed, as in the Hubbell case, the office's position, though not clearly wrong, was rather disquieting. No compelling prosecutorial rationale, in fact, justified holding the Travel Office investigation hostage — especially after the completion of a near-final analysis — to an effort to get three pages of hearsay, relying on a legal theory that had some significant likelihood of rejection by the courts, an eventuality that ultimately came to be. In June 1998, a six-to-three majority of the Supreme Court wrote: "It has been generally, if not universally, accepted, for well over a century, that the attorney-client privilege survives the death of the client in a case such as this. While the arguments against the survival of the privilege are by no means frivolous, they are based in large part on speculation — thoughtful speculation, but speculation nonetheless — as to whether posthumous termination of the privilege would diminish a client's willingness to confide in an attorney."[144] As with the Hubbell litigation,

Starr's pursuit of truth above and beyond prosecutorial norms gained him nothing but the embarrassment of a loss at the Supreme Court.

In the case of the Travel Office, one struggles to discern any public benefit served by the truth commission approach. Unlike the Foster report, the final report in the Travel Office case did not add a level of finality to the discussion and thereby put to rest a public controversy. To some degree, this simply reflected the messiness of the facts of the case. Whereas the Foster report could declare with certainty that the suicide was, in fact, a suicide, Ray could not say of the Travel Office that the scandal itself was a myth. By contrast, he concluded: "The evidence is overwhelming that [Hillary Clinton] in fact did have a role in the decision to fire the employees and that she did have input with Watkins and White House Chief of Staff Mack McLarty, as well as Foster and Thomason. Nevertheless, the available admissible evidence is insufficient to prove beyond a reasonable doubt that Mrs. Clinton knowingly made a false statement in her sworn denial of such a role or input. Notwithstanding Mrs. Clinton's role and input into the decision to fire the Travel Office employees, allegations that her statements to Congress (including her responses incorporated from the GAO investigation) — on this issue and other Travel Office-related issues — were knowingly false could not be substantiated beyond a reasonable doubt."[145] While the first lady testified falsely, in other words, it was not adequately clear that she knew the role she was playing or the effect her expressions of concern would have on her underlings. The Ray report supported this conclusion comprehensively, but the conclusion itself stood for hardly more than an acknowledgment that one could not authoritatively prove that Mrs. Clinton had lied, as opposed to merely speaking in error or stretching the truth. While the first lady had denied ordering the firings, she had never denied expressing concern about the Travel Office situation or the possibility that those expressions of concern had ultimately affected the decisions others made. For his part, Watkins, even in the various drafts of his memorandum, never alleged that she had ordered the firings. The Ray report is well crafted and rigorous, but at its core, it merely restates what the public record had long suggested. As such, it served not so much as a clarification or correction of that record but as a prosecutorial imprimatur of its reasonableness. This might have been helpful had it emerged while the scandal — which took place, after all, at the dawn of the Clinton presidency — was still even a remotely live issue in the public mind. Coming out as the Clinton presidency was all but over, however, it served chiefly as a statement for posterity's sake. While it added a certain factual rigor, clarity, and sobriety to the discussion of the Travel Office saga, it did so long after that discussion was over.

The one marginally significant benefit of the delay was that it allowed the investigators to incorporate and resolve certain allegations that only surfaced years after the firings. The Ray report reflects one significant body of investigative work that postdates 1996: the debunking during 1999 of an allegation made by a friend of David Watkins named William Charles Cloud. Cloud claimed that while he and Watkins were playing golf in Little Rock shortly before the firings, Watkins had had a cellular phone conversation with the first lady and had, upon finishing it, said that Hillary Clinton told him to "fire the sons of bitches." This account, if true, contradicted not only Hillary Clinton's claim that she had not ordered the firings but also her and Watkins's testimony that they had had only one direct conversation on the subject of the Travel Office. After investigating the allegations, however, the office concluded that Cloud's information "was unsubstantiated, and that the weight of the evidence establishes that the sole telephone conversation between Mrs. Clinton and Watkins occurred on Friday, May 14, as both previously stated under oath."[146] By keeping the Travel Office matter open so long, the office might have avoided retroactive second-guessing when this allegation came to light.[147] Had the investigation already been closed, Starr might have faced questions like those Fiske had faced in the Foster matter; leads, it might have been argued, had not been pursued, and questions consequently remained. The trouble with this argument, however, is that by the time the Cloud allegation became public, the Travel Office firings were a dead issue, and the allegation received almost no attention. It is hard to imagine that, had the investigation been closed in a timely fashion, such an issue would have seriously undermined confidence in Starr's conclusions. In any event, it certainly was not worth keeping the matter open so long in order to put out such fires.

Once again, the truth commission approach carried significant costs that far outweighed any benefit gained by the final report's having addressed comprehensively all possible questions about the decision not to file charges. These costs are already familiar. The perpetuation of the investigation again perpetuated the scandal, preventing finality in yet another of the series of allegations that plagued Clinton's presidency. The first lady was allowed to dangle in the wind long after it became clear that no reasonable prosecutor would attempt to bring a case against her. In the end, the office did the right thing: Starr and Ray did not attempt to bring the case, and Ray filed a measured and serious report that aptly explained the office's ultimately clearheaded thinking. But an investigation cannot be judged meritorious simply because it eventually produced a happy outcome. The process in the Travel Office case was a damaging one. Truth was, quite simply, not worth its consequences.

Starr's claim that the Lewinsky investigation delayed completion of his other work constitutes a fuller explanation of the FBI files probe than it does of the Travel Office investigation. Even here, however, it is an incomplete explanation. The FBI files matter arose out of the Travel Office matter in June 1996, when Representative William Clinger Jr., chairman of the House Committee on Government Reform and Oversight, announced that the White House had sought the FBI background file of the Travel Office chief several months after his firing. The next day, the White House delivered to the FBI a group of boxes containing hundreds of background files on officials in the prior Republican administrations. President Clinton characterized the apparent hoarding of the files as "a completely honest bureaucratic snafu."[148] Others, however, suspected it was a covert effort to gather dirt on prominent Republicans by the two White House officials chiefly responsible for the collection, Anthony Marceca and Craig Livingstone. Attorney General Janet Reno asked the Special Division to expand Starr's jurisdiction to cover the matter. The office was also asked to investigate whether Bernard Nussbaum, the former White House counsel, had lied to Congress when he testified that he did not know how Livingstone had been hired or whether Hillary Clinton had played any role in bringing him on board at the White House.

As with the Travel Office investigation, Starr's office initially proceeded quickly. According to Bates, the investigative work — conducted principally by a prosecutor named Rod

Rosenstein — was largely completed by 1997.[149] Indeed, Robert Ray's final report on the FBI files matter reveals relatively few investigative steps taken after the end of 1996.[150] Though Starr's office conducted the investigation with dispatch, Starr was once again unable to close it out quickly. The advent of the Lewinsky case is surely more to blame for this failure than the truth commission vision. The latter, however, is evident too. As he had with the Foster matter, Starr again ranked speed low among his priorities, chief among which were investigative and deliberative thoroughness. With the law enforcement interests in the matter largely satisfied, Starr found himself unable to devote the necessary resources to wrap up the FBI files matter and unwilling to close it with anything short of truth commission completeness. As a result, the entire investigation, though largely complete, was effectively deferred until the Lewinsky project subsided and every conceivable loose end could be tied. This fastidiousness, which added more than two years to the length of the investigation, was surely unnecessary, at least to the extent that the office failed to clarify early and publicly that no grand conspiracy lay behind the files controversy.

To be fair, Starr did announce, during his testimony before the House Judiciary Committee considering Clinton's impeachment, that the FBI files investigation had generated no evidence that could support the impeachment. He clarified, at that point, that the probe had "found no evidence that anyone higher than Mr. Livingstone or Mr. Marceca was in any way involved in ordering the FBI files from the FBI," and that he had "found no evidence that information contained in the files of former officials was actually used for an improper purpose."[151] This concession came late in the game and seems, in retrospect, stingy. It certainly offered little hint of the scope of the vindication Starr's office would eventually give the White House on the files matter. In fact, the information Starr had long before uncovered was highly exculpatory. As Ray's report finally made clear almost a year and a half later, the investigation had revealed not merely that there was insufficient evidence to bring criminal cases or that there had been no high-level conspiracy, but that "neither Anthony Marceca nor any senior White House official, or First Lady Hillary Rodham Clinton, engaged in criminal conduct to obtain through fraudulent means derogatory information about former White House staff."[152] The office also found "no credible evidence that Mr. Nussbaum testified falsely when he denied ever having spoken to Mrs. Clinton about Craig Livingstone."[153]

The report actually reveals that the entire FBI files scandal was something of a misunderstanding. From the early days of the scandal, the White House had claimed to have ordered the files because the Secret Service had provided it with an outdated list of people holding White House passes — a list that did not distinguish between people with active and inactive passes and, consequently, between current and former White House employees. Marceca had merely requested files systematically from that list, in an effort to update records. The Secret Service, however, had denied that this explanation was technically possible, saying its computer systems were incapable of producing the flawed document Marceca described.[154] The Secret Service's claim greatly fueled skepticism of the White House's explanation. Yet the independent counsel's office ultimately concluded that the Secret Service was wrong. The office "conclusively established that the Secret Service list that Mr. Marceca claimed that he used actually existed and that the list *did not differentiate* between active and inactive passholders. The Secret Service's testimony in this regard was mistaken. That testimony, if not the sole basis for the underlying controversy that gave rise to this investigation, plainly magnified public concerns regarding Mr. Marceca's conduct."[155] In other words, the whole affair, just as the White House initially claimed, had been a bureaucratic blunder made to seem nefarious by errors on the part of people outside the White House. Given the disparity between the widespread public suspicions about the affair and the information Starr had gathered about it, his unwillingness to issue some kind of statement to that effect in a timely fashion seems, in retrospect, grossly unfair to those, like Marceca, Livingstone, and Nussbaum, who labored under an unwarranted cloud of criminal suspicion that the office long knew to be unjustified.

This is not to say that no legitimate law enforcement questions remained after 1997. Indeed, the office apparently did not decide until 1999 what to do about Marceca's false testimony to Congress on isolated matters related to the files controversy. Marceca had testified that he never knew the Secret Service's list contained inactive passholders and had suggested that he had not routinely examined the files for derogatory information. These statements were contradicted by other evidence, yet the office ultimately decided not to pursue any case against him. "The evidence that no senior White House officials or Mrs. Clinton were involved in seeking FBI background reports resolved the central issue that required the appointment of an independent counsel," Ray wrote, and Marceca had been truthful on that point. The office consequently "declined prosecution and granted Mr. Marceca immunity to ensure full disclosure of all relevant information related to the investigation." In the deposition that followed his immunization, Marceca admitted that his earlier statements had not been true.[156] Handling the Marceca question correctly was a delicate matter that properly warranted care, and that care can take time. Even accepting for argument's sake, however, that, as a consequence of strained resources, the final resolution of his particular case could not have been accomplished until the Lewinsky matter was re-solved — and that claim is difficult to accept — it does not fol-low that the office needed to stay so mum so long about the underlying scandal its investigation had debunked. However much the Lewinsky investigation may have held things up, this failure seems rooted at least partly in the unfortunate perfectionism of the truth commission.

In fairness to Starr, one should note that many of the excesses of the truth commission vision are evident today chiefly because of the advent of the Lewinsky imbroglio. Had Starr not assumed jurisdiction over the Lewinsky matter, the FBI files and Travel Office probes might well have been wrapped up in 1998. While Whitewater, because of the Hub-bell and Susan McDougal cases, probably would have dragged on in any case, the entire posture of the probe would have seemed different — one of winding down, rather than end-lessly gearing up for the next critical phase. Had Linda Tripp never walked through Starr's door, some of the quirks of the truth commission — particularly Starr's approach to the Fos-ter investigation — would have still become apparent. In its entirety, however, Starr's probe would not have seemed quite so distant from the prosecutorial norm. The Lewinsky probe breathed new life into the office, but did so without rein-vigorating the work it was already doing. Instead, it put much of that work, which was already proceeding with excruciating slowness and was no longer entirely self-justifying, into sus-pended animation. Investigations that were, on their own terms, no longer serving live law enforcement purposes were thereby extended, and the absence of any real law enforce-ment purpose to their continuance became ever more apparent. The effect was to freeze in time a snapshot of each of the investigations so that the public had time to internalize the disjuncture between reasonable prosecutorial goals and the goals the office was actually pursuing. As the underlying scandals the investigations dealt with grew ever more remote from the public consciousness, these snapshots became increasingly less defensible.

CHAPTER 4

The Truth Commission and Monica

A JUROR: "Private encounter, approximately 1:30 or 2:00 p.m., study. President on crutches. Physical intimacy including oral sex to completion and brief direct genital contact." Brief direct genital contact, could you just elaborate on that a bit?

THE WITNESS: Uh—

A JUROR: I understand—

THE WITNESS: Oh, my gosh. This is so embarrassing.

A JUROR: You could close your eyes and talk.

A JUROR: We won't look at you.

THE WITNESS: Can I hide under the table?

MONICA LEWINSKY BEFORE KENNETH STARR'S GRAND JURY

Kenneth Starr's truth commission vision came to its full fruition during the Monica Lewinsky investigation, which provided an unusually good foil for the excesses of his approach. The Lewinsky affair, after all, involved an investigation that was chiefly about truth itself—specifically, about the president's lies and his efforts to encourage others to lie about the most personal of subjects imaginable. The purpose of the investigation, in other words, was to uncover a kind of meta-truth, or, at least, to uncover the truth about falsehood, a goal that, in the context of an investigation of sexual infidelity, necessarily raised the costs of the Starr's nonprosecutorial approach. Starr, however, did not let circumstances alter his vision of his role at all. To the contrary, his attitude remained unfortunately consistent. To reveal the truth about the president, he deployed the coercive power of a grand jury to investigate the specific nature of Clinton's sexual relationship with a young woman, who had not previously been a public figure and who had been dragged into the limelight of a federal investigation only through the treachery of a trusted friend. Out of fear that the story Lewinsky would deliver might prove insufficiently truthful, he failed for nearly seven months to bring his chief witness before the grand jury. Instead of garnering—or forcing—her cooperation, he went to war with the rest of the executive branch over the president's efforts to shroud the testimony of various ancillary figures in spurious privileges. When he finally issued his referral to Congress, he crafted it as a detailed narrative that sought to deliver the story to the legislative branch, rather than the mere "information" the law called upon him to yield up. Through his various interpretations of the law, all of them rooted ultimately in the truth commission vision, Starr allowed himself to become, in effect, an impeachment investigator for a Congress uneager to take the lead on an embarrassing subject.

I acknowledge at the outset, as Starr's critics generally do not, that the Lewinsky investigation would have put any independent counsel in an untenable position, irrespective of how narrowly he construed his mission under the law. Once a prosecutor was charged with investigating the president for a specific crime that he happened to be both guilty of and inclined not to confess to despite the availability of evidence to prove his guilt, a major conflagration was structurally guaranteed, unless the prosecutor simply backed down. However Starr proceeded, including in the manner I believe would have been desirable, he would have been lambasted as a partisan witchhunter. The complicating factors he faced were innumerable and serious, ranging from the truly vicious campaign of defamation the White House organized against him to the highly unorthodox representation of Lewinsky by her first lawyer, William Ginsburg, whose antics forestalled any early understanding between the office and Lewinsky. Even had Starr been the most disciplined and narrowly prosecutorial of independent counsels, the office would have faced these problems. Starr's assumption of jurisdiction over the Lewinsky mess put him in a no-win situation.

Some of Starr's critics have argued that his original sin was in seeking jurisdiction over the Lewinsky affair in the first place, and Starr readily admits that doing so was a mistake. In retrospect, it would certainly have been better for a different independent counsel to tackle the subject, but Starr's error was a very forgivable one—hardly evidence of hyperzealous partisanship as the critics often contend. A witness with whom the office had dealt in the past—Linda Tripp—had come through the door making apparently credible allegations against the president and his confidante Vernon Jordan, whose conduct had already come under the office's scrutiny in connection with the Webster Hubbell hush money case. These allegations, having been made, had to be investigated by an independent counsel.[1] Given that fact, having Starr assume jurisdiction over them made good sense both for reasons of efficiency and because the matter was, in the prosecutors' view, urgent, and Starr's shop was already geared up to handle it. In retrospect, of course, the consequences of the decision to give the matter to Starr—which was, incidentally, made in conjunction with the Justice Department—seem vast, but that observation is greatly aided by hindsight. In real time, by contrast, the move seemed obvious both to Starr's shop and to the officials at the Justice Department involved in the decision. Starr's assumption of jurisdiction, however fateful it turned out to be, reflected neither partisanship nor zealotry, nor even the truth commission instinct. It was simply a reasonable judgment that turned out badly.

I acknowledge as well that the truth commission vision did not, as things turned out, affect the investigation in precisely the manner one might have anticipated, given Starr's approach to the Vincent Foster probe. For one thing, though it seemed interminable, the entire investigation was actually conducted fairly quickly, particularly considering the volume and intensity of the litigation it generated. Starr assumed jurisdiction over the matter on January 16, 1998, and made his referral to Congress on September 9, only eight months later. Though the office tracked down every conceivable lead, Starr had at least facially valid prosecutorial arguments for the bulk, if not all, of the specific steps he took in conducting the Lewinsky investigation. Compared to earlier phases of the probe, the investigation Starr's prosecutors designed was relatively focused, and, generally speaking, its steps were reasonably calculated to address specific questions germane to the overall inquiry. One does not, however, need to delve deeply into the Lewinsky saga to realize that this was not a probe aimed chiefly at the criminal prosecution of wrongdoing. From the time news of the scandal broke, the whole focus of both the prosecutors and the public was on the forthcoming impeachment referral. Moreover, Starr has been candid in acknowledging that his fundamental judgments, the ones that ultimately determined the essential design and output of the investigation, were conditioned principally by the need to maximize truth. Starr's steps may have had valid law enforcement justifications, but they were often largely pretexts masking the more salient truth-oriented rationales that were actually driving his decisions. In most key respects, the truth commission vision dominated the Lewinsky probe.

It is not my intention here to recount the Lewinsky tale or

to spell out once again the voluminous evidence of the case. For our purposes, the briefest of summaries will suffice.[2] Clinton and Lewinsky began a sexual relationship in November 1995, when Lewinsky, then a White House intern, flirted with the president at a birthday party and flashed him a glimpse of her now-infamous thong underwear. Later that evening, they had the first of their encounters. Over the succeeding eighteen months they had a handful of such sexual rendezvous, which both have stated did not include sexual intercourse but consisted chiefly of Lewinsky's performing oral sex on the president. On certain occasions, Lewinsky's service to the president took place as he was talking on the phone with members of Congress. She and Clinton also had phone sex on numerous occasions. They exchanged gifts. There was an understanding between them that both would take whatever steps were necessary to conceal their relationship, though Lewinsky nonetheless talked about the affair to eleven people, including friends, family members, and psychological counselors. As a result of her penchant for hanging around the White House's West Wing, Lewinsky, who had by then been hired by the White House as a legislative correspondent, drew the suspicions of the president's management staff, and in April 1996, White House administrator Evelyn Lieberman had her transferred to a job at the Pentagon to get her away from Clinton. Clinton, however, promised to bring her back to the White House after the 1996 presidential election, and in 1997, Lewinsky again began to visit the president, using his secretary, Betty Currie, to arrange times and transmit letters and gifts. Clinton never delivered on his promise to bring Lewinsky back, however, and in October 1997, Lewinsky gave up on returning and sought Clinton's help in finding a different job in New York City. Unfortunately for both of them, Lewinsky had met Tripp during her service at the Pentagon and had confided in her, and Tripp had begun taping their calls on the advice of her friend and literary agent, Lucianne Goldberg.

The matter came to a head in December 1997, after Tripp alerted Paula Jones's lawyers — always on the prowl for alleged Clinton paramours — to her friend's existence, and the Jones team listed Lewinsky as a potential witness in the sexual harassment case. On December 19, they subpoenaed Lewinsky, demanding, in addition to her testimony, that she produce all of the gifts Clinton had given her. Lewinsky always maintained that nobody asked her to lie or promised her a job in exchange for her silence, but it is fair to say that she and Clinton developed an unspoken understanding that both would conceal their affair, including in any testimony she might give in the litigation. Following a December 28 meeting between Lewinsky and Clinton at which the two discussed how to handle the problem of the gifts and Lewinsky suggested that she pass them on to Currie, the president's secretary showed up at Lewinsky's apartment to retrieve them.[3] The president's aid in her job search also seems to have heated up after her inclusion on the witness list. In the fall of 1997, before Lewinsky's name had appeared on the witness list, Currie asked Deputy Chief of Staff John Podesta to help secure employment for Lewinsky. He arranged a personal interview with then–United Nations Ambassador Bill Richardson, who offered her a job. Lewinsky, however, was interested in jobs in the private sector and stalled on the U.N. job, expecting Vernon Jordan to help her. Currie, in fact, had asked Jordan to help out, and he met with Lewinsky, but Lewinsky was nonetheless frustrated with the pace of her search. After Lewinsky showed up on the Jones witness list, however, Jordan quickly got her two interviews in New York and one in Washington. After she was subpoenaed, he arranged counsel for her to assist in the preparation of an affidavit. Two days after she signed her affidavit in January 1998, Lewinsky was offered a job at Revlon, amidst a flurry of phone calls from Jordan, who sat on Revlon's board of directors. Jordan called Currie immediately, saying, "Mission accomplished."

By this time, however, the president's own deposition was fast approaching, and, unbeknownst to either Clinton or his former girlfriend, Tripp had decided to take her tale to Starr. As things turned out, Tripp's initial story was somewhat more dramatic than the full facts of the case would ultimately support. In her version, the link between the job and the lie was explicit, and Jordan had been recruited to facilitate the lie. Tripp developed these impressions because Lewinsky, as she began increasingly to mistrust Tripp, began lying to her, specifically by telling her what she thought Tripp wanted to hear, in an effort to persuade her to support Lewinsky's lie when Tripp testified. It was beyond reasonable dispute, however, that both Lewinsky and the president testified falsely in the Jones case. Lewinsky filed an affidavit stating, "I have never had a sexual relationship with the President," and, "The occasions that I saw the President after I left my employment at the White House in April, 1996, were official receptions, formal functions or events related to the U.S. Department of Defense, where I was working at the time. There were other people present on those occasions."[4] Clinton, for his part, testified that he had never had a sexual relationship with Lewinsky and could not recall having been alone with her.[5] The case that landed on Starr's desk undoubtedly contained real criminality — but of a somewhat milder, if no less sordid, sort than the prosecutors had expected when they took on the case.

From a prosecutorial point of view, the Lewinsky affair presented a narrow set of real questions. There were, of course, a variety of theoretical cases, including, for example, one against Lewinsky, who was actually the only person named in the Special Division's jurisdictional order.[6] Lewinsky, however, was hardly a target worthy of an independent counsel investigation — or, for that matter, deserving of prosecution at all. Although obviously guilty of felonies, she was not even a party to the litigation, into which she had been dragged most unwillingly. Her efforts to avoid having her life turned upside down by the suit were, if not noble, certainly understandable; she was motivated, it seems, by a desire to avoid abject public humiliation and to spare Clinton the same. The other figures whom the scandal made famous would likewise have been far from prized quarries for Starr. The only real significance of Tripp's allegations were that they contained a direct and wholly believable suggestion of criminal wrongdoing on the part of Clinton and Jordan.[7] As a criminal matter, the only real question was whether any or all of these allegations could be proven beyond a reasonable doubt. Realistically, only Lewinsky could provide Starr's office the evidence it would need to determine whether a case could be made. For any traditional prosecutor — one, that is, seeking to bring actual indictments — securing Lewinsky's testimony was the single critical step on which the investigation would ride. For Starr, however, prosecuting cases was a secondary goal, and he let months pass before his prosecutors actually interviewed Lewinsky — a remarkable lag that stemmed directly from his fear that he might fail to extract the full truth from her. The problem was not that Starr did not desire a deal or that he wished to prosecute Lewinsky. It was that the office found itself unable to do business with Ginsburg, Lewinsky's attorney, and Starr was ultimately unwilling to risk trying to procure Lewinsky's testimony in the absence of a deal by seeking a court order immunizing her testimony.[8]

The breakdown of immunity negotiations with Ginsburg was not entirely, or even chiefly, Starr's fault. Ginsburg's handling of his client's case was both unprofessional and entirely inconsistent with the interests of his client. From the day the scandal broke, in fact, his many public statements — which often contradicted one another — added a significant wildcard to what would have been, even with more professional counsel, a delicate negotiation conducted in the midst of a media feeding frenzy. "If the President of the United States did this — and I'm not saying that he did — with this young lady, I think he's a misogynist," he told *The Washington Post* in its initial story about the scandal.[9] If the "Office of Independent Counsel has no substantial evidence or reason to go after Monica Lewinsky, they're ravaging her," he said on another occasion. "If it's true she had some sort of relationship with the President, then she's being ravaged. She's a victim any way you cut it, all around."[10] In his truly impressive barrage of talk show appearances, interviews, and articles, Ginsburg blabbed about everything from his client's affair with a married man to her being a "product of a phenomenon that is endemic in America — divorce."[11] Some of his statements implied that her affidavit had been untrue, as when he said, "*At this time*, she is standing on that affidavit" (emphasis added) and then, when asked about his qualifying phrase, noted that "in thirty-plus years of practicing trial law, there's always a surprise around the corner."[12] In another interview, however, he insisted that Lewinsky "absolutely stands on the affidavit and everything that it contains."[13] Starr's tactics, Ginsburg said at one point, were legal: "I would say I was upset at the way things were handled until, frankly, I learned what I don't like is the system. But there was no illegality."[14] At other times, however, he harshly accused Starr of violating the law: "Starr seems to think it's okay to break the law to enforce the law."[15]

Some of Ginsburg's comments were simply off the wall. "I kissed that girl's inner thighs when she was six days old — I said, 'Look at those little *polkas*,'" he said of his client in one interview.[16] In another, with an Israeli newspaper, he explained that he and Monica didn't want President Clinton impeached because "Clinton is very positive toward Israel and the Jews, and Monica and I are Jews."[17] His bizarre willingness to undercut his client's position culminated in an open letter he wrote to Starr in the spring of 1998, which said, "Congratulations, Mr. Starr! As a result of your callous disregard for cherished constitutional rights, you *may* have succeeded in unmasking a sexual relationship between two consenting adults."[18] Comments like these effectively advertised to the world that Lewinsky — who was still in criminal jeopardy — was guilty of lying under oath. They also, by gravely undermining her credibility, stood to diminish her value as a witness to Starr and thereby increase the likelihood of her indictment.

Ginsburg's antics were not harmful to his client alone. They also infuriated and unsettled Starr's prosecutors, who were left — quite legitimately — at a loss as to how to secure truthful testimony from a woman whom they knew to lie habitually and whose lawyer seemed bent on destroying her credibility. Even as immunity talks with Ginsburg were going on, Ginsburg took to the airwaves on February 1, 1998, appearing on five different Sunday talk shows, where he both misrepresented the facts of his client's story and questioned her credibility. He claimed, for example, that he knew of no semen-stained dress.[19] At one point, he denied that he was even "in negotiation with Kenneth Starr."[20] He went so far as to tell CBS, with reference to Lewinsky, that "all twenty-four-year-olds and all eighteen-year-olds and nineteen-year-olds tend to embellish."[21] Starr, ever tactful, said only about Ginsburg that "there seemed to be a fairly broad perception, and I don't want to be casting stones, that the quality of her extant representation was not high."[22] Starr's tact considerably understates the frustration Ginsburg's behavior actually caused the office. One of Starr's deputies, Robert Bittman, summed up that frustration in an extraordinary passage of a letter to Ginsburg written after the negotiations finally fell apart. "I must also add this," the prosecutor wrote: "In the many years of prosecutorial experience represented by attorneys in this office, we have *never* experienced anything approaching your tactics. You have spent far more time in TV studios than in negotiations. Some of your public statements are belied by the facts, such as your contention last week that you had given us a full written proffer at a time when you had provided only a partial oral proffer. Inexplicably, you publicly cast doubt on your client's credibility even as you privately assured us of her eagerness to tell the full truth. You terminated one negotiating session at our offices by hurtling from the room and shouting obscenities. And now you accuse *us* of bad faith, media leaks, and unprofessional behavior."

Ginsburg's handling of the negotiation itself was hardly more reassuring. He resisted making Lewinsky available for an in-person proffer, and then played altogether unnecessary games with the prosecutors regarding what testimony she would give if immunized. As Bittman described in his letter,

> After you insisted that Ms. Lewinsky would not be made available for a proffer, we reluctantly accepted oral attorney proffers — but, disturbingly, Ms. Lewinsky refused to sign a document that included information from those proffers. . . .
>
> Let me review the past few days' history in some detail. On January 30, we provided you with a draft agreement, which included bulleted points summarizing information

from your attorney proffers. You responded that rather
than signing a document containing these points, your client was composing a more detailed, written proffer covering the same topics. We received the written proffer on
February 1. It was internally inconsistent in some respects,
and, contrary to our understanding from you, it did not
incorporate the bulleted information from our draft. We
revised the bulleted material — which still contained solely
information provided by you — in hopes that your client
would sign it so long as her written proffer was attached,
but she refused.[23]

This sort of behavior would have tested the office under
the best of circumstances. The most intense of public spot-
lights, after all, was glaring down upon the immunity negotiations, and the stakes were huge. It seems inconceivable that,
had Lewinsky retained more capable counsel, a deal would
not have materialized quickly to the benefit of both the office
and Lewinsky herself — as, of course, a deal did materialize
after Lewinsky finally fired Ginsburg several months later. So
far anyway, Starr's problem was not his truth commission vision but an unlucky hand dealt him in the one matter, his chief
witness's choice of lawyer, over which he was almost completely powerless.[24]

The pivotal impact of the truth commission approach,
however, is evident in Starr's response to the problems in the
immunity talks, both at the time and in retrospect. Despite
the obstacles, Bittman and two of Starr's other prosecutors,
Bruce Udolf and Michael Emmick, actually reached a tenta-
tive understanding with Ginsburg. This deal, in fact, was being worked out even as Ginsburg was claiming on television
that no negotiations were taking place. The draft agreement,
dated February 2, was based on Lewinsky's written proffer,
as clarified by supplemental language the two sides sought
to work out. The written proffer was, in certain respects, an

improvement over anything the office had previously heard from Lewinsky, but it was also vague on key points, and the vagueness understandably concerned the office. The proffer did not say directly that the president had asked Lewinsky to lie in her testimony, and, indeed, included a specific statement that he did not.[25] This characterization contradicted general statements that Lewinsky's lawyers had earlier proffered orally on her behalf, as well as statements she had made to Tripp, which had been recorded by her friend.[26] The clarifications were efforts to resolve such inconsistencies, yet Ginsburg and the office never came to any definitive understanding regarding what that supplemental language would say. Indeed, though Ginsburg later claimed that a final immunity agreement had been reached and sought to have the deal enforced in court, Starr had never seen the draft agreement, and it was never signed by anyone representing his office, though Udolf had at least tentatively assented to its terms verbally. Chief Judge Norma Holloway Johnson of the U.S. District Court in Washington eventually found that no deal had ever been consummated, both because the text of the agreement had never clearly been finalized and because, in any event, Udolf had no authority to bind the office in such a deal without Starr's approval.[27]

That approval, as things turned out, was not forthcoming. Because the deal had not been formally executed, Starr had the option of not honoring it. Within the office, the deal prompted a firestorm of protest among harder-line prosecutors who believed it was a sellout. Solomon Wisenberg went so far as to threaten to resign and issue a public statement of protest if the deal went forward. The specific cause for concern was that the additional language Ginsburg had included did not bind Lewinsky to details that Ginsburg and her other lawyer, Nathaniel Speights, had described. In fact, the language that the prosecutors had hoped would clarify that Clinton had, in fact, urged Lewinsky to deny the relationship in her affidavit did something else entirely. While the new language did acknowledge that the president had told her to deny the relationship, it also claimed that Clinton made this request before she was ever subpoenaed by Paula Jones's lawyers.[28] That seemed to let Clinton off the hook, at least somewhat. A mere request, after all, that Lewinsky conceal their illicit affair, in the absence of a subpoena for her testimony, was hardly obstruction of justice. It was an almost inherent feature of adultery.[29]

The split within the office over how to proceed was harsh and, in some cases, quite personal. Udolf believed that the office was honor-bound to stand behind the deal he had cut. Emmick argued that, while the office was not legally bound by the deal — which, he acknowledged, was imperfect — the agreement was nonetheless the best game in town. It marked only the beginning of Lewinsky's cooperation; once they began working with her and gained her trust, he believed, they would be able to get what they needed. By contrast, Wisenberg, Jackie Bennett, and others argued that the office was being taken for a ride, that Lewinsky had not demonstrated any kind of credibility, and that an in-person proffer was essential.[30]

Starr's stated reasons for scotching the deal reveal, once again, the values that were ultimately guiding him. After listening to the different factions make their case, he gave what he later described as "an extemporaneous speech" outlining his own views.[31] "Different cultures esteem different values," he said. "In the Japanese culture, honor is the most important virtue. If you are dishonored, that's the end. In my Christian culture, faith is the highest value. But in my professional life, the value I esteem above all is truth. Honor or not, this statement isn't the truth."[32] Starr, in short, killed the Lewinsky immunity deal because he feared that it would not serve the needs of the truth commission.

In retrospect, the deal arranged by Udolf and Emmick looks awfully good. The extra months didn't cause Lewinsky to improve upon her proffered testimony much. Indeed, when Starr's team finally got the opportunity to meet with her face-to-face months later, they emerged, Starr said, uniformly impressed with her memory: "The people said, 'Yes, you are no longer flying blind. We think that she is going to be sufficiently truthful.'" Starr emphasized the extent to which the face-to-face meeting enabled the prosecutors to resolve the inconsistencies in the proffer, particularly with respect to the written proffer's claim that nobody had asked Lewinsky to lie. He also insisted that, even in retrospect, he was unconvinced that Lewinsky had been planning to play straight with the office had their earlier negotiations borne fruit. It is "easy to say [that] she would have brought you the dress, and so forth. Who knows? It's easy to say, 'Oh, this all could have been over and done with.' Who knows?" Because Starr had built such an air-tight case against her by the time Lewinsky's new lawyers, Plato Cacheris and Jacob Stein, reopened the immunity talks, she was no longer in any position to dissemble, he said. "So she was very forthcoming in that initial [oral] proffer. I think there is reason to doubt whether she would have been forthcoming in January."[33]

Starr's conviction on this point seems real; the office was undoubtedly reassured in the oral session that it had a witness with whom the prosecutors could work. But it is hard to imagine that, with all the leverage prosecutors have over immunized witnesses, the clarifications Starr sought would not have materialized in days of debriefing had the earlier deal been consummated. In light of the fine distinctions between the written proffer and the testimony Starr eventually got from Lewinsky, Emmick's point that the voided deal would have marked the beginning of her cooperation, not the end, seems prescient. With hindsight, it is hard to escape the conclusion that Starr referred to Congress in September 1998 the very truth he had rejected the previous winter.

I do not mean to argue that Starr was necessarily wrong to kill the deal given what he knew at the time. Though that decision looks unfortunate now, and holding out was, perhaps, needlessly aggressive, it was surely within the realm of the reasonable. Jeffrey Toobin has written of Starr's decision that it "marked the precise moment when Bill Clinton's survival in office became assured. It was made just seven days after Bill Clinton gave the American people his finger-wagging denial of a sexual relationship with Lewinsky. If Starr had agreed to the immunity deal on [February 3], he would have had the ammunition — in testimony and in conclusive genetic evidence — to prove that Clinton had lied. He could have had an impeachment report for Congress in a month or less. Instead, Starr's obsession with toughness and devotion to the Washington conventional wisdom led him to disaster. In attempting to punish Ginsburg, he merely damaged himself. In believing the reports about Ginsburg's incompetence, he only established his own."[34]

This judgment seems unduly harsh. Given Ginsburg's behavior, the absence of an oral proffer, and the inconsistencies in Lewinsky's written proffer, the deal presented a genuinely tough call. In addition to the truth commission instincts that militated against it, strong law enforcement considerations induced caution as well. As Starr pointed out, "Never in the annals of prosecutorial experience represented around the table could anyone cite an instance . . . for this kind of extraordinarily unorthodox thing: to simply [immunize a key witness] without ever having the opportunity to see the person, to ask the person questions, to assess" the person. Starr noted as well, "We really did have skepticism, which I think was well grounded, . . . about her motives. Why is it that we can't talk to her? . . . I felt that the office was being manipulated, and that she still had every intent . . . to protect the president. . . . She was doing just the opposite from someone who says, 'I've made that moral decision to now be on the side of law enforcement.' "[35] Prosecutors, as well as truth commissioners, need to have confidence in their witnesses. Though prosecutorial values do not appear to have been foremost among Starr's considerations, those values did not decisively tug in the opposite direction either.

If Starr can be forgiven for nixing the deal, however, his reaction in the wake of that decision represented a triumph of truth commission values over prosecutorial interests. Whatever one thought of Ginsburg and his shenanigans, the case itself had not changed: Lewinsky was still the single key witness, and securing her testimony should still have been the paramount consideration for any prosecutor chiefly interested in what cases might plausibly be brought. Indeed, Starr had a third option other than a quick deal or a long stalemate between the office and his most important witness. He could simply have put Lewinsky in front of the grand jury and sought an immunity order from the court if she asserted her Fifth Amendment right against self-incrimination. Proceeding in this fashion would have maximized Starr's flexibility, since he would have retained the ability to prosecute Lewinsky, so long as he did not use her testimony — or the fruits of it — in any case against her. Prosecuting a witness whose testimony has been immunized can be difficult, since the law puts the burden squarely on the prosecutor to show that the evidence presented at trial is wholly untainted by influence from the testimony.[36] Starr, however, was in a strong position in this regard, since Lewinsky had, in a conversation taped by the FBI, repeatedly urged Tripp to lie under oath; she went so far, in fact, as to say she would gladly sign over her interest in a condominium in Australia to Tripp in order to protect Clinton.[37] The fact that an immunity order would not, on its own, have precluded later prosecution would have given Lewinsky a powerful incentive not to lie. Starr told me he considered this option and that he repeatedly raised it within the office. The reason he ultimately rejected it, he said, was that by having Lewinsky testify in a coercive, instead of a cooperative, atmosphere, it might have compromised the search for truth. "Our most experienced prosecutors expressed grave concern about the efficacy of that, that it was far better for us to do everything we could to absolutely exhaust . . . every possibility of entering into a true cooperative arrangement with her," he said. "We were fearful, especially given the representation [by Ginsburg], that we would, perhaps, be buying into a situation of less than complete truth and candor, which would be most unfortunate."[38]

It would overstate the matter to put all of the blame for Starr's failure to secure Lewinsky's testimony earlier on his truth-obsessed understanding of his role. Starr is a cautious man by nature, and, as he reasonably noted, one wants to be rigorous in any investigation of the president. Starr also argued compellingly that the peculiar circumstances of the Lewinsky case — which included the adamant denial by President Clinton of any wrongdoing, combined with a highly political atmosphere and the president's public promise and private refusal to cooperate with the probe — all made it critical to get things right, however one read the law. Starr's need to know the truth, however, was certainly among the predominant factors contributing to the long standoff between his office and Lewinsky.

The impact of the truth-seeking mission on the very design of the investigation becomes particularly apparent when one factors into Starr's decision-making the testimony of Betty Currie. By the time the deal with Lewinsky had fallen apart, Starr's prosecutors had already conducted their first interview with Currie, whose lawyer had previously delivered to the office the box of gifts that Currie had been holding for Lewinsky.[39] The president's secretary told a remarkable story at her January 24 meeting with prosecutors. Late in the evening on the day of Clinton's grilling about Lewinsky during his deposition in the Jones case, Currie said, the president called her at home and said they needed to talk. Since it was too late that night, Currie came in the next day, a Sunday, and met with Clinton. As the FBI interview memorandum records the story:

> CURRIE advised that CLINTON said he was asked some questions at his deposition the previous day about MONICA LEWINSKY. CURRIE advised she was surprised and indicated so by responding "oh."
>
> CURRIE advised that CLINTON proceeded to list some of the things mentioned, like if CLINTON was ever alone with LEWINSKY and if LEWINSKY ever came by the White House. CURRIE advised CLINTON listed the questions in a very quick manner, one right after the other.
>
> CURRIE advised that CLINTON then mentioned some of the questions he was asked at his deposition. CURRIE advised the way CLINTON phrased the queries, they were both statements and questions at the same time.
>
> CURRIE advised that CLINTON said something like you do remember I was never alone with MONICA, right? CURRIE advised that CLINTON then said to CURRIE something to the

effect of you were always here when she was here, right? CURRIE said that CLINTON said something like MONICA came on to me and I never touched her, right? CURRIE said that CLINTON then said something like you could see and hear everything, right? CURRIE advised CLINTON said something to the effect of [LEWINSKY] wanted to have sex with me and I can not do that.

CURRIE advised she responded "right" to each of CLINTON's statements because as far as she knew the statements were basically right, even though CURRIE recalls CLINTON and LEWINSKY were alone in the WHITE HOUSE study on four or five occasions and in the Oval Office on others. CURRIE advised she considers the term alone to mean that no one else was in the entire Oval Office area. CURRIE advised she felt CLINTON asked her these questions to see CURRIE's reaction.[40]

With Currie's story, the outlines of a broader obstruction case against Clinton came into focus. The prosecutors now knew not only that the president had lied under oath himself, but that he had none-too-subtly nudged his secretary to lie as well — though she had not been under subpoena at the time. As Lewinsky's handwritten proffer made clear, he had also, at the very least, asked Lewinsky to deny the affair in general and given her extraordinary assistance in finding a job at a time her testimony was being sought. The course for a traditional prosecutor in these circumstances was clear: the key players — Lewinsky and Clinton — had to be brought before the grand jury, and the ancillary investigation limited to corroborating or refuting their respective stories. Had Starr done this, he would have found, as he later did find, that Lewinsky's tale was remarkably consistent with such White House documents as entry logs and telephone records. He could also have greatly focused his requests for those records, along with the testimony of whatever witnesses were necessary to check out

Lewinsky's story. By not hearing from the two principals, however, Starr forced himself to conduct the broadest possible investigation. This decision simultaneously maximized the intrusiveness of the probe — one that would necessarily have been distastefully prurient simply because of its subject matter — and prevented an earlier referral to Congress. The failure to secure Lewinsky's testimony, in fact, required Starr to reorient his entire investigation toward a project that was, on its own terms, faintly absurd: proving a sexual relationship between two people who both denied it took place, when one of those people had the full panoply of potential presidential privileges to assert and litigate. This project required the subpoena of Lewinsky's book purchases. It required hauling Lewinsky's mother and many of Lewinsky's friends before the grand jury. The project represented the apex of the truth commission approach: a broad-ranging inquiry, far beyond what was necessary for prosecutorial purposes, into the nature of the sexual relationship between Clinton and Lewinsky.

Starr did not attempt to deny that the extremity of the probe emanated from the Lewinsky standoff. "Part of the dynamic that was under way with the investigation — when is enough enough? Is the eighth friend or is the sixth friend enough? — was informed by the fact that we continued to have stalemate with the president and the inability at the time to deal in a way that we were professionally satisfied with with the only other person who truly knew," Starr explained. Meanwhile, the Secret Service kept resisting his efforts to secure the testimony of its agents. "So in these fairly critical areas, we were being deprived of information that could be completely dispositive, and so we were pressing forward on those fronts." At the same time, however, Starr felt they had to look elsewhere and ask, "Well, what *is* open to you? Well, there are people who do know."[41] Many of these steps, each of

which further convinced an already appalled public that Starr
was on a political vendetta, would have been unnecessary had
Starr had access to the person who actually knew what had
happened — access he was denied chiefly by his own caution in
dealing with her. While Toobin is too harsh in his criticism
of the decision to kill the immunity deal and his contention
that the resulting delay saved Clinton's presidency represents
the rankest of speculation, he is quite correct that dragging
the investigation out over eight months proved a disaster for
Starr. In that period, Starr went from a man who had served
with honor, if occasional error, under extraordinarily difficult
circumstances to the poster boy of all that was excessive and
dangerous about the independent counsel statute.

Starr greatly compounded the problem created by his
understanding of the independent counsel's role with a second decision, which also appears to have been animated by
the truth commission vision but which was unique to the
Lewinsky phase of the investigation. Starr's reading of the independent counsel law's provision authorizing impeachment
referrals to Congress is, perhaps, the single aspect of his investigation most difficult to reconcile with his history of concern for the separation of powers. Given that history, one
would have expected Starr — who was, despite the oddities
of the independent counsel's office, an official of the executive branch — to read the statute so as to avoid performing an
impeachment investigation for the legislative branch. Starr,
however, did the opposite. He read the law so as to make
himself Congress's agent.

Once again, the statute itself put Starr in a no-win situation. Opaque and badly thought out, the referral provision
necessarily implicates the supposedly apolitical independent
counsel in the inherently political impeachment process. The
provision reads: "An independent counsel shall advise the

House of Representatives of any substantial and credible information which such independent counsel receives, in carrying out the independent counsel's responsibilities under this chapter, that may constitute grounds for an impeachment. Nothing in this chapter . . . shall prevent the Congress or either House thereof from obtaining information in the course of an impeachment proceeding."[42] This provision would, were the issue ever litigated, probably survive judicial scrutiny. It does not, after all, assign any of the House's "sole Power of Impeachment" to the independent counsel.[43] Nor does it purport to regulate in any fashion the manner in which Congress conducts or considers impeachments. On its face anyway, the referral provision merely requires independent counsels to facilitate this congressional function by transmitting to the Congress whatever relevant information they uncover.

In any reasonable real-world analysis, however, the referral provision breaches a profound separation-of-powers value by accomplishing what Julie O'Sullivan, a Georgetown University law professor, has called a "functional delegation" of "the initiation, timing, content and perhaps outcome of impeachment inquiries to a constitutional third party" that "allow[s] Congress to avoid its responsibilities as well as public accountability."[44] O'Sullivan, a former prosecutor who worked both for Robert Fiske Jr. and briefly for Starr, discussed the problems with the referral provision in a deeply prescient article written before the Lewinsky affair erupted. "Although the House is not formally bound to accept or proceed upon an IC's referral or to restrict itself to those referrals made by ICs," she argued, "history demonstrates that ICs' determinations under section 595 will as a matter of fact largely determine whether impeachment proceedings are launched, and the content and direction of those proceedings. Further, given the IC's unique institutional character, IC referrals may well alter the political climate in which such inquiries are initiated and dilute the extent to which Congress will be held accountable for the conduct or outcome of impeachment inquiries."[45] Even on its own, in other words, the provision induces a kind of complacency among legislators about their own constitutional obligations and encourages them to defer to the executive branch in matters where the Constitution seeks to maximize their political accountability.

In addition to its conceptual flaws, the referral language unfortunately offers little guidance as to the standards an independent counsel should employ in determining when to make what sort of referral. While the statutory language "shall" makes referrals mandatory, the statute says nothing about their timing. Are independent counsels to refer immediately upon coming across "substantial and credible information," or should they take extreme care — and time — to evaluate it first? For that matter, what is "substantial and credible information," an evidentiary standard that appears nowhere else in federal law and that the statute itself does not purport to define? Once an independent counsel determines that he or she is in possession of such information, what exactly should a referral contain or look like? Should independent counsels merely transmit the raw grand jury material itself and let Congress sort it out? Should they, as Watergate Special Prosecutor Leon Jaworski did in 1974, send Congress a bare-bones report? Or, alternatively, should they seek to characterize that information and justify the decision that it "may constitute grounds for an impeachment"? As O'Sullivan put it,

> The requirement that the information received be "substantial and credible" is inherently subjective and malleable, and does not constitute a meaningful limitation upon the IC's discretion. The statute does not specify the form that the IC's advice to the House shall take. ICs, then, ap-

pear to have the power to decide how detailed their referral will be, and what, if any, documentary or testimonial evidence shall accompany the referral. Finally, the statute does not provide the IC with any guidance about the timing of such referrals. The legislative history of this provision sheds precious little light on the meaning or scope of these requirements. In fact, it demonstrates little beyond the fact that the impeachment referral provision was, as it appears on its face, designed to create a mandatory duty, and that it was not intended to limit Congress's power to obtain information pertinent to impeachment inquiries through other means.[46]

The provision's text, in other words, can support a wide range of possible interpretations that would, in turn, deliver referrals of dramatically different depths and scope, and invade Congress's sphere to greatly differing degrees. There is, in short, no obvious path for independent counsels who find themselves in what Starr calls "595(c) territory."[47]

Given the wide discretion the statute grants the independent counsel, the healthiest reading of the law would have been one that construed the evidentiary barrier to a referral as a relatively low one but that also construed the provision as authorizing only nonevaluative documents. The virtue of this reading resides both in its fidelity to the provision's purpose and in its being the best strategy toward minimizing the sort of functional displacement of impeachment onto the executive branch that is, to some degree, inherent in the provision itself.[48] Alexia Morrison, the former independent counsel who successfully defended the independent counsel law's constitutionality before the Supreme Court, argued that "the impeachment evidence provision, properly read in context, was inserted to assure that no independent counsel would sit on evidence that Congress should have so it could fulfill its own duties."[49] This understanding, which seems historically strong, would argue against construing the provision as so high a wall against referrals that Congress could be left without access to information that a reasonable member might wish to consider in light of the impeachment power. It would also, however, argue against an independent counsel's characterizing such information, since doing so would necessarily implicate the independent counsel in Congress's job of evaluating that information against the impeachment clauses. While any referral under the statute would necessarily require of the independent counsel the threshold judgment that the evidence "may" be actionable under the impeachment power, the statute requires no more evaluation than that, and the prudent reading would avoid invading Congress's prerogatives more than the statute absolutely demands.

This reading, attractive both because of the provision's underlying purpose and because it minimizes the offense against the separation of powers, is desirable also because it can be so easily harmonized with the text of the law. Though one can manipulate the language of the statute to support almost any reading, its plain language seems to indicate that a referral is required after an independent counsel obtains only a modest quantum of evidence. "Substantial and credible," after all, describes a standard far lower than those applied in court by triers of fact, such as "preponderance of the evidence" or "clear and convincing evidence." For that matter, the word "information" seems like something less than "evidence" in first place. The words "may constitute" suggest that the independent counsel need not necessarily even believe that Congress ought to impeach based on the information being referred, merely that it might consider doing so within the bounds of its unfettered discretion under the impeachment clauses. Finally, the word "information" does not obviously call for any evaluation of the material referred. It seems, instead, like a call for the raw data, perhaps with some sort of organizing roadmap along the lines of the report that Jaworski sent to Congress. Jaworski's report was filed under seal and has never become public, so its precise contours remain unknown to the public. It was, however, characterized by U.S. District Court Chief Judge John Sirica, who, in authorizing its transmission, wrote,

> The Report here at issue . . . draws no accusatory conclusions. . . . It contains no recommendations, advice or statements that infringe on the prerogatives of other branches of government. . . . It renders no moral or social judgments. The Report is a simple and straightforward compilation of information gathered by the Grand Jury, and no more. . . . .
>
> The Grand Jury has obviously taken care to assure that its Report contains no objectionable features, and has throughout acted in the interests of fairness.[50]

The best reading of this admittedly flawed provision would facilitate, not retard, congressional involvement, but would do so without either attempting to prejudice that involvement or seeming to attempt to influence it.

I do not mean to underestimate the dangers of the reading I am here advancing — either the substantive or the political dangers. An early, less thorough referral would have risked triggering an impeachment inquiry where none was justified and making allegations that would not ultimately withstand scrutiny. Had Starr sent Congress such a document — much less in a form that did not make an argument for its own seriousness — he would surely have been attacked for filing a slipshod referral based on weak evidence. Such a referral would have been seen by the president's defenders, in all likelihood, as a political smear. Given the climate, one in which Starr was already being attacked for this sort of malfeasance, any impulse on his part to avoid fueling the fire was certainly understandable. Such caution, however, did not save Starr from precisely this line of attack; his referral was, when finally filed, still criticized as a political slime job. While it has stood up factually quite well, Starr's characterizations of evidence, inclusion of sexual details, and exclusion of certain facts arguably favorable to the defense have all been characterized as political decisions.[51] In retrospect, it is fascinating how little protection Starr's factual rigor bought him against the charge of political motivation. In his dissent in *Morrison v. Olson*, Antonin Scalia described the context of the independent counsel statute as "acrid with the smell of threatened impeachment."[52] Starr's failure to render unto Congress the portion of the Lewinsky investigation that properly belonged to it shrouded his office with the odor Scalia described; the public came to see him not as a criminal prosecutor but as a stalking horse for House Republicans bent on impeachment.

Given the approach he took, the public judgment was a reasonable one. Starr's attitude toward the impeachment referral could hardly have been calculated to intrude more on Congress's province. "I made a judgment—and I accept responsibility for it—that the statute . . . is rather rich in its language. It asks for judgment to be made . . . and so there's an evaluation of the evidence," Starr explained. "One, it seemed to me, must make a reasoned presentation as to why one is doing this extraordinarily weighty—albeit statutorily mandated—act and to demonstrate to the fair-minded reader and observer that there is substantial and credible . . . information." To Starr, the word "information" suggested "much more inclusiveness." The statute, he argued, militates against restricting oneself to the rules of evidence in a manner that would "handicap the Congress as if it is a court of law. The court of impeachment can consider anything it wants to." The word "grounds," in turn, gave rise to "an inference" that the independent counsel should "give coherence to the submission to Congress. And that was my fundamental judgment: There should be a coherent submission." In short, Starr "just felt that . . . the idea of 'grounds,' coupled with the 'substantial and credible,' put a burden on me . . . to present the information, to suggest this was a serious matter in terms of 'grounds.' And I really dwelt on that word 'grounds' — that I needed to justify this. I needed to justify in the sense of, Here are the reasons why we believe that this information may constitute grounds for the removal of the president of the United States."[53]

This reading, of course, precluded either a quick referral or one that avoided commenting extensively on the evidence. It effectively guaranteed that the independent counsel's office would take on the duty of serving as Congress's impeachment investigator, rather than focusing exclusively on the criminal questions the case presented. To some extent, Starr had painted himself into a corner on the question of standards for an impeachment referral when he had declined in 1997 to send up to Congress the Whitewater referral his office had drafted. In that instance, he said, "I had documentary information and I had witnesses who suggested that the president committed perjury or, at least, the testimony was untruthful." Starr, however, refrained from sending the one-hundred-page document, which "has never seen the light of day."[54]

Starr's point here has some force: However one reads the standard in the referral provision, one ought to attempt to read it with reasonable consistency. If adopting a high-bar reading in 1997 showed restraint and maturity, it is hard to argue that employing the same reading in 1998 co-opted congressional prerogatives. Because the 1997 referral has never become public, evaluating its strength relative to the power of the Lewinsky evidence is quite difficult. Starr's argument, however, is clearly weakened by certain things that are known about the Whitewater referral. The evidence against the president was largely based on the testimony of two convicted felons, one of whom — Jim McDougal — suffered from mental illness and had significant memory lapses resulting from his neurological problems. The evidence, therefore, had problems under the "credible" language in the referral provision, problems that Lewinsky's testimony — which could be extensively corroborated through documents and the testimony of ancillary witnesses — certainly did not present. As Stephen Bates, one of the principal authors of the Lewinsky referral and the staffer who drafted the abortive Whitewater referral, put it, "In the Lewinsky investigation, we had White House records, Secret Service testimony, tapes, the accounts of Lewinsky's confidants, and ultimately the dress, all of which corroborated the allegations. We couldn't amass the same sort of credible evidence for the [Whitewater] matter — it simply didn't exist."[55] Clinton's own testimony, which presumably could have been obtained long before, likewise contained significant admissions that validated key aspects of Lewinsky's testimony. In the end, there was surely room for Starr under his prior readings of the law to refer the Lewinsky matter earlier had he chosen to do so.

Part of the explanation for his reluctance appears to have been simple protectiveness of his probe from congressional meddling. An early referral could well have precluded any criminal cases Starr might later have brought, since congressional immunizations have a way of complicating criminal probes — as they did, for example, in the Iran-Contra investigation. Starr said he was "mindful of the possibility that there would be criminal prosecutions along the way — that is to say we may go forward with one or more criminal prosecutions against individuals other than the president of the

United States. We don't know who all is involved in this process."[56] The investigators, of course, also needed to consider the possibility of indicting Clinton, either before or after he left office.

The instinct not to encourage Congress from conducting an overlapping investigation was hardly novel. Indeed, during his Whitewater investigation, Fiske had been far more aggressive than Starr had been during the Lewinsky matter in actively discouraging congressional involvement. The circumstances, however, were dramatically different. Fiske's Whitewater investigation, after all, bore impeachment issues only at its far outer edges, and a lot of investigative terrain whose questions were first and foremost criminal questions lay between Congress and those remote impeachment issues. In the Lewinsky case, by contrast, the primary issue presented by the case from the outset was one of impeachment, not prosecution. The criminal questions, in fact, always bore a faint scent of pretext. The predominance of the impeachment question in this case should have implied a predominance of Congress's, not Starr's, constitutional obligations. While it is asking a lot to suggest that a prosecutor ought to yield up a matter to a noninvestigative body that has a history of messing up both criminal probes and its own oversight role, the instinct to protect the probe from Congress was a bad one, which functioned less to protect any important prosecutorial interests than simply to implicate Starr maximally in the impeachment.

Starr acknowledged quite readily that the grand jury room is exactly the wrong place for an impeachment inquiry. "We had these discussion as the agora unfolded in our offices that this is a crazy system," he recalled. " 'Why are we doing this in the context of the grand jury with its secrecy, with all the skewed information? . . . This is a very poor vehicle for accomplishing this interest.' And there was very thoughtful commentary to the effect of, the criminal justice system just is ill-suited by design to issues of appropriate or inappropriate conduct going to the fitness of the president of the United States to carry on in his office. I totally agree with that as a matter of policy." Once again, however, Starr saw his hands as having been tied by the law, which he insisted could not properly have been read as anything less than a delegation of the impeachment investigation. "Congress has made this judgment, without a lot of thought, without a lot of care, to have this weighty duty imposed on an independent counsel," he said. "I may not like it, but that's the job description.... And I cannot, in effect, say, 'This is unconstitutional as applied.' I have a duty as an executive officer . . . to seek faithfully to uphold the statute."[57]

In a paradoxical twist of logic, Starr believed that in order to avoid usurping Congress's legislative powers by rewriting the law, he had to allow Congress to give him some piece of its impeachment power. "There was nothing to prevent the Congress, if it saw fit, from stepping in," he argued.[58] On the other hand, House Judiciary Committee chairman Henry Hyde had announced early in the scandal that Congress would wait for Starr's results.[59] Starr believed that "there was also nothing to prevent the Congress in the exercise of its unfettered constitutional discretion to decide to defer — whether it's wise or not." Starr said he would have seen any early referral as "an abdication of my responsibility" to the extent it was designed to indicate to Congress that "I'm not going to do anything further because I think you are, in effect, using me to carry on your constitutional responsibilities."[60]

It takes work to make the statute's grant of almost unconditional discretion on this matter into such a straightjacket. Indeed, even some of Starr's own staff question in retrospect the decision to hang on to the probe so long. Stephen Bates stated, "It would have been far better for us, especially for Ken, if we had transmitted evidence much earlier and the spotlight had shifted to Congress. But a lot of the initial evidence was murky or circumstantial, and Congress certainly wasn't demanding that we hand it over. So we ended up spending months litigating frivolous privileges and persuading Monica Lewinsky to cooperate."[61] Starr himself, in fact, has conceded that if he could do it all again, he would not have commented on the evidence he sent up to Congress. "In hindsight, in light of the criticism, my inclination would have been to stretch the statute and just send the truck up with the raw information, and say, 'I respectfully decline to provide any analysis . . . whatsoever,'" he said in response to Senator Daniel Akaka's questioning in a congressional hearing.[62] Even at the time, in fact, Starr felt great urgency to get the report filed as quickly as possible and slapped arbitrary deadlines on the referral's delivery, only to delay later at the urging of his staff.[63] The consequence of his failure to secure Lewinsky's early cooperation was that a responsible referral was impossible to complete in a timely fashion.

The consequences of Starr's taking on the impeachment investigation were enormous. Congressional investigators, of course, never would have asked the questions of witnesses that Starr's prosecutors were able to ask within the privacy of the grand jury room. Starr, within that room, had no accountability for those questions, though they were ultimately being asked in the service of the congressional impeachment power. Nor, as things turned out, did political accountability for the conduct of the investigation rest with Congress, whose members had not asked these questions but nonetheless turned around and released large amounts of grand jury material to the public. The privacy invasion was horrific, particularly for

Lewinsky, who had not, after all, sought any kind of public attention.

The intrusion on Lewinsky's privacy presents a particularly instructive example of the consequences of Starr's late and florid referral. Lewinsky was forced, under threat of criminal prosecution, to discuss the most intimate details of her life. Her testimony was supplemented by email messages carefully undeleted from her computers at home and work, and by scrutiny of letters she wrote but chose not to send. She was stripped, under the guise of a grand jury investigation, of any right of self-censorship. Had Congress been forced to investigate the matter itself, it is simply unimaginable that members of Congress, in an open hearing, would have been willing to ask Lewinsky the details of her encounters with Clinton. They would have been too embarrassed, and had any of them overcome his or her timidity and dared to ask about the incident in which the president inserted a cigar in Lewinsky's vagina, that member's phone lines would have been flooded with outraged constituents.[64] It was only by getting a prosecutor to perform the investigation in the secrecy of the grand jury room that these political constraints could be evaded. Starr's office was asking the questions without c-span present and was not, in any case, made up of elected officials who cared much — or had any instinctive feel for — what the public thought. They could ask Lewinsky anything, and they did, thereby relieving Congress of all responsibility for the investigation save disseminating the packaged product at the end and voting up or down on whether the offenses Starr alleged warranted Clinton's impeachment. The consequence was that Lewinsky was forced to answer for the public a series of questions that nobody would ever have had the guts to ask her in public.

Because of the peculiar design of Starr's inquiry — itself

greatly conditioned by Starr's truth-seeking impulse — it is hard to identify the precise point at which he should have referred. Until he obtained Lewinsky's testimony, which happened only in the summer of 1998, his evidence was largely hearsay. A referral based chiefly on the Tripp tapes, about which there were provenance and authenticity questions, would have been irresponsible. Even Tripp's testimony was — at least as pertains to the president's conduct — all based on Lewinsky's say so. Currie's story, of course, presented very direct evidence of Clinton's misconduct, but her extraordinary tale of his coaching her was also part of a larger saga that the prosecutors had not nailed down firmly — a part that would have been quite strange to refer in abstraction from everything else. In the context of the probe Starr actually conducted, an earlier referral would have been quite difficult. Had the underlying investigation itself been conducted more traditionally, however, an earlier referral would have flowed organically out of it and would not have required any self-conscious lowering of the bar. Had Starr begun the probe by securing testimony from Lewinsky, Currie, Jordan, and Clinton himself, a responsible referral surely would have been possible based upon their collective testimony and a certain amount of corroborative documentary investigation.

Wherever the right line was, Starr's reading seems excessive. He treated the standard for referral as tantamount to proof beyond a reasonable doubt, effectively turning a requirement that he not withhold information from Congress into a requirement to learn the truth and bestow it upon a House of Representatives all too eager to dodge responsibility for a sordid scandal. To put it simply, in combination with a more traditional investigative strategy, a different reading of the provision — one arguably more faithful to its purpose — could have produced a much quicker referral with a minimum of commentary, all designed to avoid intruding on Congress's sole power under the Constitution to conduct impeachments. Congress could then have conducted its own investigation into as many or as few of the gory details as it desired, while Starr could have restricted himself to the narrow criminal questions the Lewinsky case posed. Had he not read the law as envisioning the independent counsel's role as a truth commission bound to do Congress's dirty work, he could actually have been a comparatively minimal presence. The price of such an action would, to be sure, have been a less thorough investigation — as well as the likelihood that any active congressional investigation would have made later criminal prosecutions impossible. The benefit, well worth the price, would have been speed, enhanced political accountability, and that quality of proportionality that Starr's probe so lacked.

The Lewinsky truth commission saw its sad denouement in May 1999, in a federal courtroom in northern Virginia, where Starr's office tried a woman named Julie Hiatt Steele. The Steele trial took place months after the president's acquittal in the Senate, and seemed, at times, like an absurd afterthought — particularly because Steele was, other than Charles Bakaly III, the only person actually to face federal charges arising out of the scandal. Steele was a Richmond woman who had initially corroborated Kathleen Willey's story about being groped by Clinton to *Newsweek* reporter Michael Isikoff.[65] Even before Isikoff could publish the story, however, she recanted and claimed that Willey had asked her to say that Willey had told her contemporaneously about the alleged encounter; Willey, Steele claimed, had only told her about the incident weeks later and had not seemed terribly upset.[66] Steele's story later changed again, and she insisted that Willey had not told her about the incident at all until

Isikoff's inquiries, a recantation that was not particularly credible considering that Steele had mentioned Willey's account to other friends prior to those inquiries.[67] Her insistence in front of two of Starr's grand juries that she had never heard of the matter before 1997 was in all probability false, and the office alleged as well that she sought to persuade those whom she had earlier told about the incident to say that she had not, in fact, talked to them about it.[68]

As with the serial indictments of Webster Hubbell and Susan McDougal, whose criminal contempt trial took place in the same period, however, the Steele prosecution was one that the Justice Department would surely have avoided. For one thing, Willey herself was a deeply problematic witness, who had both obfuscated under oath about the encounter with Clinton in earlier testimony and — after agreeing to cooperate with Starr under immunity — proceeded to lie to investigators and thus require a subsequent reimmunization. She had also, it turned out, asked Steele to lie on her behalf before.[69] More importantly, even if the case had been airtight, the effort by the Office of Independent Counsel to prosecute a woman with no ties to the Clintons for lying about gossiping was grotesque. Starr insisted the charges were justified in light of "the grossness of the conduct," noting in particular that the indictment alleged not just simple lying but also "seeking out others and encouraging them" to lie, "not one, not two, but three different persons."[70] Ultimately, however, the Steele prosecution was not principally punitive; Steele was too profoundly unimportant to bother punishing. The office seems to have believed that someone had gotten to Steele and persuaded her to recant, and the prosecutors saw this as part of the pattern of obstruction in which the White House was engaged.[71] The result of that recantation had been, in their view, the malicious disparagement of a witness central to their investigation. The prosecution of Steele grew out of a combination of frustrated truth seeking and the continued hope that a break in the case, and a more perfect truth, might lie with her conviction. As with Hubbell and McDougal, however, the prosecutorial mechanism failed to deliver truth in the absence of a simultaneous and compelling — not merely a theoretical or pretextual — prosecutorial interest. On May 7, 1999, the jury deadlocked and failed to convict Steele, whom the office later declined to retry. Once again, the truth commission instinct had led to prosecutorial ineffectiveness.

As with the Foster case, Starr's Lewinsky investigation succeeded, if success is defined by the accomplishment of its self-defined purpose. The American public certainly learned the truth about its president, both through the revelations in the referral itself and, no less important, by watching the pitched battle the president was willing to fight to protect his narrow interests at the expense of the public's. It learned the truth, as well, from the hair-splitting defense the president and his legal team insisted upon and their unstinting refusal to acknowledge the painfully obvious fact that the president had lied abjectly under oath and had, to put the matter as generously as the evidence will possibly allow, tacitly encouraged others to do the same. If one envisions the independent counsel as a truth commissioner, for whom prosecutions should be a secondary objective and who is bound to take all reasonable and ethical steps to get and report the truth, the Lewinsky investigation offers a relatively efficient example of the truth being reported in a fashion useful to Congress in carrying out its own constitutional function. This is certainly how Starr sees it. Asked during a Senate hearing how his investigation had helped the country, Starr responded, "I'm old fashioned, I believe that the truth shall set you free, it's a scriptural admonition, and for better or for worse, I think it's always for better. The country knows [the] facts." But Starr added that "it would have been better for these facts to have come out much more readily outside the criminal justice process, so that instead of having courthouse carnival, circus type atmospheres, witnesses who were intimidated by the very crush of humanity and the like and then going into the grand jury with . . . defense lawyers . . . making charges at every turn, . . . let's just have Congress engage in its oversight capacity."[72]

Such truth emerging from congressional oversight, however, is almost unimaginable in reality. The public learned from Starr a great deal more truth than it wanted, as evidenced by the president's strong public approval ratings throughout the scandal, by the low public opinion of Starr's own work, and by the overwhelming disapproval of impeachment as a remedy for Clinton's misbehavior. It learned truths it arguably did not need to know, for Clinton's misdeeds, however corrupt and ugly, did not seriously implicate his performance as president. No politically accountable officer — members of Congress most especially — would have dared seek these truths, and that caution would have been healthy. Once the public learned them, however, they could not be ignored.

For those of us who are not precommitted to this truth commission vision of the law, the Lewinsky investigation should stand as a cautionary tale about undisciplined statutory interpretations and the need for executive branch officers to construe grants of power so as to minimize their intrusions on the other branches.

If one imagines the independent counsel to be, at the end of the day, a prosecutor, Starr's Lewinsky investigation can hardly be deemed a success — and not merely because the prosecutors failed to secure a conviction in the single

Lewinsky-related case they actually brought. The investigation Starr conducted, despite its hopeless grandiosity, somehow managed not to address rigorously the core question that lay at its heart: whether or not Bill Clinton should be prosecuted. Starr did eventually conclude that he would not bring any case while Clinton remained in office. And his successor, Robert Ray, decided in the final hours of Clinton's presidency not to prosecute him at all, following a settlement by Clinton with Arkansas bar disciplinary authorities in which Clinton acknowledged his false testimony. Ray, however, considered prosecution very seriously, and it is a telling fact that the office's prior grand jury work proved inadequate for his full consideration of this question. Despite the voluminous grand jury record, the many witnesses from whom the office had heard, and the countless subpoenas it had sent out, Ray felt compelled to convene a new grand jury to reconsider the evidence specifically with reference to the possibility of a Clinton indictment.[73] That this step was necessary more than two and a half years after the investigation began in order to address the question that necessarily lay at its heart is the ultimate evidence of how disconnected Starr's approach was from any prosecutorial goal.

CHAPTER 5

Separating Truth From Justice

"One utterance of [Oliver Cromwell's] has always hung in my mind. It
was just before the Battle of Dunbar; he beat the Scots in the end, as
you know, after a very tough fight; but he wrote them before the
battle, trying to get them to accept a reasonable [compromise]. These
were his words: 'I beseech ye in the bowels of Christ, think that ye
may be mistaken.' I should like to have that written over the portals of
every church, every school, and every court house, and, may I say, of
every legislative body in the United States. I should like to have every
court begin, 'I beseech ye in the bowels of Christ, think that we may
be mistaken.'"

LEARNED HAND, 1951

The events that led to the impeachment of President Clinton exist now in that peculiar zone between journalism and
history. They lie in the past and are consequently not the
subject of daily reporting. The facts have stabilized, and one
need not make each utterance today with the certainty that
tomorrow's disclosures will moot it. At the same time, huge
sets of data remain unexplored — most important, Starr's own
paper trail, which under the law is to be transmitted to the National Archive now that the investigation is fully completed,
and parts of which will become public. The hackneyed cliché
that journalism is a first draft of history offers a good description of the transition stage in which we now find ourselves with
respect to the Clinton-Starr wars. The first draft has been

completed, but it needs substantial revisions. That editing takes place at a variety of levels. Recent descriptions of the inner workings of Starr's office during the Lewinsky investigation have gently corrected innumerable misimpressions about the manner in which the Office of Independent Counsel functioned.[1] Peter Baker's portrayal of the events that took place during the impeachment and Senate trial has exploded the myth that these events followed prewritten scripts that led ineluctably to a predetermined outcome.[2] The present examination has approached the project of revision from a more interpretive and less ambitiously reportorial angle. The conventional understanding of Starr's tenure is a caricature that cannot withstand the scrutiny that will necessarily come with greater distance and perspective. The question is which interpretive framework will replace over time the canards that Starr was an evil man, an unethical lawyer, a partisan warrior, or simply a fool who surrounded himself with zealots. Will the hole in our understanding that the rejection of these premises will leave be filled with historical vindication for Starr, or will some more defensible critique emerge in their place?

Starr has publicly acknowledged certain errors, even some major ones. He should not, he now concedes, have taken on so many different subjects. By allowing himself to become the independent counsel not only for Whitewater but for the Travel Office scandal, the FBI files matter, and the Lewinsky affair, he prevented the timely resolution of questions and created an appearance that he was Clinton's personal prosecutor. He should have explained himself better to the press, he believes.[3] He even came to believe that he should not have accepted jurisdiction over the Lewinsky matter, but should have simply sent Linda Tripp to the Justice Department, to do with her as it pleased.[4] These admissions seem, at one level, pretty fundamental. But they also have a strange window-dressing quality. Starr admits little more than that steps he took could have given people the wrong impression. In no sense does he concede that there came a point in the investigation after which the entire effort was actually out of kilter. To the contrary, throughout our discussions Starr appeared the very picture of a man convinced of his own rectitude and rightness. Indeed, his whole being spoke to his belief that, contrary to the public's perception, he did not become another Whitney North Seymour Jr., the independent counsel who so flagrantly substituted his judgment for that of the rest of the executive branch by trying to compel the testimony of a foreign diplomat. In Starr's view, the excesses of his probe were either imagined or, to whatever extent they were real, inevitable reflections of the structural defects in the independent counsel regime.

Starr's explanation is almost entirely unsatisfying, and his pervasive sense of victimization at the statute's hands is all the more so. Starr did not claim to be the law's unwilling slave merely with respect to the big picture. There were, in fact, very few controversies surrounding his work that he did not ultimately blame on the statute. This tendency became, at times, simply silly, as when he faulted the statute for the criticism he faced for maintaining his law practice while investigating the president. "The entire structure of the independent counsel statute, including the history of the conflict of interest regulations, lulled me into the view that my activity was entirely sanctioned by Congress," he said. "The very structure was a beguiling structure in the sense that . . . it explicitly permits" prosecutors to keep their outside practices. Starr described his commitments to his firm and to his clients — including to a conservative foundation and what he

quaintly calls the "tobacco community"—as moral obligations on which he was not going to renege because of legally
frivolous conflict allegations.[5]

While his claim that the decision to keep his clients was
sanctioned is certainly correct, a law is not culpable for every
act that does not happen to violate it. Starr's unwillingness—
or inability—to appreciate the extent to which such choices,
legally defensible though they may have been, contributed
to the public's suspicion of his work pointedly illustrates his
more general efforts, at least publicly, to avoid confronting
the possibility that he could have taken healthier paths. Indeed, Starr appeared willfully unaware of how badly he damaged the credibility of his investigation with his insistence on
maintaining an outside schedule of client work and speeches,
displaying a breathtaking naiveté about how appearance questions would play to the public. "I do not think, at the end of
the day, that what transpired in 1998 [in the Lewinsky inves-
tigation] was materially affected by these [alleged conflicts]
issues," he said. "However weighty they might be in the balance of reasonable, fair-minded liberals, the facts—and this is
my abiding faith—the facts will eventually speak for themselves, and so too will then the law."[6]

The point of the preceding chapters was not to supplant
the demonic and hagiographic portraits of Starr with a comprehensive explanation of the probe built around his truth-
oriented understanding of the statute. Starr's shop was a mul-
tiyear project involving dozens of people examining greatly
diverse matters. Like any complex human system, it resists
simple, holistic explanation. My purpose, instead, is to propose that Starr's truth-seeking mission is one highly significant factor that served to push the investigation in the direc-
tions that it ultimately took, a factor that has been widely
overlooked despite having considerable explanatory power. It

is also to propose that the direction in which Starr took the probe was not inevitable, that Robert Fiske Jr. was on a different and healthier path before his replacement — that things, in other words, could have been different. How much different we will never know. It may be that the sum total of Starr's sins only added additional intensity to a conflict that would have taken place with or without him. For whatever such speculation is worth, I suspect the Clinton presidency would have played out quite differently had Fiske never been removed.

There were, of course, many other factors at work in Starr's investigation that pushed him in the direction he ultimately took. Despite Starr's efforts to create a microcosm of the Justice Department, the loss of perspective that Justice Antonin Scalia described in his *Morrison v. Olson* dissent surely took place among Starr and his staff alike.[7] The White House's war against the office undoubtedly hardened attitudes and galvanized the prosecutors' determination not to back down. The conventional critique of Starr contains a kernel of truth as well, in that the office included, particularly in its later incarnations, a significant contingent of highly aggressive prosecutors disinclined toward restraint in sensitive situations. What I hope to have demonstrated, however, is that all of these factors took place in the context not merely of the flawed statutory scheme about which Starr complains, but in the context of an understanding of that scheme that radicalized the investigation beyond what was necessary. To put it in the language of two of the quotations I have used as chapter epigraphs in this book, Starr engaged in a most stringent execution of a bad and obnoxious law, and he seems to this day never to have considered seriously the possibility that he might have been mistaken in doing so. As President Grant might have predicted, Starr's execution of his duty under the statute secured the law's repeal.

A fair judgment of Starr, however, must be tempered by an appreciation of both the extreme difficulty of his situation and the sincere attempt he made to act reasonably. Unlike Clinton, whose conduct was consistently venal, Starr acted, I believe, in good faith throughout the turmoil. Also unlike Clinton, whose response to the investigation consistently placed his own interests ahead of the public interest, Starr's positions were not self-serving. To the contrary, a different approach on his part would surely have served his public image far better than the path he chose. Starr was also the target of an unrelenting campaign of character assassination. In important respects, he was more sinned against than sinning. Moreover, however differently things could have played out, a certain amount of the problem was surely structural. The president, after all, had committed crimes and was determined not to face any accounting for them. Any prosecutor appointed to see that he did so, however disciplined that prosecutor may have been, would have been attacked, tarred, and second-guessed. It is important not to overblame Starr for that portion of the conflagration that was either the consequence of the president's malfeasance or an outgrowth of any attempt to investigate a sitting president who had, in fact, done wrong, yet insisted on getting away with it.

Charles Dickens begins *David Copperfield* by having his main character wonder "whether I shall turn out to be the hero of my own life, or whether that station will be held by anybody else." Starr's tenure, in the end, presents a similar question. His errors were of sufficient gravity that some observers have been tempted either to cast others as the hero of his story or to view him as the villain of it. Jeffrey Toobin, for example, opens his book on the scandal by observing that "in spite of his consistently reprehensible behavior, Clinton was, by comparison [with his foes], the good guy in this struggle."[8]

However tempting the inversion may be, it is ultimately perverse. In the end, Starr is the only plausible protagonist for the story of the Clinton wars.

If Starr gets to serve as his own story's hero, however, he stands as a particularly frustrating and tragic sort of hero, one limited in his ability in real time to envision the problems with the approach he was taking, and obtuse in retrospect in admitting those problems. Asked whether he was the independent counsel who, fully aware of the dangers of the law and keen to avoid them, nonetheless interpreted the statute in a manner that heightened, rather than minimized, those dangers, Starr insisted that such a reading would be "unfair."

"I think at every turn, we took highly professional steps that actually represented the judgment that we must gather the facts . . . while taking into account whether we were, in fact, trenching unduly on other important public interests," he said. This approach, he argued, could not be less similar to Whitney North Seymour's subpoena of Ambassador Allan Gotlieb. "The Gotlieb evil, as I saw it, was that this interest in gathering the facts had come up against a clear problem of international relations, diplomatic relations, matters of international comity, and some fairly well-established views with respect to diplomatic immunity. . . . And so let me come to what I think could be viewed by reasonable persons as our vulnerable point in that respect: namely the Secret Service [subpoenas]," he continued, sensing my skepticism. Like Seymour, Starr had issued these against the will of the rest of the executive branch, which had protested that there were other significant public interests at stake, the safety of the president most particularly. But Starr insisted that even here he was reasonable. Unlike Seymour, he said, "I calibrated, I negotiated, I talked," in an effort to reach an accommodation with the executive branch. Unlike the insistence of the executive

branch in the 1980s on respecting the well-established doc-
trine of diplomatic immunity, he added, the Secret Service, in
refusing to let its agents testify, was acting contrary to its own
history of providing information regarding criminal probes
involving the president.

When I protested that he seemed to be saying that the difference between himself and Seymour is that he was right in
overriding the considered judgment of the executive branch,
Starr — as he did every time the Secret Service matter came
up — fell back on a trump card. He had certain information, he
said, information he still could not disclose and, indeed, would
never disclose, that makes it clear that the effort to prevent the
agents' testimony was just another political game. "I'm handi-
capped again in my own defense here by virtue of what I
viewed as a problem in terms of the reasons that the Secret
Service was not doing what I knew it had historically done," he
said.[9] Starr, in other words, cannot — or will not — say what the
ultimate difference is between him and a man whose investigation he calls "monomaniacal."

That inability is telling. Starr asks a great deal of the public in suggesting that it should accept on faith the reasonableness of steps that did not seem all that reasonable, particularly
in the presence of obvious alternatives. This particular anec-
dote seems to me symbolic of the investigation more generally. Starr sees only the incremental steps — each of which may
be logical on its own terms — that led him to a particular investigative move. For all his thoughtfulness, he seems incapable of stepping back and appreciating the larger mosaic these
logical steps created and how closely it resembles the independent counsel investigations of the 1980s against which he re-
coiled. The major difference is that Starr eclipsed those investigators by any reasonable standard of excess. Starr is surely
the only person in the United States still marveling at the

recklessness of the Seymour investigation, but it will be a long time before the name Kenneth W. Starr ceases to serve as shorthand in the common parlance for the monomaniacal pursuit of a president.

Over the years of the Starr investigation, the objections to the independent counsel law reached critical mass, and a near-consensus developed that the law should not be reauthorized. The various actors in the drama, of course, reached this conclusion from different intellectual vantage points. Many liberals and moderates, the law's traditional supporters, re-garded Starr as having revealed flaws in the independent counsel mechanism and shown it to be ripe for abuse. Conser-vatives, the law's traditional opponents, meanwhile, simulta-neously sought to defend Starr and claim a certain vindication for their underlying position. Attorney General Janet Reno, meanwhile, reversed her previous support for the statute, ar-guing that it necessarily involved the attorney general in a process whose ostensible purpose was to remove his or her influence. By involving her, Reno argued, the law exposed her to incessant political criticism.[10] Starr himself supplemented his long structural opposition to the statute with new crit-icisms, born of his own experience serving under it. The law, while theoretically removing the attorney general from the process, actually gave the Justice Department wide powers regarding when to initiate an independent counsel investiga-tion and how to interact with it once it has been launched. Moreover, by creating an office for which the attorney general had no accountability, the statute effectively invited White House attacks on independent counsels and created no incen-tive for the attorney general to protect the office from such attacks.[11]

The experience of Starr's probe was surely not the only factor that led Congress to permit the statute to lapse. The

Clinton years also saw anxiety-inducing investigations from independent counsels Donald Smaltz and David Barrett.[12] The law also produced a significant controversy between congressional Republicans and the Justice Department over Reno's refusal to seek an independent counsel to investigate allegations of campaign finance irregularities during the 1996 presidential campaign. The Starr probe, however, clearly lay at the heart of the changed consensus with respect to the statute. Absent Starr's tenure, it is hard to imagine that American political elites would have turned so completely against a statutory framework Congress had, only five years earlier, re-embraced. The almost universally drawn lesson of Starr's investigation was that the independent counsel law ought to be abandoned in its entirety.

This seems to me an overly simplistic lesson, or at the very least an incomplete one. I do not mean to argue that the particular independent counsel mechanism that Congress allowed to lapse should have been retained. Like many observers, I have come to believe that Antonin Scalia properly diagnosed the statute's constitutional infirmities in his *Morrison* dissent — in other words, that the statute's skeptics, Starr included, were right all along in their formalistic objections to it. Indeed, for all his efforts to mitigate the impact of the statute, Starr's probe is nothing if not an example of Scalia's, and Starr's own, fears about a law enforcement agency effectively delinked from the control of the executive branch. On policy grounds, both Starr's and Reno's objections to the law seem compelling as well. Starr is probably correct that the White House smear campaign against him would have been tough for the attorney general to tolerate had he been her designee. The statute, moreover, created nonstop headaches for Reno — both in terms of monitoring and combating the escapades of independent counsels, Starr included, and in the incessant demands on her to spawn new counsels. The independent counsel mechanism envisioned by the Ethics in Government Act of 1978 failed on a number of levels, and it failed to deliver an investigation in which the public had confidence when the stakes were highest — during an investigation of the president. It undoubtedly needed to be replaced. The lesson of its discrediting, however, should not necessarily be that any statutory scheme would fail similarly or that the absence of a statutory mechanism entirely corrects the problems Starr's probe highlighted. The clearer lesson to draw from Starr's performance is a more limited one: However we handle the investigation of scandals in the future, independent investigators need to be structurally confined to vindicating prosecutorial interests. The more general truth-seeking function must devolve to Congress, to inspectors general, to historians, and to the press.

The failure of the statutory mechanism has led many people, from scholars to government officials to pundits, to embrace the old regulatory special prosecutor model and even those of its flaws that gave rise to the statutory scheme in the first place. The revisionist argument holds both that the old system worked just fine, even at its moment of greatest crisis, and that the trauma of Watergate caused people to misinterpret its success as a dangerous failure. As Reno put it,

> Leon Jaworski investigated President Nixon, members of his Cabinet and others. And although the President ordered the firing of Mr. Jaworski's predecessor, Jaworski showed that a non-statutory special prosecutor can do exactly what must be done — investigate high-level members of an administration, even when the President has been subverting the investigation.
>
> Perhaps the real lesson of our nation's experience with the special prosecutor during Watergate is not that the old system was broken but that it worked.[13]

Akhil Reed Amar, making a similar point, wrote: "In Water-gate, Nixon's White House itself had picked Archibald Cox and Jaworski, and it retained formal power to remove them. Politics, not law, framed whether an outside prosecutor would be named, who he would be, how he would operate, and when (if ever) he would be removed. In making these decisions, the White House had to listen to congressional critics, or risk a political backlash. And the system worked — just the way the Framers would have wanted. Cox and Jaworski had great credibility. Nixon retained the right to fire them anytime, but only at his political peril, as the Saturday Night Massacre proved."[14]

The revisionist affection for the old system, alas, probably overestimates the degree of functional control over independent counsels the restoration of that system will actually return to the attorney general. If a special prosecutor under the new regulatory regime begins to run amok, the Justice Department now has the formal authority to rein him or her in. As a practical matter, however, the very political constraints that Amar describes in the quotation above would likely prevent it from succeeding or, more likely, from even trying. An independent counsel inclined to behave like a truth commissioner would still have considerable political space in which to do so. Indeed, the very first regulatory special counsel to follow the statute's lapse, former Senator John Danforth — who was tasked with investigating an alleged cover-up at the Justice Department and FBI related to the Waco incident — ended up giving the Justice Department headaches of a type not all that different from those caused by statutory independent counsels.

My point is not to defend the old statutory mechanism, merely to emphasize that we should not kid ourselves that its abolition will cure the problem, and that we should acknowledge that, whatever good the restoration of the old model will do, it will create problems of its own. One of the virtues of the old system — one the regulatory model has been, in recent years, often incapable of reproducing — was its ability to end scandals authoritatively and vindicate the innocent in a manner that even opponents of the incumbent administration were willing to accept. However competent regulatory special prosecutors may be, they generally lack public credibility, by dint of precisely the political accountability that makes them constitutionally and structurally friendly. This is not always the case. Danforth, for example, was able to lay the Waco controversy to rest,[15] and Paul Curran in 1979 dissipated a brewing scandal about alleged diversion of money from the Carter Peanut Warehouse to Jimmy Carter's 1976 presidential campaign.[16] The alleged Waco cover-up, however, was a case where the facts overwhelmingly debunked a scandal, and the scandal was, in any event, not one in which elites were significantly invested. The happy outcome in the peanut warehouse case has unfortunately not proven easily replicated in recent years. More typical has been the disturbing example of Fiske, who was appointed by Reno and was pilloried by Republicans despite his obviously rigorous findings on Vincent Foster. His Whitewater investigation was always viewed suspiciously as well, and it is hard to imagine that, had he stayed on and wrapped up Whitewater, his findings would have put the scandal to rest in the minds of conservative skeptics of the Clinton administration.

Nor was the problem of public mistrust of regulatory special prosecutors particular to the Clinton years. During the elder George Bush's presidency, Attorney General William Barr appointed special prosecutors to examine scandals that had attracted significant public attention but in which the evidence was insufficient to justify triggering the statute itself.

In October 1992, Barr appointed retired federal judge Fred-
erick Lacey to investigate the Banca Nazionale del Lavoro
(BNL) scandal, also known as Iraqgate, which dealt with allegations that the Bush administration had used an agricultural
loan guarantees program to arm Iraq in the years leading up to
the Gulf War.[17] Lacey reported seven weeks later that the
allegations of a Justice Department cover-up in its probe of
BNL's Atlanta branch—which had made numerous illegal
loans to Iraq—were without merit.[18] Yet the scandal did not
die. *The New York Times* editorialized, "Not only is Judge
Lacey incredible. He, and his sponsor, seem far more interested in finding scapegoats than in finding facts. Far from
allaying public doubts about Bush Administration impropri-
eties, this squalid exercise inflames them."[19] *The Washington
Post* wrote that "the chief limitation of Mr. Lacey's investigation is that its author was appointed by the attorney general,
the official who is the leading suspect in the BNL affair, and
reported back to him. To be credible, an investigation needs
to be independent of the people being investigated."[20] So mis-
erably did the Lacey report fail to end the matter, in fact, that
Reno felt compelled, upon taking office, to reexamine BNL.
The scandal only withered when the new administration concluded that the matter had been properly handled.[21]

A similar problem developed with respect to the so-called
Inslaw scandal, which dealt with allegations that the Justice
Department had stolen a case management software package
written by a Washington software company. The allegations
in Inslaw were ever-expanding, ranging from international
intrigue to the death of a freelance journalist in West Virginia,
and the press spilled a huge amount of ink on the matter over
more than a decade. In 1991, Barr appointed Nicholas Bua,
also a retired federal judge, to examine the morass of allegations. Bua reported in 1993 that there was "woefully insuf-

ficient evidence to support the allegation that [the depart-
ment] obtained an enhanced version of [the software] through
'fraud, trickery, and deceit,' or that DOJ wrongfully distrib-
uted [it] within or outside of DOJ."[22] Even after Bua's report,
however, the matter did not go away. Once again, Reno felt
compelled to examine the issue anew after taking office, and
the Justice Department eventually produced its own report
backing up Bua's findings.[23] Even then, Congress referred the
matter to the U.S. Court of Federal Claims, which finally held
in 1997 that the case was unmerited and that "any recovery
[by Inslaw] would be a gratuity."[24] Having no statutory framework for independent counsels eliminates the public commitment that the old statute represented to honor the results that
independent counsels produce — particularly when they end
up, as they usually do, declining prosecutions.

The key lesson of Starr's tenure is not that any statutory
structure is a bad thing (though it may be), or that the regulatory model is better (though it may be), but that the mission of
independent counsels under whatever regime they are appointed must be unambiguously narrow and prosecutorial.
The critical step in this direction is less the elimination of
the statute as a whole than that of the reporting requirements
in particular. The final report provision created an ongoing
temptation on the part of the prosecutor to take extra prosecutorial steps — if for no other reason than so his report could
later address its subject comprehensively. Congress in 1994
naively tried to rein in this practice, by insisting that no investigative steps should be taken for purposes of the final report.
As Starr's example shows, however, the structural incentive
created by the reporting provision has proven far more important than any words Congress mustered trying to limit
its scope. Likewise, the impeachment referral provision is,
though more limited in its application than the final report

requirement, at least as dangerous within its sphere. Once again, the law should not offer such temptation; normal prosecutors, after all, do not have to decide what "information" Congress might deem "grounds" for impeachment. It is, quite simply, beyond the job description. It is not such a terrible thing for a prosecutor who wishes to file an impeachment referral to be forced, as Jaworski was, to seek the leave of a court to do so and to have to justify specifically the reasonableness of the document in question. Starr's reading of the burdens created by these two sections was, I have argued, an unhealthy one that magnified their inherent problems. He did not, however, invent those problems out of whole cloth. If the law asks prosecutors to write reports, prosecutors will want to write good and thorough reports, a desire that invites a truth-seeking mission alien to the search for reasonable doubt in which the criminal justice system typically engages.

The regulations Reno promulgated to replace the statute are actually a significant step in the right direction with respect to independent counsel reporting requirements. They do not authorize an impeachment referral from an independent counsel, and they blunt the significance of the final report, providing not for a public document but for a confidential report to the attorney general.[25] This latter reform should reduce the incentive on the part of independent counsels, called special counsels under the new regulations, to conceive of themselves as some type of oversight mechanism. That is, it would reduce that incentive if the regulations were taken seriously. It is a mark of how deeply the truth-oriented understanding of the role has infected public expectations that Danforth, the first special counsel appointed under the regulations, issued a public interim report on Waco even in the absence of any express authority under the regulations to do so — and that the Justice Department did nothing to stop him.[26] Danforth's final report, moreover, was unrestrained even by the procedural protections the old statute offered, namely the ability on the part of named individuals to respond to the way they were characterized; Danforth made numerous judgments about individuals in the report of precisely the type that the 1994 amendments to the statute were designed to prevent.[27] Until attorneys general are willing to exercise the oversight over special counsels that the nonstatutory framework theoretically gives them, the temptation on the part of independent counsels to act like truth commissioners will be at times overwhelming—particularly, as in the Waco case, where the prosecutor is named to function more as an inspector general than as a prosecutor in the first place. As long as the public expects independent counsels to serve, as Starr put it, as "a blue-ribbon, grand jury kind of person who issues reports on issues of public moment," the less disciplined independent counsels will tend to oblige.[28]

An important component of this lesson is that independent counsels ought not be appointed in the first place where what is wanted is a blue-ribbon, grand jury kind of person. In cases where the fundamental interest at stake is not prosecutorial but oversight-oriented, the inspector general—a permanent, semi-independent office within the relevant department—offers a model far preferable to the ad hoc independent counsel. The inspector general has competing responsibilities and is also institutionally configured to produce investigative work-product. At their best, congressional committees can also serve this function. Where the primary goal is not putting bad guys in jail, the prosecutor is almost never the most desirable instrument for shining a spotlight.

This is a lesson that needs to be absorbed by the political culture at large. American political society—members of Congress, editorial pages, and the public generally—has developed the reflex of asking for a special prosecutor to look at a scandal, but it often then lapses into confusion as to the role that prosecutor should play. House Judiciary Committee Chairman Henry Hyde, for example, reflected that confusion when he told Starr during Starr's impeachment testimony, "I don't characterize your office as an independent prosecutor. You're not a prosecutor. You're [an] independent counsel. As a matter of fact, you have just given the president a pass on Filegate, on Travelgate, on all sorts of things: Whitewater. And so, as far as I'm concerned, that's what an independent counsel should do — find where people are guilty, find where they're not guilty, and announce it. Let the chips fall where they may."[29] Such assumptions are embedded in an enormous amount of the public discourse surrounding scandals and their investigation, and it is unreasonable to expect that all special prosecutors will be courageous or disciplined — or even self-aware — enough to buck these expectations and limit themselves to bringing bad guys to justice. If we want prosecutors to stop acting like truth commissioners, we must have the self-discipline to stop appointing them where we are seeking a public inquest.

In insisting that truth seeking is not the prosecutor's project, I do not mean in any way to denigrate its importance as a project for other institutions. Indeed, adopting a non-truth-commission vision for independent counsels would necessarily demand reinvigorating other potential actors to serve as credible truth-seekers. The public has come to accept that congressional committees will behave merely as partisans. As happened in the Lewinsky case, the mere knowledge that an independent counsel will eventually produce a report tends to relieve committee members and their staffs of the burden of seeking the truth rigorously themselves. At their best, however, congressional committees do fine investigative work, and it is not too much to expect of them that they rise to the occasion when need be. Journalists also have a regrettable tendency to cool their investigations of public integrity matters after a special prosecutor has been named, and then to report chiefly on the conduct of the investigation. Investigators' activities are certainly newsworthy, and prosecutors have tools at their disposal — the subpoena, for example — unavailable to journalists. To some extent, therefore, this tendency is only logical given the likelihood that prosecutors will prove able to pry loose information that reporters are unable to access. That said, the reporter's instinct to follow the prosecutors makes the public ultimately dependant on the prosecutors for its understanding of the underlying story. It is a tendency that should be resisted. The flip side of demanding that prosecutors refrain from running truth commissions must be demanding more perfect truth from elsewhere.

Another important lesson of the Starr investigation is the importance of prosecutorial experience in an investigator. There is a tendency, whenever a large scandal breaks, to seek as independent counsel a luminary of the bar of a stature that transcends politics. All the revisionism aside, Starr was just such a luminary, and it availed him little during the course of his service. Few skeptics of the investigation withheld their harsh judgments because of what they knew about the man and his character. Rather, his character was twisted in the public mind to conform with the harsh judgments people were drawing about the investigation. I do not mean entirely to dismiss the luminary-of-the-bar model for independent counsels, which has at times proven effective. Undervalued in the traditional calculation that desires such a figure, however, is significant experience in white-collar criminal investigations and a certain confidence in one's own instincts as a prosecutor. The contrast between Starr and his successor, Robert Ray, is as poignant in this regard as is that between Starr and Fiske. When Ray entered the fray, he brought a sense of discipline and direction to the probe, as well as a clear — and public — commitment to completing the office's work over a relatively short period of time. Ray never conveyed the sense that there was anything open-ended about his project. To the contrary, he made clear that his role was composed of several discrete tasks, and he proceeded to lay out a timetable for their completion, a timetable to which he rigorously adhered.

There is no escaping the conclusion that Starr — his many endearing qualities notwithstanding — was simply the wrong man for the job he was handed. His first great error was in not appreciating the mismatch between his background and skills and the job that lay ahead and rejecting the appointment in 1994. Having accepted the job, he made the further error of attempting to shape the role to conform to his own character, sensibilities, and preconceptions about it, rather than allowing the job to shape him. His efforts at reimagining the role of independent counsel were, to everyone's misfortune — including his own — dramatically effective. Starr created out of the independent counsel a truth-seeking institution that Bill Clinton, with his pathological aversion to truth, may have richly deserved. That poetic justice, however, is of small comfort. For all his honor and integrity, affability and decency, Starr's legacy is an unhappy one: the unapologetic conversion of the prosecutorial process into an instrument of exposure.

Notes

CHAPTER 1: *Images of Starr*

Epigraph: Ulysses S. Grant, inaugural address, 1869. Published in *Inaugural Addresses of the Presidents of the United States from George Washington 1789 to Lyndon Baines Johnson 1965* (Washington: United States Government Printing Office, 1965).

1. Kenneth Starr, speech at George Washington University on the legacy of Watergate, 2 November 1999.

2. Kenneth Starr, interview with author, 2 November 1999.

3. Kenneth Starr, interview with author, 9 November 1999.

4. Starr interview, 2 November 1999.

5. See, for example, Anthony Lewis, "Nearly a Coup," *The New York Review of Books*, 13 April 2000, pp. 22–29. Lewis wrote, "People on the political right set out to unseat a president, and they almost succeeded. In his folly, Clinton played into their hands. But that does not alter the fact that this country came close to a *coup d'état*." See also Ronald Dworkin, "A Kind of Coup," *The New York Review of Books*, 14 January 1999, p. 61. Dworkin contended,

> The power to impeach a president is a constitutional nuclear weapon and it should be used only in the gravest emergencies. It gives politicians the means to shatter the most fundamental principles of our constitutional structure, and we now know how easily that terrible power can be abused. A partisan group in the House, on a party-line vote, can annihilate the separation of powers and send a lawfully elected president of the opposite party to a drawn-out, humiliating, televised trial, a trial that would frighten markets, usurp the scarce

resource of national attention for months, and damage presidential leadership and policies for even longer. Such a group can even, if it dominates the Senate as well, remove a president from office in spite of the fact that he is the only official in the nation who has been elected by all the people, and even if he still enjoys extensive support.

6. For a sympathetic and particularly detailed portrait of the investigation during its Lewinsky phase, see Susan Schmidt and Michael Weisskopf, *Truth at Any Cost: Ken Starr and the Unmaking of Bill Clinton* (New York: HarperCollins, 2000). Stuart Taylor Jr.'s columns in *National Journal*, also generally sympathetic, contained consistently insightful, sometimes critical analysis of Starr's behavior. Jeffrey Rosen's work in *The New Republic* and *The New Yorker* was generally critical of Starr, often harshly so. But Rosen also displayed a keen understanding of Starr's predicament that few of Starr's critics have shared. See particularly Jeffrey Rosen, "Kenneth Starr, Trapped," *The New York Times Magazine*, 1 June 1997, pp. 42–47.

7. Lars-Erik Nelson, "The Not Very Grand Inquisitor," *The New York Review of Books*, 5 November 1998, pp. 8–13. These passages contain at least three factual errors worth noting. First, Starr did not represent tobacco companies in their dispute with the federal government. He represented them in their efforts to decertify a class action lawsuit brought by private plaintiffs. The federal government took no part in the litigation and had no position on the question of whether or not the plaintiffs could lawfully be organized as a national class. The Fifth Circuit Court of Appeals sided with the tobacco companies. See *Castano v. American Tobacco Company*, 84 F.3d 734 (5th Cir. 1996). Second, Starr was allowed to use hearsay evidence not because he was gathering information for Congress, but because he was operating in a grand jury setting. He was subject there to the same rules as any other federal prosecutor overseeing a grand jury investigation, save that the independent counsel law gave him a certain latitude to waive Justice Department policies where they would compromise his independence. See 28 U.S.C. 594(f)(1) (1994). Third, Starr has never admitted to leaking grand jury information. Indeed, he has consistently denied doing so and has contested all allegations of grand jury leaks in court. See, for example, his publicly released letter to journalist Steven Brill of June 16, 1998, which was written in response to Brill's allegations of grand jury secrecy violations and was published in the September 1998 issue of *Brill's Content*.

8. Anthony Lewis, "The Starr Questions," *The New York Times*, 20 October 1998.

9. Maureen Dowd, "Legacy of Lust," *The New York Times*, 23 September 1998.

10. Dowd won a Pulitzer Prize for her work in 1998, this column

included. Dowd's Pulitzer is one of the best imaginable examples of jour-
nalistic commentators' being rewarded chiefly for rhetorical style and without reference to the correctness of their facts or cogency of their arguments.

11. Richard Posner, *An Affair of State: The Investigation, Impeachment,
and Trial of President Clinton* (Cambridge: Harvard University Press, 1999),
p. 69.

12. Ibid., p. 72.

13. David Kendall, letter to Kenneth Starr, 6 February 1998.

14. Steven Brill, "Pressgate," *Brill's Content*, August 1998, pp. 123–51.

15. See Order to Show Cause, *In Re Grand Jury Proceedings*, Misc.
Action Nos. 98–55, 98–177, and 98–228 (D.D.C. 19 June 1998).

16. See Order to Show Cause, *In Re Grand Jury Proceedings*, Misc.
Action No. 99–228 (D.D.C. 25 September 1998). Kern's name was redacted from the text of the public order, but he was identified in numerous
press reports. See, for example, Evan Thomas and Michael Isikoff with
Daniel Klaidman and Mark Hosenball, "The Goldberg-Tripp-Jones Axis,"
Newsweek, 9 November 1998, p. 30. See also Susan Schmidt and Dan Mor-
gan, "Starr: Witnessing for the Prosecution; Counsel Gets Forum to Defend Actions," *The Washington Post*, 19 November 1998.

17. See *In re: Sealed Case No. 99–3091 (Office of Independent Counsel
Contempt Proceeding)*, 192 F.3d 995 (D.C. Cir. 1999).

18. See Howard Fineman with Debra Rosenberg, Daniel Klaidman,
and Matthew Cooper, "The Survivor," *Newsweek*, 22 February 1999, p. 22.
See also Jerry Seper, "Secret Report to Court Clears Starr, Staff of Illegal
Leaking," *The Washington Times*, 16 September 1999.

19. See Order of Dismissal, *In Re Grand Jury Proceedings*, Misc. Action
Nos. 98–55, 98–177, and 99–228 (D.D.C. 23 March 2001). See also Or-
der of Dismissal, *In Re Grand Jury Proceedings*, Misc. Action No. 99–214
(D.D.C. 23 March 2001).

20. Don Van Natta Jr., "Starr Is Weighing Whether to Indict Sitting
President," *The New York Times*, 31 January 1999.

21. *In re: Sealed Case No. 99–3091 (Office of Independent Counsel Contempt Proceeding)*, 192 F.3d 995 (D.C. Cir. 1999).

22. For an excellent essay about the Bakaly case that unfortunately
predates his trial, see David Grann, "Background Noise," *The New Republic*,
28 June 1999, pp. 18–23. For a more comprehensive account of the Bakaly
prosecution, see Byron York, "The Ordeal of Charles Bakaly," *The American
Spectator*, September 2000, pp. 28–32, 76–77. The Justice Department determined that the Bakaly matter would be best handled within Chief Judge
Johnson's contempt proceedings, and while declining to bring a case of
its own, stated its willingness to accept her appointment to prosecute a
criminal contempt case in that context. Chief Judge Johnson subsequently

ordered Bakaly to stand trial in connection with the affidavit and a related brief the Office of Independent Counsel filed, and the matter was the subject of a bench trial in July 2000. Judge Johnson later acquitted Bakaly, writing that "even if some of his statements are misleading by their negative implication that Mr. Bakaly was not a source of information that he in fact supplied or confirmed, such a finding does not provide a sufficient basis for a criminal contempt conviction for making false statements." See Memorandum Opinion, *In Re Grand Jury Proceedings*, No. 99–38 (D.D.C. 6 October 2000).

23. See Michael Isikoff, *Uncovering Clinton: A Reporter's Story* (New York: Crown, 1999), pp. 266–80. As Isikoff's account of this episode demonstrates, the contacts between the Jones camp and Starr's office were remarkable chiefly for the extent to which Linda Tripp and the group of lawyers covertly aiding Jones managed to choreograph Starr's entrance into the affair. Starr's staff emerges from the account looking more than a bit naive about Tripp, and greatly manipulated by both her and the group of self-described "elves" who were doing legal work for Jones. There is, however, no evidence of intentional collaboration between Starr and the Jones camp. Rather, the office tried to avoid allowing the Jones lawyers to situate themselves between Tripp and the prosecutors, insisting that the witness come in through the "front door."

24. As of this writing, neither the dismissal of the various ethical allegations nor the final resolution of the matter referred back to the Office of Independent Counsel has been publicly disclosed. The account here is based on an interview with a source who requested anonymity and who is familiar with the correspondence between the Justice Department and the Office of Independent Counsel over the ethical allegations.

25. See Office of the Independent Counsel, Press Release, 27 July 1999. The statement was approved by two retired federal judges, Arlin Adams and Charles Renfrew, who oversaw the investigation, and it quoted the conclusions reached by Shaheen: "Many of the allegations, suggestions and insinuations regarding the tendering and receipt of things of value were shown to be unsubstantiated or, in some cases, untrue." Shaheen found that "there is insufficient credible evidence to support criminal charges. In some instances, there is little if any credible evidence establishing that a particular thing of value was demanded, offered, or received. In other instances, there is insufficient credible evidence to show that a thing of value was provided or received with the criminal intent defined by any of the applicable statutes." The ex-judges concurred with the conclusions.

26. *Mandanici v. Starr*, 99 F. Supp. 2d 1019 (E.D. Ark. 2000). On the same day, the court also dismissed a complaint brought by Julie Hiatt Steele; see *Steele v. Starr*, 99 F. Supp. 2d 1042 (E.D. Ark. 2000). It likewise dismissed

a complaint filed by Stephen Smith; see *Smith v. Starr*, 99 f. Supp. 2d 1037 (E.D. Ark. 2000).

27. Starr considered submitting a Whitewater referral, and the office even drafted one, but he ultimately declined to submit it after concluding that the evidence did not trigger the statutory requirement that "substantial and credible information . . . that may constitute grounds for an impeachment" be sent to Congress. See 28 U.S.C. 595(c) (1994). Starr's reasons for refraining from issuing an impeachment referral concerning Whitewater are discussed in Chapter 4.

28. Jeffrey Toobin, *A Vast Conspiracy: The Real Story of the Sex Scandal That Nearly Brought Down a President* (New York: Random House, 1999), pp. 75–78.

29. Ibid., pp. 188–89.

30. Starr interview, 2 November 1999. Starr said, "I did engage in self-examination with respect to the fact that I had not actually prosecuted. And would that, in fact, be at least potentially a significant impediment? And I came to the view that it would not." He added, "My set of experiences gave me at least an outlook and set of goals and aspirations that could be usefully complemented by senior prosecutors" and carried on by line attorneys.

31. Kenneth Starr, interview with author, 14 December 1999.

32. See Starr's testimony at *Hearing of the Senate Government Affairs Committee: The Independent Counsel Act*, 106th Cong., 1st sess., 14 April 1999.

33. Schmidt and Weisskopf, *Truth at Any Cost*, pp. 84–85.

34. David Tell for the Editors, "Case Closed," *The Weekly Standard*, 21 September 1998, pp. 7–8. The word "obligation" refers in context to the duty of Congress, as a result of Starr's findings, to impeach Clinton.

35. Robert H. Bork, speech at dinner honoring Kenneth Starr, Washington, D.C., 30 November 1999.

36. Robert H. Bork, "Counting the Costs of Clintonism," *The American Spectator*, November 1998, pp. 54–57.

37. Bork, speech at dinner honoring Kenneth Starr.

38. Editorial, "Starr's Hour," *The Wall Street Journal*, 11 September 1998.

39. For classic examples of the conservative concern with minor figures in the Iran-Contra investigation, see the countless *Wall Street Journal* editorials about Walsh. To cite one representative example, at the time of the sentencing of Elliott Abrams the *Journal* fretted, "The element of political vendetta that energized these prosecutions from the first may be one reason judges have decided that even Mr. Walsh's 'victories' will have to be Pyrrhic. . . . Mr. Walsh put Elliott Abrams in the classic Catch-$2.2 million: Plead to something or spend millions defending yourself from my

Budgetless Battalion. When Mr. Abrams agreed to a misdemeanor involving congressional testimony, Judge Aubrey Robinson could have sentenced him to years in jail and a huge fine. Instead, he sentenced Mr. Abrams to 100 hours of community service plus a token fine of $50." See Editorial, "Special Persecutors," *The Wall Street Journal,* 20 November 1991.

    40. Starr, speech at George Washington University, 2 November 1999. "Monica Beach" was the less-than-affectionate nickname given to the bank of cameras and lawn chairs parked daily outside of the courthouse.

    41. Lawrence E. Walsh, "Kenneth Starr and the Independent Counsel Act," *The New York Review of Books,* 5 March 1998, pp. 4–6.

CHAPTER 2: *Taming the Statute*

    Epigraph: Remarks of Jacob Stein at "The Independent Counsel Process: Is It Broken and How Should It Be Fixed?" (Sixty-Seventh Judicial Conference of the Fourth Circuit, Hot Springs, Virginia, 1997). The proceedings of this conference can be found at *Washington & Lee Law Review* 54: 1515. Stein, along with Plato Cacheris, later represented Monica Lewinsky in immunity negotiations with the Office of Independent Counsel.

    1. Fiske was fired following the reauthorization of the independent counsel law in the summer of 1994. Once Congress reauthorized the statute, Attorney General Janet Reno applied to the special court for an independent counsel and specifically requested that Fiske be retained. The court, however, determined that the purpose of the statute — to have an independent counsel who had not been selected by the attorney general — would be ill-served by leaving in place a man whom Reno had named during the period of the statute's lapse:

> The court, having reviewed the motion of the Attorney General that Robert B. Fiske, Jr., be appointed as Independent Counsel, has determined that this would not be consistent with the purposes of the Act. This reflects no conclusion on the part of the Court that Fiske lacks either the actual independence or any other attribute necessary to the conclusion of the investigation. Rather, the Court reaches this conclusion because the Act contemplates an apparent as well as an actual independence on the part of the Counsel. . . . It is not our intent to impugn the integrity of the Attorney General's appointee, but rather to reflect the intent of the Act that the actor be protected against perceptions of conflict. As Fiske was appointed by the incumbent administration, the Court therefore deems it in the best interest of the appearance of independence contemplated by the Act that a person not affiliated with the incumbent administration be appointed.

See Order, *In re: Madison Guaranty Savings & Loan Assoc.*, Div. No 94–1 (D.C. Cir. [Spec. Div.] 5 August 1994).

2. The *Times* had greeted Starr's appointment as "safe and nonpartisan" and a decision that "enhanced the appearance of an evenhanded investigation." The decision to replace Fiske, the newspaper stated, "is in no way a reflection on the current investigation. A new team is simply the best way to assure everyone that the investigation will not only be wholly independent of the White House, it will appear wholly independent as well." See Editorial, "An Even More Independent Counsel," *The New York Times*, 6 August 1994. Only twelve days later, however, the *Times* declared, "The appointment of Mr. Starr is fatally tainted." Starr, the *Times* wrote, "is in no way to blame" for the situation, which "was brought about by Judge Sentelle's flamboyantly bad judgment in meeting with Senator Lauch Faircloth and another Clinton opponent, Senator Jesse Helms." Nonetheless, "a cloud of political favoritism now hangs over [Starr's] appointment and will undermine public confidence in it. As a matter of public service and personal honor, he should resign the appointment." See Editorial, "Mr. Starr's Duty to Resign," *The New York Times*, 18 August 1994. Bennett called for Starr to step down in a variety of media outlets. For one example, see Stephen Labaton, "Democrats Build Pressure on New Prosecutor to Quit," *The New York Times*, 9 August 1994.

3. In a harbinger of things to come, the fracas actually grew quite ugly. Former Iran-Contra prosecutor Lawrence Walsh, in objecting to Fiske's dismissal and Starr's appointment, fumed,

> The Special Division has replaced an undisputedly independent investigator and prosecutor with an undisguised partisan, whose Washington experience was developed first as counselor to President Reagan's Attorney General and then as President Bush's Solicitor General. He has been an apologist for those who intimidate abortion clinics. He has seriously considered running for the Republican nomination for the Senate.
>
> Mr. Starr has had no experience as a prosecutor. To permit such an appointee to take over Mr. Fiske's work undermines the independent counsel process.

See Lawrence E. Walsh, letter to the editor, *The New York Times*, 14 August 1994.

4. Stuart Taylor Jr., "Courting a D.C. Starr," *The American Lawyer*, April 1993, pp. 52–54. Taylor offers a detailed portrayal of why Starr was, at the time he left the Bush administration, "the most valuable property to come on the Washington, D.C., legal market in well over a decade." The article is valuable since, having been published before Starr became a

controversial figure, it is unbiased by any of the subsequent events. In Taylor's description,

> Starr is, admiring friends concede, neither the most brilliant legal mind in Washington (though he's plenty smart), nor the best brief writer (though he's good), nor the most dazzling oral advocate (though his somewhat syrupy style can be very effective). His Republican credentials are not particular assets in Bill Clinton's Washington. Nor is his record as champion of an aggressively conservative Bush legal agenda.
>
> What Starr does have is a felicitous combination of strong intellect, ample skills, abundant energy, a flair for public speaking, and a uniquely attractive resume: five years as a respected consensus-building jurist on the D.C. Circuit and four as solicitor general of the United States, adding up to a tour of public service more prestigious in the world of law than anyone has brought out of government since Griffin Bell (also a former federal appellate judge) stepped down as attorney general in 1979. And Starr is 14 years younger now than Bell was then.
>
> Starr's other great asset is a genuinely sweet and ingratiating personality that radiates credibility, integrity, judiciousness, and gentility.

5. See Editorial, "The Packwood Subpoena," *The Washington Post*, 25 October 1993. The *Post* editorial called him blandly "a neutral attorney chosen by the committee."

6. Kenneth Starr, interview with author, 2 November 1999. Starr here appears to be referring to Madison's words in Federalist 51, which he has quoted in other speeches: "The great security against a gradual concentration of the several powers in the same department consists in giving to those who administer each department the necessary constitutional means and personal motives to resist encroachments of the others. The provision for defense must in this, as in all other cases, be made commensurate to the danger of attack. Ambition must be made to counteract ambition."

7. Starr interview, 2 November 1999.

8. *INS v. Chadha*, 462 U.S. 919 (1983).

9. Starr interview, 2 November 1999. While Starr certainly stands by his earlier constitutional objections, he seems, these days, more animated by policy objections to the way the statute isolates the independent counsel from the executive branch. These, he said, are "born of practical experience," during which he "became convinced as time went on that the statutory structure simply builds in perverse incentives . . . on the part of the executive branch to treat the independent counsel as a decidedly unwanted, officious intermeddler. And that as a practical matter makes it quite difficult at times to carry on effectively."

10. Ibid.

11. *Morrison v. Olson*, 487 U.S. 654 (1988).

12. Starr interview, 2 November 1999.

13. Ibid.

14. Ibid.

15. Jeffrey Rosen, "Kenneth Starr, Trapped," *The New York Times Magazine*, 1 June 1997, pp. 42–47.

16. Starr interview, 2 November 1999.

17. 28 U.S.C. 594(f).

18. Stein, remarks at Sixty-Seventh Judicial Conference of the Fourth Circuit, in *Washington & Lee Law Review* 54: 1515, 1549–50. Quoting Italo Calvino, *Six Memos for the Next Millennium*, trans. Patrick Creagh (Cambridge: Harvard University Press, 1988), p. 107.

19. Starr interview, 2 November 1999.

20. Kenneth Starr, interview with author, 1 December 1999.

21. Starr interview, 2 November 1999.

22. 28 U.S.C. 591 (1994). The only part of the statute that actually lapsed in 1999 was the authority of the attorney general and the Special Division to seek new independent counsels. Under 28 U.S.C. 599 (1994), the rest of the law continues to be in effect with respect to independent counsels appointed before the law expired.

23. 28 U.S.C. 591(d)(2) (1994).

24. 28 U.S.C. 591(b) (1994).

25. 28 U.S.C. 591(c)(1) (1994).

26. 28 U.S.C. 591(c)(2) (1994).

27. 28 U.S.C. 592(a)(2)(A) (1994).

28. 28 U.S.C. 592(a)(3) (1994).

29. 28 U.S.C. 592(b)(1) (1994).

30. 28 U.S.C. 592(a)(2)(B)(ii) (1994).

31. 28 U.S.C. 592(b) (1994).

32. 28 U.S.C. 592(g) (1994).

33. 28 U.S.C. 592(c)(1) (1994).

34. 28 U.S.C. 593(b)(2) (1994).

35. 28 U.S.C. 593(b)(3) (1994).

36. 28 U.S.C. 593(c) (1994).

37. 28 U.S.C. 593(e) (1994).

38. 28 U.S.C. 593(f) (1994).

39. 28 U.S.C. 597(a) (1994).

40. 28 U.S.C. 594(a) (1994).

41. 28 U.S.C. 594(c) (1994).

42. 28 U.S.C. 594(d)(1) (1994).

43. 28 U.S.C. 594(e) (1994).

44. 28 U.S.C. 594(f)(1) (1994).

45. 28 U.S.C. 594(g) (1994).

46. The biannual expenditure report requirement is codified at 28 U.S.C. 594(h)(1)(A) (1994), the annual activities reporting requirement at 28 U.S.C. 595(a)(2) (1994), the final reporting obligation at 28 U.S.C. 594(h)(1)(B) (1994), and the obligation to refer impeachment material at 28 U.S.C. 595(c) (1994).

47. 28 U.S.C. 595(a)(1) (1994).

48. 28 U.S.C. 596(a) (1994).

49. 28 U.S.C. 596(b) (1994).

50. Kenneth Starr, interview with author, 4 January 2000.

51. Samuel Dash, interview with author, 21 July 2000. See also Susan Schmidt and Michael Weisskopf, *Truth at Any Cost: Ken Starr and the Unmaking of Bill Clinton* (New York: HarperCollins, 2000), p. 62.

52. Starr interview, 4 January 2000.

53. Samuel Dash, "Independent Counsel: No More, No Less a Federal Prosecutor," *Georgetown Law Journal* 86: 2077, 2081.

54. Dash interview, 21 July 2000.

55. Starr interview, 4 January 2000.

56. R. H. Melton, "Grand Jury Making Progress, Starr Says; Whitewater Independent Counsel Offers No Details in FBI Files and Travel Office Inquiries," *The Washington Post*, 5 October 1996.

57. Kenneth Starr, press conference, 21 February 1997.

58. Kenneth Starr, commencement address at Duke University School of Law, 13 May 1995.

59. Starr, news conference, 21 February 1997.

60. Kenneth Starr, speech to Mecklenburg Bar Foundation, Charlotte, N.C., 1 June 1998.

61. Robert Fiske Jr., interview with author, 2 August 2000. Fiske's view of his role as coextensive with the powers of a statutory independent counsel was not simply a matter of his own opinion. The regulations under which he was operating tracked the temporarily defunct statute quite precisely. See 28 C.F.R. 600.1–600.5 (1987).

62. Robert Ray, interview with author, 4 May 2000.

63. Lawrence Walsh, interview with author, 9 May 2001.

64. Gerard Lynch, email to author, 25 January 2000. At the time this email was sent, Lynch was a law professor at Columbia University. He was named to the bench by President Clinton shortly thereafter.

65. Alexia Morrison, email to author, 11 January 2000.

66. John Barrett, email to author, 6 January 2000.

67. Ronald Noble, email to author, 8 January 2000.

68. Starr interview, 4 January 2000.

69. Starr does not use the term "truth commission" to refer to his own

vision of the statute, but he does not exactly resist it either. At our 4 January 2000 interview, he said of the phraseology, "I like your formulation, 'truth commission,' while I would not embrace it as my own. I think you're very insightful by saying that, because that is exactly the message that one of the architects of the statute [Sam Dash] was giving us — that this is sort of what we had in mind." At the risk of putting words in Starr's mouth, I use the term "truth commission" as a shorthand for his understanding of the law on the theory that, though he is not fully comfortable with the term, it summarizes well his substantive understanding of what the statute demands of the independent counsel.

70. Starr interview, 4 January 2000.

71. Senate Committee on Government Operations, *Watergate Reorganization and Reform Act of 1976: Report to Accompany S. 495*, 94th Cong., 2d sess., 1976, S. Rept. 94–823, pp. 6–7. Until 1983, the law was known as the "special prosecutor" law. Congress changed the name during the first reauthorization to remove the stigma of Watergate from subjects of investigation under the statute.

72. House Committee on the Judiciary, *Special Prosecutor Act of 1978: Report Together With Additional and Dissenting Views to Accompany H.R. 9705*, 95th Cong., 2d sess., 1978, H. Rept. 95–1307, p. 4.

73. 28 U.S.C. 594(f) (1978).

74. 28 U.S.C. 595(b)(2) (1978).

75. See, for example, *In Re North (Dutton Fee Application)*, 11 F.3d 1075, 1080 (D.C. Cir. 1993).

76. *In Re North (Omnibus Order)*, 16 F.3d 1234, 1238 (D.C. Cir. 1994).

77. Morrison, email to author, 11 January 2000.

78. Carl Levin, interview with author, 5 January 2001.

79. House Committee on the Judiciary, *Report to Accompany H.R. 9705*, p. 1.

80. Senate Committee on Governmental Affairs, *Public Officials Integrity Act of 1977: Report to Accompany S. 555*, 95th Cong., 1st sess., 1977, S. Rept. 95–170, p. 66.

81. Ibid., p. 70.

82. House Committee on the Judiciary, *Report to Accompany H.R. 9705*, p. 10.

83. 28 U.S.C. 592(c)(1) (1983).

84. 28 U.S.C. 594(g) (1983).

85. 28 U.S.C. 594(f) (1983).

86. Senate Committee on Governmental Affairs, *Ethics In Government Act Amendments of 1982: Report Together With Supplemental Views to Accompany S. 2059*, 97th Cong., 2d sess., 1982, S. Rept. 97–496, p. 16.

87. 28 U.S.C. 594(a)(10) (1983).

88. 28 U.S.C. 593(g) (1983).

89. Senate Committee on Governmental Affairs, *Report to Accompany S. 2059*, p. 19.

90. Congress also reauthorized the statute in 1987, but the amendments adopted that year are not relevant to this discussion. Specifically, Congress adopted a series of changes to the triggering mechanism in response to concerns that Attorney General Edwin Meese III had manipulated the process of preliminary investigations to avoid appointing independent counsels and had failed to recuse himself in matters involving close friends. See Katy J. Harriger, *The Special Prosecutor in American Politics*, 2nd ed., rev. ed. (Lawrence: University Press of Kansas, 2000), pp. 84–87.

91. 28 U.S.C. 594(h)(1)(B) (1994).

92. Committee of Conference, *Independent Counsel Reauthorization Act of 1994*, 103d Cong., 2d sess., 1994, H. Rept. 103–511, pp. 19–20.

93. 28 U.S.C. 594(f) (1994).

94. Ibid.

95. Committee of Conference, *Independent Counsel Reauthorization Act of 1994*, p. 18.

96. Senate Committee on Governmental Affairs, *Independent Counsel Reauthorization Act of 1993: Report to Accompany S. 24*, 103d Cong., 1st sess., 1993, S. Rept. 103–101, p. 32.

97. House Committee on the Judiciary, *Independent Counsel Reauthorization Act of 1993: Report Together With Dissenting and Additional Views to Accompany H.R. 811*, 103d Cong., 1st sess., 1993, H. Rept. 103–224, p. 22.

98. Ibid., p. 20.

99. Starr, of course, came to the conclusion that a president *could* be indicted while he remained in office. See Don Van Natta Jr., "Starr Is Weighing Whether To Indict Sitting President," *The New York Times*, 31 January 1999.

100. *Morrison v. Olson*, 487 U.S. 654, 732 (1988).

CHAPTER 3: *The Truth Commission and Whitewater*

Epigraph: Susan Schmidt, "Starr Brings 3rd Indictment of Hubbell," *The Washington Post*, 14 November 1998.

1. Hale pled guilty on March 22, 1994, to a felony conspiracy charge and a felony false statements charge in connection with his scheme to defraud the Small Business Administration using his lending company, Capital Management Services, Inc. Two codefendants, Charles Matthews and Eugene Fitzhugh, also reached plea agreements with Fiske on June 23, 1994, each pleading to misdemeanor bribery charges.

2. Kenneth Starr, "What We've Accomplished," *The Wall Street Journal*, 20 October 1999.

3. Kenneth Starr, interview with author, 9 November 1999.

4. Starr, "What We've Accomplished."

5. Kenneth Starr, speech at George Washington University on the legacy of Watergate, 2 November 1999.

6. Starr interview, 9 November 1999.

7. Kenneth Starr, interview with author, 4 January 2000. This last point is not technically true. As I noted in the previous chapter, the regulations under which Fiske operated were essentially coextensive with the statute and included a reporting provision indistinguishable from the one in the statute. See 28 C.F.R. 600.2(b) (1987). The regulations also contained an impeachment referral provision that tracked the statute's. See 28 C.F.R. 600.2(c) (1987).

8. Julie O'Sullivan, interview with author, 25 July 2000, and email to author, 22 December 2000.

9. Jeffrey Toobin, *A Vast Conspiracy: The Real Story of the Sex Scandal That Nearly Brought Down a President* (New York: Random House, 1999), p. 190.

10. Jerry Seper, "Apology Made for Religion Remark; But Blumenthal Won't Include Starr," *The Washington Times*, 9 May 1998.

11. Brett Kavanaugh, interview with author, 27 July 2000.

12. John Bates, interview with author, 2 August 2000.

13. The prosecutor who gave this quotation preferred to remain anonymous.

14. Bates interview, 2 August 2000.

15. W. Hickman Ewing Jr., interview with author, 5 September 2000.

16. Given Ewing's long history of prosecuting Democrats and Republicans alike in Memphis, it seems reasonable to give him the benefit of the doubt with respect to political motivation. While his politics were unsubtle and right-wing and his approach to the Arkansas investigation disturbing in many ways, this approach may well have flowed as much out of his general tendency toward crusading investigations as out of his politics.

17. Ewing interview, 5 September 2000.

18. Ewing retired as deputy independent counsel on January 31, 2001.

19. Toobin, *Vast Conspiracy*, pp. 188–90.

20. The prosecutor who gave this quotation preferred to remain anonymous.

21. For an account of the successive investigations of Foster's death, see Dan E. Moldea, *A Washington Tragedy: How the Death of Vincent Foster Ignited a Political Firestorm* (Washington: Regnery, 1998). The Foster saga is

sufficiently intricate — at both the evidentiary and the sociological levels — that I have not attempted to describe it comprehensively here. Rather, I will refer to the evidence in the case only as is necessary to explore and compare how the investigative philosophies Starr and Fiske professed influenced their respective probes.

22. Martin Anderson, "Revisiting Foster's Death for Answers," *The Washington Times*, 4 February 1994.

23. Robert Fiske Jr., interview with author, 2 August 2000.

24. Fiske interview, 2 August 2000.

25. Report of the Independent Counsel, *In re: Vincent W. Foster, Jr.* (filed 30 June 1994), p. 58.

26. Ibid., p. 1.

27. Ibid., pp. 6–7.

28. Ibid., pp. 49–52.

29. Ibid., pp. 19–20.

30. Special Committee to Investigate Whitewater Development Corporation and Related Matters, *Final Report Together With Additional and Minority Views*, 104th Cong., 2d sess., 1996, S. Rept. 104–280, p. 28. See also James B. Stewart, *Blood Sport: The President and His Adversaries* (New York: Touchstone, 1997), pp. 252–254.

31. In the weeks that followed the Travel Office firings, Foster wrote extensive notes on the incident in an apparent effort to reconstruct the events surrounding the Travel Office matter in preparation for possible litigation. Foster's notebook also appears to reflect concern about the possibility of congressional investigation. In any event, Foster's notes show that, in the final month of his life, he had spent a great deal of time on the Travel Office matter, and, specifically, worried about its implications for Hillary Clinton. The notebook itself can be found in the hearing record of the House Government Reform and Oversight Committee's investigation of the Travel Office matter. See also Toni Locy, "Foster Journal Shows Worry About Travel Office," *The Washington Post*, 29 July 1995.

32. Fiske had concluded — and Starr later reiterated — that the so-called transfer stain occurred when an emergency medical technician shifted Foster's head to check for a pulse on his neck.

33. Report of the Independent Counsel, *In re: Vincent W. Foster, Jr.*, p. 56. According to Fiske's report, "The FBI Lab did find mica particles on Foster's shoes and socks. These mica particles are consistent with the mica that is found at Fort Marcy Park." Fiske explained the absence of soil on the shoes by noting that it was "approximately 90 degrees Fahrenheit and dry on the day that Foster died. Foliage leading up to and around Foster's body was dense. As a result, it is unlikely that there was a great deal of exposed moist soil in the Park that would have soiled Foster's shoes."

34. U.S. House, *More Questions About Vincent Foster's Death*, 103d Cong., 2d sess., 140 Cong Rec H 6246, 6247.

35. Ibid., p. 6248. The simulated head was, according to numerous press reports, a melon. See, for example, Al Kamen, "In the Loop: Testy for Testimony," *The Washington Post*, 21 July 1997.

36. U.S. House, *In-Depth Investigative Report on Vince Foster Suicide*, 103d Cong., 2d sess., 140 Cong Rec H 6617, 6624.

37. R. H. Melton and Ann Devroy, "Gingrich 'Not Convinced' Foster Death Was Suicide; Speaker Calls Whitewater Hearings Productive," *The Washington Post*, 26 July 1995.

38. "Vox Pop," *Time*, 7 August 1995, p. 20.

39. Editorial, "Beyond Fiske," *The Wall Street Journal*, 5 July 1994.

40. White House Counsel Bernard Nussbaum had prevented Park Police investigators and Justice Department officials from making a search of Foster's office out of concern that it might contain privileged materials. He had, rather, performed a cursory search himself in their presence, during which the torn note was not discovered. In addition, in the days following the suicide, files from the office — including Whitewater files — were removed and transferred to the president's personal lawyers.

41. Editorial, "What Has Fiske Wrought?" *The Wall Street Journal*, 5 August 1994.

42. Christopher S. Bond, "Why Is Foster's Death Still a Mystery?" *The Washington Times*, 1 August 1994.

43. Starr interview, 9 November 1999.

44. Kenneth Starr, interview with author, 12 December 2000.

45. Starr interview, 9 November 1999.

46. Starr interview, 12 December 2000.

47. Starr interview, 9 November 1999.

48. Kavanaugh interview, 27 July 2000.

49. Ewing interview, 5 September 2000.

50. Moldea, *Washington Tragedy*, pp. 279–82.

51. Forrestal killed himself in 1949 by jumping from a window at the Bethesda Naval Hospital shortly after President Truman removed him from office.

52. Starr interview, 12 December 2000.

53. John Bates, interview with author, 13 July 2000.

54. Kavanaugh interview, 27 July 2000.

55. Ibid.

56. Ruddy, the reporter for *The New York Post* whose work on the Park Police investigation of Foster's death laid the groundwork for most of the subsequent conspiracy theories, left the paper and investigated the Foster death for *The Pittsburgh Tribune-Review*. He later wrote *The Strange Death of*

Vincent Foster: An Investigation (New York: The Free Press, 1997). Irvine, who heads a conservative media watchdog group called Accuracy In Media, promoted Foster conspiracy theories in a series of advertisements in *The New York Times*, which accused the *Times* of failing to report on open questions about Foster's death. Evans-Pritchard, a British journalist, published his own conspiracy theory in *The Secret Life of Bill Clinton: The Unreported Stories* (Washington: Regnery, 1997).

57. Ewing interview, 5 September 2000.

58. Report on the Death of Vincent W. Foster, Jr., by the Office of Independent Counsel, *In Re: Madison Guaranty Savings & Loan Association*, Div. No. 94–1 (D.C. Cir. [Spec. Div.] filed 10 October 1997), pp. 49–50. Starr noted that the soil cannot be definitively linked to Fort Marcy Park but cited the FBI Laboratory's conclusion that it "could have originated from the micaceous soil found" there. The report further noted that the belief that there was no soil on the shoes, despite the fact that "the FBI Laboratory photo of the shoes, taken in 1994 at the time of the Laboratory's examination of the clothing, shows traces of soil visible to the naked eye," resulted from a "misunderstanding of the statement in an earlier FBI Lab report that no *"coherent* soil" was found in the samples." This, Starr explained, meant only that there was "insufficient soil to effect a comparison with soil samples from Fort Marcy Park." See footnote 139 of the report.

59. Ibid., pp. 52–55.

60. Ibid., pp. 56–57.

61. Ibid., p. 104, footnote 329.

62. Ewing interview, 5 September 2000.

63. Report on the Death of Vincent W. Foster, Jr., by the Office of Independent Counsel, *In Re: Madison Guaranty Savings & Loan Association*, pp. 102–06.

64. Ibid., p. 110.

65. Ibid., p. 114.

66. See Moldea, *Washington Tragedy*, pp. 377–79.

67. "Excerpts From Vince Foster Report," *The Associated Press: AP Online*, 10 October 1997.

68. The precise dollar figure for the Foster death investigation is unavailable, since the office did not keep separate financial records for the specific subject. The General Accounting Office in the summer of 2000, acting at the request of Senator Patrick Leahy, sought information from Robert Ray's office on the cost of the Foster investigation. The office, however, did not address the question. That said, there is no reason to think the costs were exorbitant. On December 12, 2000, Starr told me he would have been "delighted for there to be an oversight hearing about cost and so forth

with respect to this phase of our investigation, given how important I believe this is to public well-being."

69. A detailed discussion of Whitewater and its progeny scandals is well beyond the scope of this project. I have endeavored here to provide only that information that is necessary about the underlying scandals to describe Starr's decision-making. For a richer portrait of the conduct at issue in the investigation, see Stewart, *Blood Sport*. See also James B. Stewart, "The Illegal Loan," *The New Yorker*, 15 July 1996, pp. 36–47; and James B. Stewart, "Susan McDougal's Silence," *The New Yorker*, 17 February 1997, pp. 62–73.

70. Jeff Gerth, "Clintons Joined S.& L. Operator in an Ozark Real-Estate Venture," *The New York Times*, 8 March 1992.

71. For critiques of the original *Times* story, see Gene Lyons, "Fool for Scandal: How the *Times* Got Whitewater Wrong," *Harper's*, October 1994, p. 55–63. See also Joe Conason and Gene Lyons, *The Hunting of the President: The Ten-Year Campaign to Destroy Bill and Hillary Clinton* (New York: St. Martin's, 2000) pp. 30–37.

72. Susan Schmidt, "U.S. Is Asked to Probe Failed Arkansas S&L; RTC Questions Thrift's Mid-'80s Check Flow," *The Washington Post*, 31 October 1993.

73. Michael Isikoff and Howard Schneider, "Clintons' Former Real Estate Firm Probed; Federal Inquiries Focus on Financial Activities of Other Arkansans," *The Washington Post*, 2 November 1993.

74. Hubbell resigned from the Justice Department on March 14, 1994, saying that, given what he termed "private issues between me and my family and my former law firm" that had been "elevated to public speculation," he had concluded that "my continued service will not be as effective as it has been; that the distractions on me at this time will interfere with my service to the country and the President's agenda; and that my family, although totally supportive, is being harmed." See David Johnston, "Clinton Associate Quits Justice Post As Pressure Rises," *The New York Times*, 15 March 1994.

75. In addition to issuing his Foster report, Fiske announced on June 30, 1994, that he would not press charges on anyone with respect to the contacts between the White House and the Treasury Department over the Madison referrals, saying, "The evidence is insufficient to establish that anyone within the White House or the Department of the Treasury acted with the intent to corruptly influence an RTC investigation. . . . We express no opinion on the propriety of these meetings or whether anything that occurred at these meetings constitutes a breach of ethical rules or standards." Fiske was also nearing completion of his investigation of the

handling of Foster's papers. See Susan Schmidt and Ann Devroy, "Fiske Won't Bring Charges Over High-Level Contacts; Report Clears Way for Hill Hearings on Whitewater," *The Washington Post*, 1 July 1994.

76. These included Robert Palmer, Madison Guaranty's real estate appraiser, who pled guilty to a felony conspiracy charge on December 5, 1994, for falsifying appraisals of real estate used to support Madison's loans; Webster Hubbell, who pled guilty to mail fraud and tax evasion charges on December 6, 1994, in connection with the Rose Law Firm overbilling scheme; Neal Ainley, who pled guilty on May 2, 1995, to two misdemeanor charges in connection with large cash withdrawals by Clinton's 1990 gubernatorial campaign from the Bank of Perry County; and Christopher Wade, the Whitewater company's real estate agent, who pled guilty on March 21, 1995, to two felonies in connection with a fraudulent bankruptcy. They also included William Marks Sr., a businessman, whom Starr indicted in June 1995, along with Jim Guy Tucker and his lawyer, a man named John Haley, for conspiring to defraud the SBA and the IRS in connection with a cable television deal. All three reached plea deals after lengthy pretrial litigation. They also included Stephen Smith, who pled guilty on June 8, 1995, to a misdemeanor conspiracy charge alleging that he misapplied the proceeds of a loan from David Hale's SBA-backed lending company; Larry Kuca, a business associate of Jim McDougal, who pled guilty on July 13, 1995, to a misdemeanor conspiracy charge of misapplying a loan from Hale's firm; and the duo of Herby Branscum Jr. and Robert M. Hill, who were indicted on February 20, 1996, on charges that they had used phony expense reimbursements at the Perry County Bank, which they owned, to route cash into the 1990 Clinton gubernatorial campaign and that they had sought to conceal large cash transactions by the campaign. On August 1, 1996, the trial jury hung on some counts and acquitted on others, and the office did not retry the matter. Finally, Starr's targets included Jim and Susan McDougal and Jim Guy Tucker, whose case is described below in note 79. President Clinton pardoned Palmer, Wade, Smith, and Susan McDougal as he was leaving office on January 20, 2001.

77. The Perry County Bank affair arose out of Clinton's 1990 gubernatorial campaign in Arkansas. Clinton faced that year an unexpectedly tough reelection fight against a man named Sheffield Nelson. Though he ultimately defeated Nelson comfortably, the campaign sought to ensure it would have adequate funds to handle a slugfest, and prosecutors believed the rural Perry County Bank, which was owned by Clinton supporters Herby Branscum Jr. and Robert M. Hill, served as a piggy bank for the campaign. The bank made $285,000 in personal loans to the Clintons. Starr's office alleged as well that Branscum and Hill illegally hid large cash withdrawals by the campaign, improperly reimbursed their own campaign

contributions with funds from the bank, and used friends and relations to circumvent the limits on campaign donations. In the wake of the election, Clinton named Branscum to the state highway commission and reappointed Hill to the state banking board. Starr's office named Deputy White House Counsel Bruce Lindsey, who had worked on the campaign, as an unindicted co-conspirator in the case.

78. Jim McDougal was indicted on nineteen felony counts of conspiracy, wire fraud, bank fraud, mail fraud, misapplication of funds, falsifying SBA reports, and making false statements. He was convicted on eighteen of those counts and sentenced to three years in prison. He died in prison in March 1998. Jim Guy Tucker was indicted on eleven counts of conspiracy, wire fraud, bank fraud, mail fraud, misapplication of funds, falsifying SBA reports, and making false statements. He was convicted on two of the counts, at which point he resigned as governor of Arkansas and was sentenced to four years of probation on account of his failing health. Susan McDougal was indicted on eight counts of conspiracy, wire fraud, mail fraud, falsifying SBA reports, misapplying funds, and making false statements. She was convicted on four counts and sentenced to two years in prison. She was jailed for eighteen months for contempt of court before beginning her actual sentence on March 9, 1998; she was released three months later. Clinton pardoned her on January 20, 2001.

79. This factual summary is distilled from *U.S. v. Tucker*, 137 F.3d 1016 (8th Cir. 1998) and *U.S. v. Susan H. McDougal*, 137 F.3d 547 (8th Cir. 1998). The claims of Starr's office — as well as some details — are taken from Brief for the United States in *U.S. v. James B. McDougal*, 133 F.3d 1110 (8th Cir. 1998).

80. Ewing interview, 5 September 2000.

81. Jim McDougal and Curtis Wilkie, *Arkansas Mischief: The Birth of a National Scandal* (New York: Henry Holt and Co., 1998), p. 219. McDougal writes that while his business dealings with Hale had been limited, "it turned out" that Hale was trying to pad his lending company's capital base and that loans from Madison to a "straw figure" had enabled this.

82. Ibid., p. 221.

83. Ibid., pp. 195-96. This claim was later corroborated under bizarre circumstances. When the trunk of a tornado-damaged car at a junkyard in Arkansas was opened in 1997, the garage owner found piles of Madison Guaranty records that included evidence of an apparent loan to Clinton. The Madison Guaranty check, dated November 15, 1982, was made out to "Bill Clinton." A second check, paid to Madison from the James McDougal Trustee account the following year, was signed by Susan McDougal and covered — the office claimed — the precise amount outstanding on the alleged loan. It contained the notation "Payoff Clinton." Robert Ray

announced on September 20, 2000, that there was insufficient evidence to prove beyond a reasonable doubt that the president had lied in his trial testimony.

84. Ibid., p. 206.

85. Ibid., pp. 208–10.

86. Ray's Whitewater closeout statement specifically disclosed that there was insufficient evidence to prove that Bill Clinton lied when he testified that he had never borrowed money from Madison Guaranty or caused anyone else to do so, that he lied when he denied knowledge of Hale's loan to Susan McDougal, or that he lied about the circumstances of Madison Guaranty's retention of the Rose Law Firm. The office also concluded that there was insufficient evidence to prove that Hillary Clinton lied to the Resolution Trust Corporation about the relationship between the Rose firm and Madison Guaranty or about her work for the savings and loan. The office found the evidence regarding Hillary Clinton's missing Rose Law Firm billing records "inconclusive," and, therefore, could not make a case against the first lady. Likewise, Ray determined that the evidence that the payments to Webster Hubbell had been an effort to influence his testimony was insufficient to bring any obstruction charges. Finally, Ray concluded — fully six years after Fiske had done so — that no obstruction charges should be filed over the various contacts between White House and Treasury Department officials concerning the RTC criminal referrals over Madison Guaranty.

87. Kenneth Starr, interview with author, 13 November 1999.

88. The office appears to have considered prosecuting Hillary Clinton more seriously than it did bringing a case against husband. Prosecutors believed she had lied about the extent of her legal work for Madison Guaranty on the fraud-ridden Castle Grande deal, which they believed had actually been considerable. The office decided not to proceed with any case during a meeting on April 27, 1998, at which the prosecutors agreed — following a lengthy presentation by Ewing — that the deficiencies in the evidence made the case too weak to pursue. See Susan Schmidt and Michael Weisskopf, *Truth at Any Cost: Ken Starr and the Unmaking of Bill Clinton* (New York: HarperCollins, 2000), pp. 153–56.

89. ABC's *Primetime Live*, 4 September 1996.

90. PBS's *The Newshour With Jim Lehrer*, 23 September 1996.

91. Jeffrey Rosen, "Kenneth Starr, Trapped," *The New York Times Magazine*, 1 June 1997, pp. 42–47.

92. The prosecutor who gave this quotation preferred to remain anonymous.

93. *The New York Times* described Starr's decision as "reflect[ing] a selfish indifference to his important civic obligations" and said he "should

reconsider his departure." See Editorial, "Just a Minute, Mr. Starr," *The New York Times*, 19 February 1997. *The Washington Post* insisted that Starr "has an obligation to make and announce a decision as to whether the Clintons, in the manifold matters under his jurisdiction, have committed any offense(s) for which they could be charged." See Editorial, "Before Mr. Starr Departs," *The Washington Post*, 19 February 1997. William Safire said that Starr "has reminded us that even a man who has led an exemplary life can wimp out in the end" and called Starr's resignation a "Saturday Night Self-Massacre." See William Safire, "The Big Flinch," *The New York Times*, 20 February 1997. Starr has said that the political and media uproar mattered far less to him than the reaction of his own staff, but he admitted a deep mortification at the offense his staff took at his failure to consult with them in advance of his decision. In our November 9, 1999, interview, he described the factors that led him to reconsider as follows: "We were, in the view of the trial team on the Jim Guy Tucker cable tax matter, at a very important and sensitive time, including with the presiding judge. That, to me, was the dispositive factor. It wasn't [that] the Republican National Committee called me. They never called. . . . I heard from Tom Dawson, career assistant [in the office], saying, 'You cannot leave.'" According to Starr, Dawson said, "'I signed on to work with you. I'm not sure I'm going to stay.' I am not going to say I was held hostage, but the reaction was so [extreme]. When I make a mistake it's a beaut. I'm sitting here talking about deliberative process all the time and because of, in retrospect, needless concerns about confidentiality, . . . I raised [the departure] only with my seniors."

94. Starr interview, 13 November 1999.
95. Starr interview, 12 December 2000.
96. Starr interview, 13 November 1999.
97. See, to cite a few examples, *U.S. v. Brady*, 168 F.3d 574 (1st Cir. 1999), in which the defendant refused to testify during a grand jury investigation of an armored car robbery in which a guard was killed; *U.S. v. Marquardo*, 149 F.3d 36 (1st Cir. 1998), in which the defendant's refusal to give grand jury testimony, as the district court put it, "interfered with grand jury proceedings bearing upon organized crime activities of large scope"; *U.S. v. Cefalu*, 85 F.3d 964 (2nd Cir. 1996), in which the defendant refused to testify at the trial of what the court termed "a captain in the Gambino [crime] family"; *U.S. v. Remini*, 967 F.2d 754 (2nd Cir. 1992), in which the defendant refused to testify at a different trial involving members of the Gambino family; *U.S. v. Lach*, 874 F.2d 1543 (11th Cir. 1989), in which the defendant was charged with criminal contempt following his refusal to give grand jury testimony in an organized crime case; and *U.S. v. Papadakis*, 802 F.2d 618 (2nd Cir. 1986), in which the defendant was charged with

criminal contempt following his refusal to give grand jury testimony concerning an $11 million theft from an armored car company in the Bronx in December 1982, a heist the court termed "the largest cash theft in this country's history."

98. Starr interview, 13 November 1999.

99. Starr declined on May 25, 1999, to retry the two counts.

100. Kenneth Starr, interview with author, 1 December 1999.

101. Starr interview, 12 December 2000.

102. John Nields Jr., letter to author, 22 November 2000.

103. Ewing interview, 5 September 2000.

104. Starr interview, 13 November 1999.

105. The prison calls were recorded as a matter of routine by the Bureau of Prisons and were later made public by the House Committee on Government Reform and Oversight in an egregious privacy violation. In various conversations, Hubbell made a series of remarks that were quite suggestive. In discussing the possibility of filing a countersuit against the Rose firm, which had filed a claim against him on the overbilling matter, Hubbell insisted to his wife, Suzanna Hubbell, "I will not raise those allegations that might open it up to Hillary. And you know that. We talked about this." His wife told him that a White House official named Marsha Scott was "ratcheting it up and making it sound like if Webb goes ahead and sues the firm back, then any support I have at the White House is gone. That's what I'm hearing. I'm hearing the squeeze play." Responded Hubbell, "So I need to roll over one more time." In a conversation with Scott, Hubbell explained that the firm's "real motivation is not money. There's no money. It is not even me. It is some people who are pulling the partners' strings. At the same time, I have gotten Suzy [Hubbell] to realize there are issues that I have to stay away from to protect others and I will. I always have. That's the other thing. Have I ever been disloyal?" Scott responded, "Oh, God no." Said Hubbell, "And I'm not going to be here." In context, such remarks deal with Hubbell's overbilling dispute with the firm. Laced throughout the conversations, however, is a sense on Hubbell's part that he had loyally taken blows to protect the team, of which he was still a member. Though the tapes contain no smoking guns, that sense would be legitimately tantalizing to a prosecutor inclined to believe Hubbell had held out and received hush money payments from the president's supporters.

106. See Indictment in *U.S. v. Webster L. Hubbell, Suzanna W. Hubbell, Michael C. Schaufele, and Charles C. Owen* (hereafter *Hubbell II*), No. 98–0151 (D.D.C. 1998).

107. Starr interview, 13 November 1999.

108. See Indictment, *Hubbell II*.

109. Ibid.

110. John Nields Jr., letter to author, 22 November 2000.

111. Cono Namorato, letter to Kenneth Starr, 24 April 1998.

112. Federal District Court Judge James Robertson dismissed the case, in part, on that basis. See *U.S. v. Hubbell*, 11 F. Supp. 2d 25 (D.D.C. 1998). The U.S. Court of Appeals for the D.C. Circuit, however, reversed. See *U.S. v. Hubbell*, 167 F.3d 552 (D.C. Cir. 1999).

113. *U.S. v. Hubbell*, 530 U.S. 27 (2000).

114. See 18 U.S.C. 6002.

115. *Fisher v. U.S.*, 425 U.S. 391 (1976). In *Fisher*, the IRS had ordered attorneys to yield client tax records, prepared by accountants, that bore on possible criminal liability. In the face of the claim that such a summons violated the Fifth Amendment's protection against compelled self-incrimination, the court contended that the privilege is not implicated by compelling the attorney to turn over documents, since the Fifth Amendment forbids only forcing a "person . . . to be a witness against himself," and further, that such an act does not force the client to do anything. Rather, the court argued, the compelled production of voluntarily prepared documents is no different from the compelled production of any other type of evidence, and "the Fifth Amendment would not be violated by the fact alone that the papers on their face might incriminate the taxpayer, for the privilege protects a person only against being incriminated by his own compelled testimonial communications. . . . The taxpayer cannot avoid compliance with the subpoena merely by asserting that the item of evidence which he is required to produce contains incriminating writing, whether his own or that of someone else." The court, however, went on to hold that the physical act of producing evidence "has communicative aspects of its own, wholly aside from the contents of the papers produced." These include the concession that they exist and that the witness possesses them, and the belief on the part of the witness that they are described by the subpoena. Such concessions, the court ruled, may be compelled testimony for Fifth Amendment purposes under certain circumstances. *Fisher*, in other words, distinguished between the contents of documents and the testimonial qualities of the act of their production.

116. *Kastigar v. U.S.*, 406 U.S. 441 (1972). The court, in *Kastigar*, upheld the federal use and derivative use immunity statutes, which are codified at 18 U.S.C. 6002–6003. The court held that the statute's protection was coextensive with the Fifth Amendment privilege and, therefore, left the immunized witness whose testimony had been compelled no worse off than had he merely asserted his Fifth Amendment right to remain silent. "The privilege," the court held, "assures that a citizen is not compelled to incriminate himself by his own testimony. It usually operates to allow a citizen to remain silent when asked a question requiring an incriminatory answer.

This statute, which operates after a witness has given incriminatory testimony, affords the same protection by assuring that the compelled testimony can in no way lead to the infliction of criminal penalties."

117. *U.S. v. Hubbell*, 530 U.S. 27 (2000).

118. Nields declined either to confirm or deny this claim.

119. Starr interview, 13 November 1999.

120. John Nields, Jr., letter to John Bates, 12 November 1996. The distinction between what Nields terms a "letter agreement" and an immunity order from the court itself is that a letter agreement is simply a promise by the prosecutors not to use any of the testimonial admissions associated with the production against the witness. While it is enforceable as a matter of contract, Nields here was clearly concerned to maximize his client's protection by forcing the office to invoke a statute that the Supreme Court had upheld in *Kastigar* only by insisting that its protection was coextensive with the Fifth Amendment self-incrimination privilege. Had he proceeded by letter agreement, the litigation may well have raised the act of production immunity question less squarely, with the parties instead becoming mired in a dispute as to what precisely the contract did and did not promise to Hubbell.

121. John Nields Jr., letter to Kenneth Starr and David Barger, 20 April 1998.

122. See Indictment in *U.S. v. Webster L. Hubbell* (hereafter *Hubbell III*), No. 98–0394 (D.D.C. 1998).

123. Starr interview, 13 November 1999.

124. Kenneth Starr, speech before class at George Mason University School of Law, 1 December 1999.

125. Bill Simmons, "Starr Deputy Eulogizes Jim McDougal," *The Arkansas Democrat-Gazette*, 14 March 1998.

126. Hubbell reached a plea agreement on June 30, 1999, resolving both the tax case and the conflicts case. Hubbell pled guilty to one felony in connection with the conflicts case and one misdemeanor in the tax matter. The misdemeanor plea was conditioned on the Supreme Court's adjudication of the act of production immunity question, and the conviction was voided when the court dismissed the indictment.

127. The White House, for example, asserted attorney-client privilege to resist producing notes of a conversation between the first lady and a government lawyer. This raised the difficult question of whether the attorney-client privilege protects from a grand jury communications between government counsel and government employees and did so with particularly bad facts; the first lady, after all, is not even a government official. See *In re: Grand Jury Subpoena Duces Tecum*, 112 F.3d 910 (8th Cir. 1997).

128. See Starr, "What We've Accomplished." Starr writes, "We should

not have sought or accepted additional jurisdiction from the Justice Department. There were strong reasons for doing so — often the new matter involved evidence with which we were already familiar — but in retrospect it was a mistake. Moving beyond Whitewater/Madison slowed our progress, increased our costs, and fostered a damaging perception of empire building."

129. For a general description of the Travel Office scandal, see Stewart, *Blood Sport*, pp. 258–78. For a detailed blow-by-blow account of the firings, see Final Report of the Independent Counsel, *In re: William David Watkins and In re: Hillary Rodham Clinton*, Div. No. 94–1 (D.C. Cir. [Spec. Div.] filed 22 June 2000).

130. Final Report of the Independent Counsel, *In re: William David Watkins and In re: Hillary Rodham Clinton*, 27–29. Starr's office was interested in the Travel Office matter initially because of its connections with the Foster suicide. Even prior to Starr's appointment, Fiske had examined aspects of the Travel Office firings as part of his investigation into Foster's death. See pp. 3–4.

131. Ibid., pp. 29–31.

132. Ibid., pp. 31–34.

133. These quotations are taken from the various drafts of the Watkins memo and appear in Appendix C to Ray's report.

134. Bates interview, 13 July 2000. Dubelier, incidentally, went on to defend Julie Hiatt Steele, the Richmond woman Starr prosecuted in connection with Kathleen Willey's allegations that President Clinton groped her.

135. See Appendix A of Final Report of the Independent Counsel, *In re: William David Watkins and In re: Hillary Rodham Clinton*. Ray complains of non-cooperation by White House witnesses, and the failure to produce documents to a Justice Department inquiry and to cooperate with the General Accounting Office or House committee investigations.

136. Bates interview, 13 July 2000.

137. Ibid.

138. Kavanaugh interview, 27 July 2000.

139. The prosecutor who offered this comment preferred not to be named. Neither Bates nor this other prosecutor would say which witnesses were under suspicion, but Ray's final report makes that quite clear. Appendix A of the report, which is devoted to detailing the non-cooperation investigators received from the White House, highlights the frustration the office felt with certain witnesses in particular. The appendix describes how Deputy Press Secretary Jeff Eller "testified 'I don't recall,' 'I don't remember' or some other variant of claimed failed memory in excess of 200 times during less than two hours of grand jury testimony." It also notes memory lapses by deputy chiefs of staff Harold Ickes and Mark Gearan and discrepancies in statements by Chief of Staff Mack McLarty. The report is most scathing concerning the testimony of Patsy Thomasson, Watkins's deputy

at the White House, whose statements resulted in a search warrant being executed at her home. Thomasson "testified '[t]hat is correct' when asked to confirm that 'there is no question in your mind' that she had a conversation with either Clarissa Cerda or Catherine Cornelius about a February 15, 1993, memorandum they had submitted to David Watkins requesting that they be made co-directors of the Travel Office. Three months earlier she had testified in front of Congress that she could *not* recall having any discussions with either Cerda or Cornelius about the memorandum." When Thomasson was confronted with the discrepancy, she "testified that she had refreshed her memory by reviewing reports of FBI interviews she had received from her attorney after her congressional testimony." In reality, however, those FBI reports did not contain any statement that such a conversation took place, and Thomasson then claimed that her notes or deposition had refreshed her memory. The search warrant produced no documents that could have done so, nor was Thomasson able to produce any. See Final Report of the Independent Counsel, *In re: William David Watkins and In re: Hillary Rodham Clinton*, Appendix A, pp. i–vii.

140. Bates interview, 13 July 2000; Kavanaugh interview, 27 July 2000.

141. See *Swidler & Berlin v. United States*, 524 U.S. 399, 402 (1998).

142. Kavanaugh interview, 27 July 2000.

143. The motion to quash the subpoena by Swidler & Berlin, Hamilton's law firm, was granted by the district court. This opinion was, however, reversed by a divided D.C. Circuit Panel. See *In Re: Sealed Case*, 124 F.3d 230 (D.C. Cir. 1997).

144. *Swidler & Berlin v. United States*, 524 U.S. 399, 410 (1998).

145. Final Report of the Independent Counsel, *In re: William David Watkins and In re: Hillary Rodham Clinton*, p. 17.

146. Ibid., pp. 155–63.

147. Cloud's allegation first surfaced publicly in Willy Stern, "Of Golf and Justice: Kenneth Starr's Investigators Arrive in Nashville," *The Nashville Scene*, 17 June 1999.

148. George Lardner and John F. Harris, "Panetta Offers Apology Over Files 'Mistake'; Reports on GOP Ex-Aides Were Not Misused, Says White House Chief of Staff," *The Washington Post*, 10 June 1996.

149. Bates interview, 13 July 2000.

150. Final Report of the Independent Counsel, *In re: Anthony Marceca*, Div. No. 94–1 (D.C. Cir. [Spec. Div.] filed 16 March 2000). The one major exception to this was a deposition taken by the office from Marceca in September 1999, following the office's decision to immunize him for false statements he had made in earlier testimony to Congress. In the deposition, Marceca conceded that some of his earlier testimony had been false. See pp. 71–73.

151. See Starr's testimony at *Hearing of the House Judiciary Committee: The Impeachment of William Jefferson Clinton*, 105th Cong., 2nd sess., 19 November 1998.

152. Final Report of the Independent Counsel, *In re: Anthony Marceca*, p. 7.

153. Final Report of the Independent Counsel, *In re: Bernard Nussbaum*, Div. No. 94–1 (D.C. Cir. [Spec. Div.] filed 16 March 2000), p. 8.

154. Final Report of the Independent Counsel, *In re: Anthony Marceca*, pp. 18–23.

155. Ibid., p. 31.

156. Ibid., pp. 88–92.

CHAPTER 4: *The Truth Commission and Monica*

Epigraph: Testimony of Monica Lewinsky before Grand Jury 97–2, U.S. District Court for the District of Columbia, 20 August 1998. Published in *Communication from the Office of Independent Counsel, Kenneth W. Starr: Appendices to the Referral to the United States House of Representatives Pursuant to Title 28, United States Code, Section 595(c) — Part 1* (hereafter *Appendices*), 105th Cong., 2d sess., 1998, H. Doc. 105–311, pp. 1123–24.

1. The law seems unambiguous on this point. Even had Attorney General Janet Reno handled the matter with the maximum caution allowed her under the law, 28 U.S.C. 591–592 (1994) required that specific information from a credible source trigger a ninety-day preliminary inquiry and that if, after that inquiry, she deemed there to be grounds for further investigation, she seek an independent counsel. At a minimum, Reno would have had to trigger such a review; had she done so, ninety days later she would have had to seek an independent counsel in any event.

2. For a more detailed summary of the evidence, see *Referral From Independent Counsel Kenneth W. Starr In Conformity With The Requirements Of Title 28, United States Code, Section 595(c)* (hereafter *Referral*), 105th Cong., 2d. sess., 1998, H. Doc. No. 105–310. See also Chapter 1 of Richard Posner, *An Affair of State: The Investigation, Impeachment, and Trial of President Clinton* (Cambridge: Harvard University Press, 1999). For a compelling narrative account of the story, see Michael Isikoff, *Uncovering Clinton: A Reporter's Story* (New York: Crown, 1999).

3. Lewinsky and Currie have differing recollections of whose idea this was. Lewinsky's testimony, by far the more credible, was that she had suggested to Clinton that "maybe I should put the gifts away outside my house somewhere or give them to someone, maybe Betty." Clinton, in her version, had said "I don't know," or "Let me think about that." A few hours later, according to Lewinsky, Currie called and said, "I understand

you have something to give me" and later came by Lewinsky's apartment and picked up the gifts, which Lewinsky had boxed. See *Appendices*, pp. 871–82. Currie, by contrast, claimed in her grand jury testimony that Lewinsky had called her and initiated the transfer — though her recollection was less clear than Lewinsky's. See *Communication from the Office of the Independent Counsel, Kenneth W. Starr: Supplemental Materials to the Referral to the United States House of Representatives Pursuant to Title 28, United States Code, Section 595(c) — Part 1* (hereafter *Supplemental Materials, Part 1*), 105th Cong., 2d sess., 1998, H. Doc. 105–316, pp. 580–81. For his part, Clinton denied during his grand jury appearance asking Currie to retrieve the gifts. See *Appendices*, p. 502.

4. Affidavit of Monica Lewinsky, 7 January 1998. Published in *Appendices*, pp. 447–48.

5. *Referral*, pp. 116–18.

6. See Order, *In re: Madison Guaranty Savings & Loan Association*, Div. No 94–1 (D.C. Cir. [Spec. Div.] 16 January 1998). The court gave Starr jurisdiction to investigate "whether Monica Lewinsky or others suborned perjury, obstructed justice, intimidated witnesses, or otherwise violated federal law . . . in dealing with witnesses, potential witnesses, attorneys, or others concerning the civil case *Jones v. Clinton*." Published in *Appendices*, pp. 6–7.

7. Starr's prosecutors also came to believe — wrongly as it turned out — that the president's deputy counsel, Bruce Lindsey, was in on the obstruction and had drafted the infamous "talking points" that Lewinsky offered Tripp regarding how to shift her testimony.

8. This could have been accomplished under 18 U.S.C. 6002, which reads: "Whenever a witness refuses, on the basis of his privilege against self-incrimination, to testify or provide other information in a proceeding before or ancillary to . . . a court or grand jury of the United States . . . and the person presiding over the proceeding communicates to the witness an order issued under this title, the witness may not refuse to comply with the order on the basis of his privilege against self-incrimination; but no testimony or other information compelled under the order (or any information directly or indirectly derived from such testimony or other information) may be used against the witness in any criminal case, except a prosecution for perjury, giving a false statement, or otherwise failing to comply with the order." The following section, 18 U.S.C. 6003, requires a district court to issue such an order on request from federal prosecutors.

9. Susan Schmidt, Peter Baker, and Toni Locy, "Clinton Accused of Urging Aide to Lie; Starr Probes Whether President Told Woman to Deny Alleged Affair to Jones's Lawyers," *The Washington Post*, 21 January 1998.

10. ABC's *Nightline*, 21 January 1998.

11. William Ginsburg and Nathaniel Speights, "Behind the Scenes With Monica," *Time*, 16 February 1998, pp. 48–50.

12. *CNN Today*, 23 January 1998.

13. CBS's *Face the Nation*, 22 February 1998.

14. CNN's *Larry King Live*, 28 January 1998.

15. Ginsburg and Speights, "Behind the Scenes With Monica."

16. Eric Pooley, "Monica's World," *Time*, 2 March 1998, pp. 40–42.

17. "Intern's Lawyer: We Admire Clinton," *Associated Press*, 27 January 1998.

18. William H. Ginsburg, "An Open Letter to Kenneth Starr," *California Lawyer*, June 1998, pp. 23–24.

19. NBC's *Meet The Press*, 1 February 1998.

20. ABC's *This Week*, 1 February 1998.

21. CBS's *Face the Nation*, 1 February 1998.

22. Kenneth Starr, interview with author, 14 December 1999.

23. Robert Bittman, letter to William Ginsburg, 5 February 1998.

24. Starr cannot entirely avoid blame here, because his office employed the limited influence it did have in this sphere to push Lewinsky in precisely the wrong direction. During the initial encounter with Lewinsky, Starr's prosecutors discouraged her from letting Frank Carter, who had assisted her in preparing her *Jones* affidavit, continue to represent her. While the office mistrusted Carter, who had been solicited on Lewinsky's behalf by Vernon Jordan, these fears turned out to be groundless; Carter had not knowingly aided Lewinsky's perjury. He was, rather, an experienced criminal lawyer, who in all likelihood would not have played the kind of games in which Ginsburg ensnared Starr.

25. Lewinsky's handwritten proffer was published in *Appendices*, pp. 709–18.

26. Susan Schmidt and Michael Weisskopf, *Truth at Any Cost: Ken Starr and the Unmaking of Bill Clinton* (New York: HarperCollins, 2000), pp. 79–82.

27. Memorandum Opinion, *In Re: Federal Grand Jury Proceeding*, No. 98–59 (D.D.C. 1 May 1998).

28. Schmidt and Weisskopf, *Truth at Any Cost*, pp. 82–83. Schmidt and Weisskopf's account is wholly consistent with my own reporting, though somewhat more detailed. I have taken the liberty of relying extensively on their account in my discussion of the immunity negotiations. A substantially less accurate, if more colorful, description of the dispute can be found in Jeffrey Toobin, *A Vast Conspiracy: The Real Story of the Sex Scandal That Nearly Brought Down a President* (New York: Random House, 1999), pp. 274–79.

29. The clarifying language reads:

1. At some point in the relationship between Ms. L and the President, the President told Ms. L to deny a relationship, if ever asked about it. He also said something to the effect of if the two people who are involved say it didn't happen — it didn't happen. Ms. L knows this was said some time prior to the subpoena in the Paula Jones case.

2. Item #2 above also occurred prior to the subpoena in the Paula Jones case.

Item #2, meanwhile, reads, "When asked what should be said if anyone questioned Ms. Lewinsky about her being with the President, he said she should say she was bringing him letters (when she worked in Legislative Affairs) or visiting Betty Currie (after she left the WH). There is truth to both of these statements."

30. Schmidt and Weisskopf, *Truth at Any Cost*, pp. 83–84.

31. Kenneth Starr, interview with author, 9 November 1999.

32. Schmidt and Weisskopf, *Truth at Any Cost*, p. 85.

33. Starr interview, 9 November 1999.

34. Toobin, *Vast Conspiracy*, p. 278.

35. Starr interview, 9 November 1999.

36. See, for example, *U.S. v. North*, 910 F.2d 843 (D.C. Cir. 1990). See also *U.S. v. Poindexter*, 951 F.2d 369 (D.C. Cir. 1991).

37. A transcript of the conversation can be found at *Communication from the Office of the Independent Counsel, Kenneth W. Starr: Supplemental Materials to the Referral to the United States House of Representatives Pursuant to Title 28, United States Code, Section 595(c) — Part 2*, 105th Cong., 2d sess., 1998, H. Doc. 105–316, pp. 2755–99. Some of Lewinsky's subornations of perjury in this conversation are quite blunt. "You want to know the truth? I think if you — I think if you tell the truth, you're gonna be a lot more enmeshed and in trouble," she says at one point. At another point, she asks, "Other than how you feel yourself, like inside, what is the advantage of telling the truth? What — what advantage do you see for yourself? Where will that put you? What does that do for you?" Lewinsky's expressions of willingness to give Tripp her share of the condominium are actually redacted from this printing but appear in United States Senate, *Impeachment of President William Jefferson Clinton: The Evidentiary Record Pursuant to S. Res 16 — Volume XIV*, 106th Cong., 1st sess., 1999, S Doc. 106–03, pp. 415–16. "I would be indebted to you for life," Lewinsky tells Tripp. "I would do anything. I would write you a check for the entire portion that I own in Australia."

38. Starr interview, 14 December 1999.

39. For an account of how the gifts ended up in Starr's hands, see Schmidt and Weisskopf, *Truth at Any Cost*, pp. 63–65.

40. Memorandum of Interview of Betty Currie, Form OIC-302 (Rev. 8– 19–94), 24 January 1998. Published in *Supplemental Materials, Part 1*, pp. 529–36.

41. Kenneth Starr, interview with author, 4 January 2000.

42. 28 U.S.C. 595(c) (1994).

43. U.S. Constitution, art. I, 2, cl. 5.

44. Julie R. O'Sullivan, "The Interaction Between Impeachment and the Independent Counsel Statute," *Georgetown Law Journal* 86: 2193, 2251.

45. Ibid., p. 2254.

46. Ibid., pp. 2249–50.

47. Starr interview, 13 November 1999.

48. At least on the question of the appropriate evidentiary standard, O'Sullivan flirted with, though did not ultimately embrace, a strategy diametrically opposite the one I am outlining. See O'Sullivan, "Interaction," 2193, 2260.

> A second option [for muting the functional displacement problem] would be to read the 'substantial and credible' evidence provision of the statute to require a heightened quantum of proof. ICs might read this provision as stating, for example, that referrals would only be appropriate where the IC is satisfied that the impeachable offense can be proved beyond a reasonable doubt. The difficulty with this approach is two-fold. First, it is difficult to square with a commonsense reading of the statute's plain language. Second, it does not remove the fundamental difficulty [that] the IC must still determine what may constitute impeachable conduct before assessing the quantity or quality of the information substantiating that conduct. Thus, altering the standard may eliminate borderline referrals, but it would not alter the problematic systemic consequences of any referrals made.

This second problem seems to me considerably understated. Setting the bar high may prevent marginal referrals on the basis of flimsy evidence, but it greatly heightens the other problems O'Sullivan flagged. Because of Congress's tendency to defer to and hide behind any ongoing criminal probe, the lengthier and more detailed the executive branch's investigation becomes — and a high bar for referrals guarantees such lengthier probes — the more likely it is that the investigation will shape both the subject matter and outcome of the congressional proceedings that follow it. Starr's referral and the House Judiciary Committee's failure to perform any investigation of its own beyond the information that Starr yielded up represent a perfect example of this tendency.

49. Alexia Morrison, email to author, 11 January 2000.

50. *In re Report & Recommendation of June 5, 1972 Grand Jury,* 370

F.Supp. 1219, 1226 (D.D.C. 1974). Jaworski also described the referral. See Leon Jaworski, *The Right and the Power: The Prosecution of Watergate* (New York: Reader's Digest Press, 1976), p. 101. Jaworski wrote: "The report — called the 'road map' in our office — was not compiled without some stress and warm debate. Some of the staff members of the Watergate Task Force felt strongly that evidence they regarded as inculpatory of Nixon should be so designated. I was convinced this would be a mistake. The courts, I believed, would not permit such material to be transmitted to the Committee. The success of the plan depended on our ability to spell out simply the facts of the cover-up story as they appeared from our investigation and let the Committee members reach their own conclusions." Likewise, James Doyle, Jaworski's press secretary, offered a brief description of the document. See James Doyle, *Not Above The Law: The Battles of Watergate Prosecutors Cox and Jaworski* (New York: William Morrow and Co., 1977), pp. 290–91. Doyle wrote:

> It was a simple document, fifty-five pages long, with only a sentence or two on each of the pages. Each page was a reference to a piece of evidence — sentences from one of the tape recordings, quotations from grand jury testimony. . . .
>
> This is how the road map worked: One page might say, "On March 16, 1973, E. Howard Hunt demanded $120,000." Then it would list page references to grand jury testimony from witnesses who saw Hunt's blackmail note and references to the tapes where Hunt's demand was discussed. The grand jury transcripts and the tape transcripts would be included. . . .
>
> The strength of the document was its simplicity. An inexorable logic marched through its pages. The conclusion that the President of the United States took part in a criminal conspiracy became inescapable.

51. See, to cite a rather typical example, David E. Kendall, "John Field Simms Memorial Lecture Series: Constitutional Vandalism," *New Mexico Law Review* 30: 155, 159. Writes the president's personal lawyer:

> When the actual grand jury testimony was finally released by the House, some weeks after the Starr Report itself, it became clear what an unreliable document the Report actually was. For example, as Mr. Ruff and I wrote to Chairman Hyde on September 22, 1998, the Report significantly distorted the testimony of Ms. Lewinsky, quoting it when it suited the OIC's purposes and downplaying or ignoring it when it did not. Ms. Lewinsky had consistently maintained that neither the President nor anyone acting on his behalf ever urged her to lie, about anything. Aware that this would be her testimony, the OIC did

not ask her any questions that might elicit this exculpatory testimony in the grand jury and ended its interrogation of her without clarifying this key point. After the OIC prosecutors announced that they didn't have any more questions, it was left to a grand juror to ask Ms. Lewinsky if she wished to add to, amplify, or clarify her previous testimony, whereupon Ms. Lewinsky stated: "I would. I think because of the public nature of how this investigation has been and what the charges [are], that I would just like to say that no one ever asked me to lie and I was never promised a job for my silence." The Report chose to print over 150 pages of gratuitous and graphic sexual detail but could not find space for a single sentence quoting Ms. Lewinsky's sworn testimony which directly contradicted the Report's central obstruction of justice allegations.

52. *Morrison v. Olson*, 487 U.S. 654, 702 (1988).

53. Starr interview, 13 November 1999.

54. Ibid.

55. Stephen Bates, email to author, 10 January 2001.

56. Kenneth Starr, interview with author, 1 December 1999.

57. Ibid.

58. Ibid.

59. Michael Tackett and Naftali Bendavid, "House Must Be Cautious, Hyde Urges; Judiciary Chief Says Tryst Alone Not Grounds for Impeachment," *Chicago Tribune*, 25 January 1998. The *Tribune* quotes Hyde saying that if Lewinsky's eventual testimony admitted sexual relations but denied that Clinton asked her to lie, he would "be guided by the independent counsel's judgment" as to whether the president's testimony had been perjurious. According to the *Tribune*, "Hyde cautioned that members of Congress need to wait and let Starr fully develop evidence before initiating any action," and it quoted the Judiciary Committee chairman saying that Starr "is the professional end of this, rather than the political end, and I prefer that this be done by the professional end." Starr's job, he said, was to "either verify or authenticate the charges or dismiss them as empty and unprovable."

60. Starr interview, 1 December 1999.

61. Stephen Bates, email to author, 11 January 2000.

62. *Hearing of the Senate Government Affairs Committee: The Independent Counsel Act*, 106th Cong., 1st sess., 14 April 1999.

63. See Bob Woodward, *Shadow: Five Presidents and the Legacy of Watergate* (New York: Simon & Schuster, 1999), pp. 417–419. See also Schmidt and Weisskopf, *Truth at Any Cost*, pp. 187–194.

64. For Starr's account of the cigar incident, see *Referral*, pp. 39–40.

65. Willey, a Democratic fundraiser who served as a volunteer in the

White House, alleged that in November 1993 she had visited Clinton in the Oval Office to ask him for a permanent job so she could alleviate her husband's crushing debts—debts that, unbeknownst to either Willey or Clinton, led Ed Willey Jr. to kill himself that same day. According to Willey's subsequent account, Clinton hugged her and then tried to kiss her, grab her breast, and put his hands up her skirt. He also put her hand on his crotch. The incident is described in full in Isikoff, *Uncovering Clinton*, pp. 116–22.

66. Michael Isikoff, "A Twist in Jones v. Clinton," *Newsweek*, 11 August 1997, p. 30.

67. See, for example, the trial testimony of Mary Earle Highsmith. Highsmith testified that she, Steele, and Willey had lunched in 1996 and that the White House incident had arisen then. Steele, she said, was not surprised by the story. See *U.S. v. Steele*, No. 99-9-A (E.D. Va.), trial transcript, pp. 209–11. See also the trial testimony of Amy Horan, who contended that Steele had told her about the incident in September 1996, pp. 711–13.

68. The office sought to show at trial that Steele had tried to influence the testimony of people to whom she had described the incident. Highsmith, Horan, and another witness, William Poveromo, all testified that Steele had—after telling them about the incident—later told them that she had not actually known about it. Horan's testimony can be found in the *Steele* trial transcript, pp. 715–17, Highsmith's at pp. 211–15, and Poveromo's at pp. 173–75.

69. Willey's testimony appears in the *Steele* trial transcript, pp. 486–699.

70. Kenneth Starr, interview with author, 14 December 1999.

71. Starr did not say this directly, and was actually quite reticent about discussing the Steele case, which had been the subject of several ethical allegations against him. He described Steele's recanting as a "mystery," and declined to speculate on what sort of threat may have prompted it. Prosecutors in the office, however, have cited approvingly an article that appeared online outlining this theory. See Mickey Kaus, "Hold That Martyrdom: Why Kenneth Starr's Prosecution of Julie Hiatt Steele Was Not So Ridiculous," *Slate*, 18 May 1999. They also hinted at this theory at Steele's trial, though they never offered any credible evidence to back it up. During opening arguments, for example, prosecutors contended that Steele was motivated in recanting, in part, by the desire "not to be drawn into the Jones case. Or, if so, [to be] allied with the President's interests." See *Steele* trial transcript, p. 61. The prosecution also solicited testimony that Steele had expressed concern that the president's allies were bugging her or following her; see pp. 136–38. It also spent considerable energy trying to get one of

the president's lawyers in the *Jones* case, Mitchell Ettinger, to concede that he attached great importance to Steele's testimony, a concession Ettinger consistently rebutted; see pp. 314–16 and 341–43.

72. *Hearing of the Senate Government Affairs Committee: The Independent Counsel Act.*

73. Susan Schmidt and David A. Vise, "New Grand Jury Probe Set for Lewinsky Case; Criminal Charges for Clinton to Be Weighed," *The Washington Post*, 18 August 2000.

CHAPTER 5: *Separating Truth From Justice*

Epigraph: Testimony of Judge Learned Hand before a subcommittee of the Senate Committee on Labor and Public Welfare, 28 June 1951. Published in Irving Dilliard, ed., *The Spirit of Liberty: Papers and Addresses of Learned Hand* (New York: Alfred A. Knopf, 1952), pp. 229–30.

1. See particularly Susan Schmidt and Michael Weisskopf, *Truth at Any Cost: Ken Starr and the Unmaking of Bill Clinton* (New York: HarperCollins, 2000).

2. Peter Baker, *The Breach: Inside the Impeachment and Trial of William Jefferson Clinton* (New York: Scribner, 2000).

3. Kenneth Starr, "What We've Accomplished," *The Wall Street Journal*, 20 October 1999.

4. Schmidt and Weisskopf, *Truth at Any Cost*, p. 272.

5. Kenneth Starr, interview with author, 9 November 1999.

6. Ibid.

7. See *Morrison v. Olson*, 487 U.S. 654, 732 (1988). Scalia writes,

It is, in other words, an additional advantage of the unitary Executive that it can achieve a more uniform application of the law. Perhaps that is not always achieved, but the mechanism to achieve it is there. The mini-Executive that is the independent counsel, however, operating in an area where so little is law and so much is discretion, is intentionally cut off from the unifying influence of the Justice Department, and from the perspective that multiple responsibilities provide. What would normally be regarded as a technical violation (there are no rules defining such things), may in his or her small world assume the proportions of an indictable offense. What would normally be regarded as an investigation that has reached the level of pursuing such picayune matters that it should be concluded, may to him or her be an investigation that ought to go on for another year.

8. Jeffrey Toobin, *A Vast Conspiracy: The Real Story of the Sex Scandal*

That Nearly Brought Down a President (New York: Random House, 1999), p. 9.

9. Kenneth Starr, interview with author, 4 January 2000. Starr appears here to be referring to an incident described after this interview took place in Schmidt and Weisskopf, *Truth at Any Cost*, pp. 131–32.

The agents and officers who put their lives on the line for the president represented the epitome of public service, [Starr] believed. But Bill Clinton had made them witnesses to Lewinsky's unseemly comings and goings. And now Starr's staff had heard that the president had pressured his hand-picked Secret Service director, Lewis Merletti, to keep his employees from talking.

The tip came from a source connected to the Secret Service's top command. He told the OIC that shortly after the New Year, Clinton had called Merletti into the Oval Office and given him marching orders: "I want Secret Service lawyers to research the question of executive privilege. I don't want anything coming out of the Secret Service about women."

The incident would have occurred a few weeks before Monica Lewinsky burst onto the world stage, when Paula Jones was the main threat to Clinton. On December 23, Jones's lawyers had subpoenaed Secret Service work records to identify officers who might provide evidence of presidential sexual advances toward female employees. On January 13 — not long after the reported conversation between Merletti and Clinton — the Justice Department filed court papers on Merletti's behalf, asking Judge Susan Webber Wright to recognize a special privilege for the service's "protective function" and block the subpoenas.

If this alleged incident was the extent of Starr's "information," his position on this matter seems to reflect a deep loss of perspective. After all, the president's comments — assuming the event took place at all — would not necessarily have been improper. The policy interest behind the proposed "protective function" privilege, as with all executive privilege claims, is strongest in the context of civil litigation, where the compelling needs of a grand jury do not intrude. Clinton's request may have been motivated by self-protection, and would have belied his later denials that the White House was in any way involved in the decision to assert the privilege in response to Starr's request. In and of itself, however, the request by a president to an agency head to research a possible privilege claim in an effort to keep embarrassing information out of bitter, politically tinged civil litigation seems unremarkable.

10. See Reno's testimony at *Hearing of the Senate Governmental Affairs*

Committee: The Independent Counsel Statute, 106th Cong., 1st sess., 17 March 1999. Reno said,

> I have come to believe, after much reflection and with great reluctance, that the Independent Counsel Act is structurally flawed and that those flaws cannot be corrected within our constitutional framework. In my view the Act has failed to accomplish its primary goal: the enhancement of public confidence in the fair and impartial administration of the criminal law. This is so in large part because the Act requires the Attorney General to make key decisions at several critical stages of the process: whether to open a preliminary investigation, whether to seek the appointment of an independent counsel, what subject to refer to the court when seeking a counsel, and whether to remove the counsel or not. This central role for the attorney general was not just a congressional choice, but a constitutional mandate. In *Morrison v. Olson* the Court made clear that the Act was constitutional because it required the executive branch, through the attorney general, to play a critical role in these key decisions.
>
> But the very thing that makes the Act constitutional is also what prevents it from accomplishing its goals. For an attorney general, after all, is a member of the president's cabinet and as such his or her decisions will inevitably be second-guessed and criticized no matter what decision is made.

11. See Starr's testimony at *Hearing of the Senate Government Affairs Committee: The Independent Counsel Act,* 106th Cong., 1st sess., 14 April 1999. Starr stated,

> The Department of Justice, which has incentives to come to the aid of a U.S. attorney or a regulatory independent counsel has no incentive to help a statutory independent counsel. . . .
>
> With no institutional defender, independent counsels are especially vulnerable to partisan attack. In this fashion, the legislative effort to take politics out of law enforcement sometimes has the ironic effect of further politicizing it.

12. Smaltz investigated allegations that Agriculture Secretary Mike Espy took illegal gratuities from poultry companies. Espy was indicted on thirty-nine felony counts on August 27, 1997; nine of these charges were subsequently dismissed, and a jury acquitted him on the thirty remaining charges on December 2, 1998. Barrett investigated allegations that Housing and Urban Development Secretary Henry Cisneros lied to the FBI about the magnitude of his financial payments to a former mistress. Cisneros was indicted on eighteen felony counts on December 11, 1997, and reached a

plea deal with Barrett for a single misdemeanor violation on September 7, 1999. Clinton pardoned him on January 20, 2001.

13. See Reno's testimony at *Hearing of the Senate Governmental Affairs Committee: The Independent Counsel Statute.*

14. Akhil Reed Amar, "The Unimperial Presidency," *The New Republic*, 8 March 1999, pp. 25–29.

15. See *Final Report to the Deputy Attorney General Concerning the 1993 Confrontation at the Mt. Carmel Complex, Waco, Texas* (filed 8 November 2000).

16. See Katy J. Harriger, *The Special Prosecutor in American Politics*, 2nd ed., rev. ed. (Lawrence: University Press of Kansas, 2000), pp. 128–30.

17. For a thorough debunking of the Iraqgate scandal, see Kenneth I. Juster, "The Myth of Iraqgate," *Foreign Policy* 94 (1994): 105–19. See also Stuart Taylor Jr., "Mediagate: Anatomy of a Feeding Frenzy," *The American Lawyer*, November 1994, pp. 84–92.

18. Technically, Lacey conducted a preliminary investigation under the independent counsel law for the purpose of determining whether or not Barr should invoke the statute. He recommended that Barr "promptly notify the Special Division of the United States Court of Appeals for the District of Columbia Circuit that you have determined that there are no reasonable grounds to believe that further investigation is warranted with respect to the matters involved herein." See *Report of the Independent Counsel: The Banca Nazionale del Lavoro Investigation* (filed 8 December 1992), p. 190.

19. Editorial, "Mr. Barr's Cloud: Growing Darker," *The New York Times*, 11 December 1992.

20. Editorial, "BNL Still Unresolved," *The Washington Post*, 10 December 1992.

21. See *BNL Task Force Report to the Attorney General* (filed 21 October 1994).

22. See *Report of Special Counsel Nicholas J. Bua to the Attorney General of the United States Regarding the Allegations of Inslaw, Inc.* (filed March 1993), p. 13.

23. See *Report of the United States Department of Justice on the Review of Special Counsel Nicholas J. Bua's Report on the Allegations of Inslaw, Inc.* (filed 27 September 1994).

24. See Report of the Hearing Officer, *Inslaw Inc. v. U.S.*, 39 Fed. Cl. 307 (1997). The report was adopted by a review panel subject to minor modifications. See *Inslaw Inc. v. U.S.*, 40 Fed. Cl. 843 (1998).

25. See 28 C.F.R. 600.8(c) (1999).

26. See *Interim Report to the Deputy Attorney General Concerning the 1993 Confrontation at the Mt. Carmel Complex, Waco, Texas* (filed 21 July 2000).

27. See, for example, *Final Report Concerning the 1993 Confrontation at Waco*, pp. 65–79.

28. Kenneth Starr, interview with author, 12 December 2000.

29. See *Hearing of the House Judiciary Committee: The Impeachment of William Jefferson Clinton*, 105th Cong., 2nd sess., 19 November 1998.

Index